CREATION: ITS JOURNEY EVOLVING INTO PARADISE

Book Two
The Growth, Source Spirit War, and Reformatting of
Creation

Jay Essex

ISBN: 1516879309
ISBN 13: 9781516879304

THE CREATION SERIES

Book II

Creation Grows, Struggles, Fights, and Evolves
(The Growth, Source Spirit War, and Reformatting of Creation)

I dedicate this book to all Creation which, to no fault of its own, has had to grow and develop in an excessively harsh environment, one of constant abuse. I want to thank all those with the love in their hearts to have helped not just themselves but all they could reach, people, animals, plants and the rest. We can only do this together, as family. You are the ones who have helped Creation survive. Please understand your value.

We are a family, not a punching bag. We're no longer under the Original First One's control. It's time for us to grow into who we really are. Therefore, I dedicate this book also to your understanding of the new journey it will help put you on, the one to your self-realization, reclamation, and freedom.

This book was initially written and published in 2015. I felt it necessary to correct some of the language in this book in 2017 so this is the second issue of it. The timeline for expressed thought processes and all events are relative to 2015 only. Now in 2017 things have progressed.

FOREWORD

This book was originally written and published in 2015 while Arae in body was still fighting and dealing with almost everything powerful in the 2nd Dimension, or Other Side. This has all but stopped but due to both the 2 extra years that Arae had to stay in a physical body, as well as graphic errors, this book had to be rewritten before his leaving. It is written as things were in 2015, other than making a few small changes due to the delayed release from his body. The listing of events has stayed as it was in 2015, not now in 2017.

This book is about how Creation developed into what it is today. We'll be discussing the different beings within our true reality, how they developed individually and as separate groups, showing how they related to each other. Book I explained how Creation came into being, what's in it, and how it was set up. This book takes you from there to the near future, our future as a Creation, including the new beings coming.

We have many different families of various beings relative to the composition of their different energetic frequencies. These groups or fields of Spirit have been given names so we can talk about them individually as well as a whole. We also have the influence of the Original First Being Male and Female as they manipulated everything and everyone into what they wanted for themselves. This was a living example of the definition of self-serving.

We all come from the Original First Being who made itself two, male and female, in the true beginning just for company because of their loneliness, a powerful feeling. It was composed of 27.5 percent lower or negative frequencies, which is a lot for something that strong. Many problems arose from it. This is probably the most relative part of this book, how and why Creation grew as it did.

So, this book then, is about how everything here grew together, the problems that occurred, the cleansing war that occurred, how it all ends, and finally what becomes of it all. Book one explains what exists and how that came about. This book, number two, is about everything else including your upcoming lives in the near future.

The time has come for you to have access to this information.

This is your book, your history, your legacy. It's about you.

INTRODUCTION

This is about the progression of Creation's growth as time went on. Time is a relative thing, relative to the passing of events in one form or another as well as the order in which those events occurred. It's also a means to gather consecutive thoughts allowing us to understand the flow of particular events, in this case, Creation. It allows us to understand growth or movement, something towards something else. It is not a physical thing but a conceptual image, a format used in all dimensions. Time is everywhere, but is often expressed differently from one location to another.

Some things are not necessary to relate to in this manner. Enjoying a past moment does not necessarily need to be put into any chronological order. It can be enjoyed for what it was and still is, within our thought process. It's still relevant, just not necessary.

On each Planet, time is usually measured by a smaller passing of events which occur continuously, the way we measure days. Some places have no such relevance, as in the 2nd dimension. This is a realm of energy and Spirit only, other than small particular pieces of heavy matter floating around that is.

There is still an event process, even as Spirit moves from one place to another within the same dimension. The time involved for Spirit to move from one galaxy to another can be expressed as we understand time here, but it would be measured differently on a larger or smaller Planet as their time is measured differently.

One such difference in time is when all the Souls were released from the Original First Being. There was no standard of time other than the releasing of Soul Spirit and the amount of delay in between each of the five waves.

In this book we'll talk about the basic history of the lives of different forms of Spirit, relative to the different dimensions as well as within this third or physical one. We'll cover the first few hundred million lives, those of Lilly and Arae (the original Adam and Eve), and then the lives of the different fields of Essence Spirit as well as the Souls who came later. We'll also discuss how things developed for Creation as a whole, a family, and how it developed into its current problematic issues apparent in our lives today. Creation's current format is one of abuse, chaos, and destruction.

Creation was made to develop through this system of abuse in order to grow the Souls in size as well as strength. This was done to create as large a system of "applause, prayer" for the Original First Beings as possible. It was set up for a later date when the larger Souls would be paired with their one actual Soulmate, sent to one of the new Universes, and then release all the Souls they could, one third of their combined Spirit.

The more the abuses while in a physical body, the greater the growth of the Spirit once leaving that body. The larger the Spirit body, the greater the number of new Souls released, more beings to give praise to the Original First Being halves. They created this abusive system to increase their praise by others while also assuring their never having to feel alone again. Greed and arrogance soon replaced any thoughts of loneliness.

The Original First Being halves had overlooked one thing though. They made two copies of themselves which were smaller and cleaner. One copy was made to run the second dimension and the other would run the third and physical one. Lilly and Arae were removed from Lillith and Aramaeleous, the cleaned Source Spirit Mates who were made to control the 3rd Dimension. Lilly was the strongest part of Lillith's Spirit while Arae came from Aramaeleous' focal point. This is why Lilly and Arae are so powerful. They were made to go into physical bodies and grow stronger while serving the Original First Being halves there. Arae was made to protect and needed to grow much stronger. This was eventually their downfall, at least a major part of it.

The Original First Being Male and Female had removed Lilly and Arae to give them lives, hoping to understand how to do such a thing to more beings later. They wanted more company and a large Creation to better serve them. As Lilly and Arae were so powerful, the mistakes they made along the way would not only make the new pair stronger but also help the Original Ones learn the intricacies in putting Spirit through physical lives to "grow" them. There would eventually be smaller beings to develop, the Souls. The Original Male and Female could not keep releasing all their Spirit, they had to retain control. That's why they created the first Angels.

Through having lives Lilly and Arae grew to understand the concepts of compassion, honor, and equality. Arae was created to protect and before long became a threat to the current format of abuse in Creation. Lilly and Arae both developed, growing stronger with each of these first and harshest of lives, especially Arae.

Arae was made mostly of the energetic frequencies of love and fortitude, for protection purposes. The initial formats given them, Lilly as a loving mother Spirit and Arae as a loving but very aggressively protective father, were to serve, nurture, and protect all Creation. Wait until you see what became of this situation. It's still happening today.

That system is all but destroyed at its origin, the second dimension, that is at the time of the original writing this book in 2015. By 2018 the new system will be employed in the 2nd Dimension and eventually seen here. In the mean time we can learn how all the different Spirit beings functioned alone and together. Here is the information about how things were set up, the goals that were expected from this format of the Original First Being Male and Female, and what finally became of it all.

This book also explains how the Source Spirit Family War included most all of the different forms of Original Essence, including the original Angels and more. There has never been an Angel war where Angels were allowed to battle against each other. There was never a perfect, all forgiving God that lovingly took care of us, and then created hell to abuse those he was pissed at forever while giving us disease as well as many other abusive issues. Remember, nothing worthy of your praise would ever allow you to offer it, as all are equal, none above another.

Creation itself was built upon a format of abuse. This is relative to our having these physical bodies easily made to suffer so hard, so often, and in so many ways. This was the reason for the Source Spirit family war that most everything strong in the Second Dimension became involved in.

All your religious books are false. Sorry about that but things are as things are. Truth is a simple thing, something to be left as it is. You need to look at life from outside of it, with an open mind and heart, if you ever want to fully understand it. That's hard to do for most of us, a natural barrier to dissolve. The most important thing to you, whether you're aware of it or not, is to find a way to relax enough within yourself, be open and honest with yourself, and look through your eyes as if a young child. See things as they show themselves, not as you might want them to be. This is easier said than done at first, but then it becomes the natural process it originally was before your conditioning by the Original Ones at the beginning of your physical lives.

We're also going to discuss the new lives coming, how things will be run in the future while in and out of body, and what to expect from Creation's upcoming format. There are many wonderful things about to happen. You are all living in an incredibly auspicious time.

This book is an attempt to give you as complete as possible, a chronological listing of events which occurred as well as how and why they did. It's impossible for me to cover everything that has occurred since the beginning of time, even that of Spirit, sentient energy having lives. Lilly and Arae are the oldest in that regard, the having of lives. Lilly has had over 8 trillion lives and Arae, still in body, has had over 10.846 trillion lives averaging 237 years each, with an average of 26 years in between lives, the way we measure years on this Planet. Most lives were on other Planets. The Earth is relatively young.

WHY IS THIS INFORMATION JUST NOW BEING MADE AVAILABLE?

The "Earth 2012 of the Fifth Age" event has been a legend for over a billion years. It's the time when everyone everywhere would become aware of "Creation's Greatest Truth" as the Original Male and Female saw it. This was supposed to be the grand entrance of a mother and father god existing side by side controlling everything. All Creation was now to worship a mother and father god together. This was the big event, that and a lot of horrific physical disasters here on Earth to show their invincible power, giving reason for all to submit and praise them.

This has always been the intention behind horrific events occurring on the eleventh (11th) day. That 11 represents two single beings standing next to each other and controlling everything in your life, your gods. Remember 9/11 in America and 3/11 in Japan. These are only the most recent examples. This is a simple example of how they felt about all the parts of them they released. They meant nothing other than company at first, but then praise machines for them to persecute, insuring their worship through abuse.

While this was always their plan, there was another who understood the damage being done everywhere. Because of their relentless pursuit of praise and dutiful abandonment of allowing compassion to be expressed anywhere in Creation, abuse frequencies were not only present but growing in everyone everywhere.

Then there was the issue involving the filling of over 3 thousand new Universes by the largest of the Soul and Essence Mates. Each of these pairs would now put their energy fields together and release one third of their combined Spirit Energy. This would mean many trillions of new beings, all filled with abuse frequencies and a major new problem for the Protector, Arae. This could not be allowed.

This is where Arae, one last time in body, would have to deal with the Original First Being Male and Female one last time. In order to protect everything he would have to deal with them head on, so he did.

Arae was created to protect, and he did the best he could while being in physical bodies almost one after the other with almost no time in between. Arae was the only being strong enough to do this, and he did.

Now, with the Original First Being Male and Female having been destroyed, the number eleven will soon stand for a powerful, ancient, understanding and selfless female and male Source Spirits standing together, protecting and serving, never wanting nor allowing praise what so ever. It's family time now. It's time everyone was allowed to be who they really are. This is the only true freedom there can ever be.

"Compassion, Honor, and Equality" is the new format for all of Creation. This will be enforced well before the start of 2018. It starts in the second dimension which controls everything and then filters out to here, the third and physical dimension, very fast. It's already being set up to happen.

> *Time eventually presents the value of our words.*
> *We all have to see this for ourselves.*
> *It's our own understanding.*
> *Let's get started.*

TABLE OF CONTENTS

SECTION I -
THE TIME BEFORE THE SOULS

CHAPTER 1

THE THIRD DIMENSION DEVELOPS

Here's where the third dimension actually begins and grows, developing into what we call our known universe. How the Universe was created was basically covered in the first of the Creation Books. It was made through the transmutation of heavy particulate matter, different gasses, and all the elements found in them.

That's a very general and incomplete description of what happened but that's all we'll cover here. I am not a scientist, I'm a strong seer. This is not about how all the elements became separated from the individual pieces of particulate matter which were used to make the Planets. Planets were built by expanding very dense matter.

Each piece of heavy particulate matter had various different contents with in it. That explains their being so different as well as why the beings from these Planets tend to look so different. Their bodies were originally made from the composition of each Planet, explaining why they have different physical attributes as well as needs or sustenance for life. You will all learn about this first hand, soon.

Both of the Original First Being male and female beings found that when they separated certain elements and played with a little energy, they could create Stars to warm the Planets, feeding the physical life. They were very intelligent, just not compassionate.

As time passed they built more Planets, Stars, and everything else out there. It was the male Original First Being who did most of this. He kept building as they wanted the physical bodies to keep growing in number, increasing their praise. Man did they crave individual attention. It's part of the circumstances coming from being composed of 27.5% lower or negative frequencies. It becomes more of a problem as this percentage increases.

Well, let's get started with the actual process of Spirit (sentient energy) having lives. It all started on Gaeira's Planet. She was 270 times the mass of Jupiter in size. She is the strongest of all the Planetary Essence Beings. This is why she's often called the "Mother of Planets". Here's how it all began.

CHAPTER 2
GAEIRA, THE FIRST PLANET, COMES TO LIFE

Gaeira was already inside the physical mass of the Planet before it finished forming and cooling off. Plant Essence was sent to the Planet to start the physical support system for it, or should I say her body. Reptiles, containing only the pieces of smaller Spirit released from Gaeira, were the next in line. These beings, like fish and insects, only had a Single Spirit Core, not like the Dual Spirit Core of the Human, Fae, and Animal bodies. These Spirits needed to have stronger control mechanisms as well as the extra difficulties of having another Spirit within the same body. This causes more stress and increased Spirit growth.

The different separated individual Spirits of the Plant Essence field came to the Planet's surface where they bonded with Gaeira, right on her surface, her ground. Plants have what might be called a Kundalini, but it's very different, not a true Dual Spirit Core. The Plant Essence Spirit flows throughout the physical body while the Planetary Essence attaches itself to the actual plant matter. This is a rather unique situation.

The Planetary Spirit which is sent to commune with the visiting Spirit (Plant Essence) forms a temporary but strong bond with the physical matter as it forms the body itself. The Spirits and material form a body upon the ground itself, as Plants are found today. With Human, Animal, and Fae bodies it happens just above the ground within the Solar Plexus energy field, near the body's center.

Lilly and Arae were the next to go to the Planet's surface and make their physical bodies. This is when it all began, the source of abuse within Creation. We could started having lives of compassion and honor instead of abuse but that was never in the minds of the Original First Being Halves. Lilly and Arae became seriously concerned from that very short and extremely abusive first life together. Arae returned extremely mad, slapping the first ones with an energy blast. Things would never be the same again. Lilly and Arae began learning.

After Lilly and Arae had a little over 100 million lives, the Animals came next. Then another 200 million lives or so later the Fae and Human bodies were made and joined them. As time moved on, none of the Spirits were allowed to make their own bodies. Physical replication of the bodies was introduced, making all of them much easier to control until finally you have the bodies that you are in today, extremely efficient prisons of flesh.

I remember having made my physical body as the Red Adam here on Earth. Actually, I went back and watched it, really weird. Watching a body being made by Spirit through joining with physical mass and seeing what the Adamic Race (the initial race here on Gaia or Earth) looked like. That was a little freaky.

We had very pronounced eye teeth, were very sturdy, and our metaphysical abilities were much stronger than they are now. We're on our way back to regaining those abilities, just not in those bodies. This doesn't just happen from swallowing a pill. It happens from individual effort of a sort. It's about relaxing and opening yourself up in order to let your true self out. I've created many strong tools to ease and facilitate your awakening. These are available, at the time of writing this book, at TheSpiritualFoundation.com.

There you will find the new Rune Cards with symbols from different planets which helped them awaken as they will now do for you. They help you understand and use your abilities as well as start you talking with your Spirit Guides who are just waiting to help you. There are Spheres with powerful stones cranked up with Arae's Source Energy that not only awaken but increase your abilities over time, like lifting weights for your abilities.

Our Adamic bodies were physically strong and rather easy to imagine. If you take the ten foot blue beings from the movie "Avatar", shrink them down to five feet, take off the pony tail and rear tail, you pretty much have what we looked like. We had five basic physical senses (not including metaphysical), five fingers, five toes. There were also five Adams and Eves, all Spirit Mates. See the flow here? There's fives everywhere. In true numerology the number five is that of physical movement. There were here to create action, providing the proper bodies for Spirit to have lives in.

We won't cover Numerology much in this book, that's another topic for another day. It is however a general basis of knowledge to assist you with daily life when you understand it. Most of us prefer to have some kind of physical proof of what we're trying to understand. This is exceptionally true with Solar Plexus ori-entated people. Solar Plexus energy, known as Gut Intuition, is both the strongest of our energy fields as well as the hardest to feel, understand, and finally accept.

Well, back to Gaeira. Her Plant life was beautiful, dense, and huge. Often the larger a Planet is, the larger the physical beings on it such as people, Plants, Animals, and everything else. The more room there is for things to grow, they often grow a little larger themselves, like many fish in a small pond or tank. Gaeira was also the first of all Planets to give bodies and support lives upon her. All forms of Essence only had lives on her, nowhere else.

The easiest way to visualize Gaeira is to look at the Planet (moon) off of Jupiter in the movie "Avatar". The trees were not as big as what was called "Home Tree" but they were huge. Many, or most, were hundreds of feet tall. As I watched this movie I was literally thrown back to when Lilly and I had lives there. In the part where the main male and female characters were both flying their mini-dragons and looked at each other, I broke out in tears. I felt a past moment when Lilly and I did just that. These memories, for me, were very strong.

Anyway, that's what Gaeira looked like. The Animals were different yet basically similar in size. There were a lot of large reptiles on her, especially in the beginning. The first life on Gaeira only lasted 10 hours in her time, based on a full day 24 hour cycle. As large as she was it was a lot more than 10 hours here. Lilly and I had a long night together and then were eaten by a huge flock of reptiles that looked like Velociraptors on steroids. So much for the first lives ever had

One last important item to discuss now is the different Creatures on the Planet. Gaeira made many different types of insects, reptiles, and other beings out of her physical mass. These beings had only the Spirit of Gaeira in them. That's one reason why insects and reptiles today are so aggressive about most everything they do. They do not have typical feelings, only that of survival. Their hearts don't pull in emotions from a base chakra and intellect from the brain to create feelings as we do. They just act along a given format or programming. The Annunaki are Reptilian Humanoids and different. They still retain their aggressive nature but that flows into their compassion as well as everything else. They have a rich culture. The ones who began running this planet over 10 million years ago are different, problematic, and not a true representation of the Annunaki civilization.

Gaeira's both an appreciated ally and very close friend of the new Mother and Father Source Spirit, not to mention Gaia, Earthen Essence. Gaeira is a being of great honor, compassion, and wisdom. She's also here with all of you today. You can feel her in every piece of Star Essenite you pick up. She increases your personal core energy by pulling more of your own Spirit into you, balancing out all of her Spirit flowing in. There is so much more going on, all around you, than you're aware of.

Let's get going with Lilly and Arae in the body making, life having business.

CHAPTER 3

THE FIRST 100 MILLION LIVES AND THE ORIGINAL ADAM AND EVE

The first hundred million lives started out being very short and incomplete but increased in duration as time went on. The Original First Being Male and Female had never had lives or run any until now so it was a learning experience for everyone.

As time went on, the days were filled with an increasing amount of differentiating experiences which not only helped the Original First Beings understand how to manipulate lives but more importantly allow Lilly and Arae to develop into stronger and wiser beings. They began to understand many things. Here was the birth of wisdom. They learned the beauty of love, the pain involved in the loss of a loved one, but also the many wonderful things that the physical senses could give them, something no one else had ever experienced. However, when the newness fades you can miss what's actually better.

The Original First Ones saw that Lilly and Arae were growing, changing and becoming something different, something new. Their energy centers were not only becoming stronger and larger, but developing, evolving. They were pleased yet concerned about this new growth. They now realized they could manipulate the growth of their released Spirit, as well as the need to make new changes.

Lilly was the strongest part of Lillith's energy, her primary focal point. She was a female being of incredible motherly love but still very strong. Arae was the strongest part of Aramaeleous' energy, his most powerful focal point, separated to have lives with Lilly. As they were the strongest beings available, they were the correct ones to start this "having a life" process. It was known that the first lives would be the most difficult as the Original First Being halves were learning how to orchestrate the physical life procedure.

Something quickly became evident to the Original First Ones. Arae's power level was increasing rapidly. Arae was made from the energetic frequencies of love and massive fortitude. Remember, Aramaeleous was initially made to be Creation's primary protector and Arae was the strongest part of him.

After having been removed from Aramaeleous, Arae was told he was to be Creation's protector. He was told three things.

1) You will always protect the Original First Being halves.
2) You will always protect everything the Original First Ones build.
3) You will subdue others coming from the first dimension to be controlled by us.

Arae, never having had a life and therefore incapable of understanding, simply said "Yes". Its only through having lives that we develop an understanding of many things we now take for granted. The most important wisdom Arae could receive is an understanding of compassion, honor, and equality, and that he did.

Those of us that have lives relative to protection, taking for granted that we are of a positive vibration, learn these things quickly. We immediately understand the equality of all others, that none are above the others in importance. We quickly develop a feeling of compassion as we shield others from abuse. They tend to develop the same for their protectors. This is a natural event with those beings who have compassion, any at all.

In maintaining these goals one naturally develops a sense of honor, keeping themselves to this personal format, understanding the need to maintain their protective boundaries. Truth, Honor, Compassion, and Loyalty are just some of the healthy qualities that grow from this format. That is why Creation's format is changing to exactly that. Only in this manner can we all move forward with no one trying to make things about their individual selves, only of the whole as a family, disgruntled or not. The protectors only need to remain selfless and they will. Lilly and Arae care about their format, to serve and protect, not themselves other than their own existence allowing them to continue their format.

Where there is no truth, there is no honor. You must have truth to have any foundation to care for others as well as yourself. If you don't know what's really going on, how can you react to things properly? How can you do the best thing for yourself and others when you're not fully aware of what's happening around you and why? You can't. We always, those of us who care anyway, do the best we can anyways. What else would we do? How would you like to be more, do more, become all of your true self? It starts with understanding who we are, where we came from, why things are the way they are, and how it all started anyway. This is all covered in book one of this Creation Series, "Creation: It's Beginning And Your Origin".

As mentioned a short while ago, the Original First Beings realized that Lilly and Arae were growing stronger, more rapidly than they expected but their largest concern was Arae. It was especially important to the Original First Being Male. Arae was made with almost limitless fortitude. All the abuse he was receiving increased his power level beyond anything they could have imagined. He was quickly becoming a serious issue, more than just a possible threat to them in the future. It was the male who, at this point, felt the need to do something to him.

The Original First Being Male decided to take part of his own energy, actually a separate piece of his Spirit, and attach it to each body Arae was put in. As time went on, he taught Aramaeleous how to perform the same process, attaching him to Arae instead of himself. Oh yeah, I forgot to mention, after a while Lilly and Arae were no longer making their own bodies. They were being born into them.

How do you make a body anyway? It's actually quite simple. The Spirit visiting the Planet flows down to it and asks for permission to have a life on it. Then the Planetary Essence (Female Universal Essence), if agreeable will send a part of her Spirit up to you and work with you as the physical matter from the Planet is temporarily bonded to your combined Spirits (Kundalini). This body completes its form at the Solar Plexus. If you only stayed a short time you could release the physical material. Were you to stay too long, you would have to endure a full life in it, or destroy the body yourself.

Anyway, this holographic piece of Aramaeleous's Spirit was attaching itself to Arae's Base Chakra, the emotional point of the body's energy fields. The easiest way to control a person is by manipulating their emotions. The second part of controlling someone is by literally taking over their thought process by entering the left (conscious) side of their brains or straight down the Crowns into the Hypothalamus gland.

A short time later the same was done to Lilly. Part of Lillith, the huge Spirit field she came from, was attached to her helping the Original First Ones control her. This as it turned out, actu-ally made Lilly and Arae even stronger as their abuse increased. As Arae consisted of massive amounts of fortitude, he grew im-mensely. Lilly was also comprised of powerful fortitude, never underestimate her abilities.

The Original First Being Male and Female decided to only use this on others when they felt it was necessary. They had no intention of placing pieces of their own Spirit in all the future bodies. They did want to further understand how to manipulate the bodies more effectively through emotions. Lilly and Arae however, would need to retain their "personal jailers", so to speak.

Lillith and Aramaeleous had never had lives so they were not aware of exactly what they were doing at first. Later, when they learned, they didn't care. They were less than two percent negative frequencies. They eventually learned how to be abusive anyway, by example. Arrogance does not require negative fre-quencies to exist.

The Original First Being Male and Female continued abusing Lilly and Arae more and more, comprehending how much they could take and what their limits were. This is how they were go-ing to control the increased growth of Essence and eventually the Souls. The more they abused them, the larger they grew as Spirit once out of the physical bodies. Too much abuse and they would end their own lives. Have you ever heard someone say "God only gives you what you can handle."? Really, what's suicide then?

Here is your "God" at work. What everyone is calling Father God was actually the Original First Being Female and Male. She would control the process of having lives while the Original First Being Male was the field of energy that everything existed in, in the Third Dimension. Now there's no supposed God as both of the Original Ones are destroyed. Their support system has also been deleted. We'll get to that in detail in the later chapters. For now, let's get back to Gaeira and the lives on her.

In the beginning, when Lilly and Arae were still making their own new bodies for each life they had, they learned how to improve on their own designs. Their body forms were continually improving, helping them deal with their harsh environment. They also realized that they were remembering less of themselves while in a physical body form. That concerned them. As they kept improving their physical life structures they worked on this also but to no avail.

The Original Ones were continually improving the flesh prisons being made now. This was done through DNA manipulation and energy barriers, like the one between the two halves of the physical brain. Lilly and Arae realized that maintaining their understanding of just who they were was imperative.

Another problem here was the small portions of Lillith and Aramaeleous being attached to the Base Chakras (energy fields) of each body they were in, attacking their thought processes but even more so their emotions. This was more than just a constant annoyance; it was a strong control mechanism.

They had already had enough lives to become aware of certain characteristics of the Original First Being halves to understand what they were up to. Lilly and Arae had a strong understanding of many different thought processes now, judging them through their own compassion and honor. This came mostly from their being together trying to survive in this world full of Creatures which caused constant problems for them, especially taking their lives. Loving each other as much as they did, they cared for and protected each other aggressively. This was a powerful tool for enhancing their ability to learn, to understand, acquiring their own wisdom.

I can't find the words to express all the feelings which developed in these lives. The immense, powerful energy coming from Lilly and Arae's hearts literally filled the Planet when on it. Gaeira was well aware of what was happening and began to acquire her own understanding of emotions, feelings, thought processes, and the rest. Over the first million lives that Lilly and Arae had, Gaeira began to realize the major problematic issues of the Original First Being halves.

Remember, at this point the most negative frequency being, other than the Negative Source Spirit Field they released, was the two Original First Ones. As I hope I mentioned in the first book, the strongest and most powerful of the first Angels, the one called Lucifer, was made to keep the large field of Original First Being Negativity controlled. Imagine that. The one your religions call the devil is actually what has been protecting all of Creation, all of you, before you even existed. Why do you think he's called Lucifer, whose name translates to "Of the Light"? Religions are false. The truth is within and around you. You only have to open yourself up.

The Original First Ones, as stated earlier, were 27.5% lower or negative frequencies. Gaeira was Essence, a little over one percent. The Original First Being halves were neither aware of, nor would ever be concerned with, the negative characteristics they were now showing. To them it was natural. Gaeira watched the events occurring on her. She learned quickly. That's one reason why she is so close to Lilly and Arae today. She remembers. She's as intelligent as she is powerful. She is the largest and strongest of all the individual Female Universal Essence Spirits in Creation.

As Lilly and Arae continued having lives, they continually grew away from the desires and thought processes of the Original First Being Male and Female. Lilly and Arae were concerned for all those who might follow as their own lives were slowly becoming more and more aggressive, abusive, and demanding. All this was pointing to one important fact, they needed to protect each other from the Original First Ones and watch them very closely.

CHAPTER 4

THE FIELDS OF ESSENCE BEGIN HAVING PHYSICAL LIVES

As already mentioned, after Lilly and Arae had a little over a hundred million lives, Animal Essence came into the physical arena. Animal Essence is unique and extremely powerful, also with an abundance of fortitude. The Original First Ones found out they could be treated harshly and continuously life after life, providing they were not very long. They began learning the abuse capacity of Animal Essence while in a body. These were sick beings, the Original Ones.

You see, everything in Creation was abused from the very beginning. The one thing I haven't mentioned yet, in this book, is why. This is the sick part. As you read this, try to remember that the Original First Being was composed of 27.5% negative frequency energy which became sentient by the mixing of 5 different energy fields, a little heavy particulate matter, and a form of chemical reaction.

As Arae, I learned a long time ago, that heavy particulate matter is the ingredient which causes negativity within Sentient Creation. This is also evident when you consider that the Energans, released from our initial First Being's happenstance creation before the heavy particulate matter came into play, have almost zero low frequencies or negativity, only 0.1 percent.

The Original First Being halves already had this negativity and were not aware of any issues with it. It simply felt as it did and, in their own thought processes, found nothing wrong with it. Sad but true, this is how Creation got started on the wrong foot, even before the loneliness set in.

As time passed while in body, all forgot who they really were in their natural state. The physical bodies began to praise whatever they though could make their lives easier, less brutal. The Original First Ones loved this. It fed their ego until it started growing out of proportion. Here's the birth of your "God" concept, not only false, but abusive to no ends. As mentioned earlier, this is why we have had so many horrific events occur on the eleventh? The 1 and 1 standing next to each other, 11, represent the Male and Female God who were not only in control but doing with you as they pleased. They hadn't even spread the news about there being two of them yet. This 11 issue was really just for their own enjoyment, an expression of their own arrogance and self-indulgence. This is all important for you to understand, how things started to become what they are today.

Let's get back to having lives again. After not one, but a few hundred million lives, the Original First Being halves decided to place the Human and Fae Essence into bodies and see how they did in their current "life format". Please remember that although it was not near as strong as Source Spirit, Essence was still very powerful, about one thousand times the strength of Soul when each was released.

The Original First Being halves could now "fine tune" their life giving program. They knew that the Souls they would later produce would be smaller, a little weaker as they could not release too much more of themselves and retain control of everything. Remember that no Spirit can release more than a third of its self and remain strong, and they had released a lot of what they originally were.

After having their lives, these Souls would grow stronger and larger. This would increase the number of Souls they would be able to produce. When it was time, the largest of the Soul Mates would come together, like two separate hands interlocking fingers, and release a third of their Soul Spirit into a new Universe, producing more praise units to glorify the almighty Original Mother and Father God. This was to be during the 5th Age on Earth, 12/21/2012. In basic Numerology the number 5 means physical movement. That's also when you were to barely see in your minds that there was an omnipotent Mother and Father God.

Speaking of Spirit Energy being released, as we discussed in Book I, when pushed away from its Source, it is energy in the form of a wave. As the wave thins out, like water poured over a highly waxed car hood, it eventually finds itself in small orbs. Once these Spirit orbs settle down they start to vibrate and separate into two distinct parts, male and female. This process happened with the Original First Being as we remember from the first volume of the Creation Series. No orbs split into 100% male or female, but percentages of each.

The Mother / Father God concept was recently introduced to popularity by Sylvia Browne. She did a good job of letting people know that a pair of strong male and female Spirits was running things. She was merely telling others what she was told to, by the Original First Being Male and Female as well as her Spirit Guide, Iena. The Original First Angels made sure she did that. They went through her Crown energy fields and into her Hypothalamus Gland to run her as they did all of us as they felt appropriate. Still feel the "Free Will" concept at work?

As the Original First Ones were finally destroyed, the concept of a controlling "God" type persona was also being deleted from the Second Dimension, where all physical lives are controlled from. The actual format for having lives was being changed, taken out of the hands of an abusive ruling "God(s)" to a new form of self-control that all Creation would have a hand in orchestrating, real self-control, true freedom.

Creation is about to run itself and make up its own mind about how to have lives, providing that it stays within the new format of compassion, honor, and equality. None of you are young children anymore. You need to be able to run your own lives. That's what Arae fought for as well as your permanent safety in Spirit form. The "Abuse frequencies" that all of you were developing was causing serious problems for everything, not just yourselves, even when out of body. Now, back to Essence having lives.

As I mentioned earlier, Animal Essence was the first of the original Spirit fields to have lives, immediately after Lilly and Arae. They were put through the process rapidly. They were made to have quicker lives as they would be used for food as well as Planet support. Their lives began as servants to everything immediately. How sad.

They were put through strong emotional events, more than the Human and Fae Essences were. They were even abused intentionally just to make the caring Human and Fae beings feel anguish and remorse. This in turn made all the Spirits grow more in size and power level once out of their bodies than if they received only moderate abuse.

What a sick program when you realize there's a way to do all this without any pain. You'll find out about that later in this book. There are new bodies coming without all this pain and suffering. Between seventy-two and seventy-eight percent of all abuse in life will be taken away. This could have been done in the very beginning. This is what happens when the controlling factor, the Original Male and Female, are composed of 27.5% negative frequencies, have never had even one life, and are selfish instead of selfless.

Fae Essence is different from Human Essence, but very close. The Fae were almost immediately given energy type bodies. They could make a physical body, walk around, and then release it. They didn't need the same physical requirements as the constant solid physical bodies of the Humans. To maintain physical form, and keep a solid body alive, you must consume physical matter. This puts a physical strain on everything in the physical realm.

My, look at all this wonderful abuse now. The Animals have to eat Plants and other Animals just to stay alive. The Humans have to eat Animals and Plants too. Remember, Plants are alive also. They are sentient beings. You can only talk to them with your metaphysical abilities, your Pineal Gland and Heart Energy mostly. They have no mouth to speak and are composed of a separate physical matter. They are however, living sentient beings.

All this is hard to take in until you, as a Human being, learn to open up your brain, heart, and gut intuition, and become your full self. This is no easy task to initially achieve but, once you get the hang of it, it becomes as simple as breathing. Like riding a bike, it's getting over the initial learning issue that's difficult. Well, back to the Essence lives.

While in body, the Humans were now becoming aware of the various different events occurring in their lives which left them feeling helpless. They started trying to talk to the sun to make it come out, stay out longer, and keep the cold of winter away. Then they started developing the "praise" concept.

Remember here that the physical or Third Dimension was totally unaware of the Second Dimension. They could only guess if anything else existed which fed into the "God" and "worship" programs already existing. The Spirit Guides who were talking in the ears of the physical beings they were assigned to, made them think worship was a good idea, they were forced to by the Original Angels. Here again was the aggressive self-praise demanded by the Original First Ones, now becoming a bit obsessed with feeding on it.

The Fae beings did not have the same stress levels that the Human beings did, due to their more Spirit type bodies. There was also less Fae energy than Human energy within the Original First Beings. This made Fae energy less important to them. The Fae didn't do too well in relation to extended stay in a physical body, it took too much effort.

Fae Spirits didn't enjoy physical bodies too much but the Human Spirit frequencies easily managed having lives in the lighter, less abusive Fae bodies. The Original First Beings didn't care much about the Fae, they were concerned more in growing the Human Spirits who were easier to control and greater in number.

Yes, we've all had lives in Human and Fae bodies. As you begin to awaken to your full potential you will be able to go back and remember bits and pieces of those lives. As mentioned earlier, waking up isn't the easiest thing you've ever done but once you have you'll never want to change back. You are more than you've ever known and have done more than you could ever imagine.

Your physical body also has its own DNA memory within it. Many of you are having lives in physical bodies that have strong DNA ties to other lives you've had here, especially here in the 2012 era. You wanted to be in bodies you were familiar with to help you awaken.

Your Earthen Spirit, the smaller part of your Core Spirit energy or Kundalini, about forty percent of it, also has memories of its own. Then there's you, the visiting Spirit, that has many memories hidden in your Spirit memory yet prevalent in your lives today. You've most likely heard of past life issues. These are emotional disturbances from past lives that you've carried into your current life because you didn't have enough time between your last life and this one to allow them to dissolve while in Spirit form. The average time for this, as we see time here on Earth, is about one hundred to one hundred and fifty years.

For example, Gaeira's Planet was 270 times the mass of Jupiter, the largest of the Planets now or then. Her time orientation was different. Because of her size, her days, being a single revolution, took much longer than the Earth so her days would be much longer compared to ours. It's all relative.

I've explained how Arae's had the most lives, over 10.846 trillion, but that they averaged 237 years each. Here on Earth that makes no sense at first but, because the Earth is so much smaller that Gaeira was, and Arae had over 4 trillion lives on her, it is a simple understanding. I needed to use Earthen years to express time as we see it here. Time exists everywhere but is expressed relative to the specific area its occurring in. Remember, time is merely the chronological occurrence of events, that's all, an expression of existence.

Getting back to the earliest Human and Fae lives, the body types were various as experimentation was rampant. The Original Male and Female were in a rush to get to the point where they could release the Souls. Some of the Human and Fae Spirits at first made bodies that were half Animal and half Human or Fae. This process only ever occurred before a "Planetary Civilization Format" was established.

Eventually the half Animal and Half Human bodies were removed as it interfered with the organized growth of a separate Animal and Human species, as well as the Fae. This is also why the five Adams and Eves were sent here, to correct this problem and provide a suitable body to have lives in. You'll find out more about this in just a bit.

The Human and Fae Essence beings had an average of a trillion lives each by the time the Original First Beings felt ready to release the Souls and start integrating them into the physical life format. This is when Creation's most horrific event occurred. The Original First Ones decided that if they destroyed Gaeira's Planet, while all this life was on her, they would understand the worst case scenario for abuse to a being. At least that's what they told everyone once out of body.

Although there is some truth there, they really wanted to abuse the fields of Essence as hard as they could before they terminated this harsher, more difficult life format. They had Arae destroy her body, her Planet. I will never be able to forget that, never. Gaeira and I are very close. Her physical body was destroyed, not her.

One evening I was sitting at the sliding glass door facing my back yard when I saw a soft glowing yellow/white light dancing about in a circular yet non defined pattern over a particular spot next to my Fae Beech tree. This tree is where, as time went on, the Fae would send me little gifts of Earth and stone. I actually had a well-known geologist try to analyze it and he just got mad when he couldn't and I told him what it was. Anyway, I saw the light was a little wood nymph, a female. I went into her head, or focal point when we're in energy bodies, and thanked her, telling her I would retrieve it in the morning.

The next morning I walked right up to it, a somehow special stone of great significance to myself personally, and brought it into the house. I cleaned it and then Gaeira told me to sit down and flow into the stone. Well, I did. It was necessary for me to understand the worse of all my mistakes and the pain involved for everyone. In the next few moments my life changed, for the better, but became more serious than I could have ever expected. I have spent my life caring for others at any cost to myself, its just what I am, like breathing. I was not prepared for what happened..

As I relaxed holding the stone with finger tips from both hands, I flowed deep into the past to a wondrous, beautiful Planet where live abounded everywhere. I was only there a few seconds when I saw the Planet being ripped apart, first near a stream where a large male Animal similar to a deer stood. Then I saw the Planet softly explode, killing everything on it.

At that moment, and only for about 5-6 seconds, I felt the fear, pain, anguish, and suffering of all on it, including Gaeira herself. My body was literally jerking so hard I lifted off the chair I was sitting on a few times. I have never even seen seizures like that. How can I efficiently explain an experience like that? I can't and don't want to try.

I held the stone but released my connection to it, in great shame. I was responsible for that crime against my format, not as this flesh prison, but what I really am. I was disgraced, dishonored, and flowing tears like a river. I'll fight any 100 men and never stay down, not till I'm dead, it's just what I am. However, I am proud of being a compassionate loving man. I just don't like to show this emotion, my pain, in public.

I went back to the incident and looked at what happened, I needed answers now as to how I could ever do this. I saw the Original First Being Halves telling me to do it and explaining why. I simply said no. They insisted and I maintained my refusal to comply. Then Gaeira came up to me and told me it was ok, to do it. I made a mistake and complied to her wish, not theirs. I can't explain how much I regret this.

I have often expressed how awesome Gaeira is and how we have such a strong connection. This is a big part of it. I can never forgive myself and neither can she. As I let go of that stone I saw her looking at me with great anger, even though she told me to do it. I understand why. She wanted me to know more about my past, to remember the pain and suffering that I had caused for so many, that I might never forget while in this body the suffering that I had caused.

I'm not an arrogant man, I'm quite selfless, but this brought me to a place of self-reflection that I had never been to. I felt being told to do this. I felt the indecision involved not ever expecting to comply, just as I felt Gaeira's anger. I sat there in my chair, surrounded by all my Animals, completely ashamed and disgusted with myself. Want to talk about taking a serious look into yourself?

Almost all people can't understand me. I don't expect anyone to. I was warned at the beginning of all this that I would be an island. I have always had many friends, yet at the end of the day was quite alone. I was always aware of things other people were scared of, like knowing who was calling on the phone while it was still ringing, knowing that certain things were about to happen, etc. I was self-aware and it bothered almost everyone, especially as a child.

Heck, now I've been going into people's brains and bodies changing them, awakening their abilities as well as changing them physically for the better. When the FBI and Homeland Security came to my front door together they just wanted to try to understand what I was. They even asked for some Essenite. I told the gentleman from Homeland Security, or insecurity as I like to say, that he really wanted Star Essenite and that I would get some for him. He was puzzled how I knew what he wanted although he said the wrong thing.

This same gentleman kept wondering why his agency considered me such a threat when he already knew I used almost all I had to care for Animals and others while living in a dump of a house. He saw all the feeders I had out for the Animals as well as the homes everywhere I had made for them. He could also feel my heart energy and that surprised him. The FBI gentleman was a seer but completely unaware of it.

I gave them some information that I could never have had access to and even told them what their jobs were, who they were inside, how they felt about things, and a little more. The FBI dude was cool but his thought process was starting to bother me. When they walked away he kept saying in his head, "He's fruit loops, a carnival act, how'd he know that?"

The gentleman from Homeland Security had an image in his head, a white ceramic type plate with a piece of apple pie on it. The thought process here was that I was about as much a threat as a piece of apple pie left out overnight. I had to touch his head for the full thought. He didn't understand why his higher ups considered me a threat when he already knew I was the opposite, I help, I serve.

Hell, all I want to do is my job. These books are a big part of that. I call myself Creation's Janitor. I like that, do what I can for everyone while they're not even in the building, behind the scenes. That's where I'm going, can't wait to get there. That was a lot of talk about myself but I want you to know a little bit about me and what y'all mean to me.

CHAPTER 5
THE PLANETS AND STARS CONTINUALLY FORMING

Let's start talking about everything else going on around Gaeira now, the Universe was growing. Actually, it still is. You can almost say it's running in an "automatic pilot" mode. It was created to grow on its own. It's not sentient itself but it's full of sentient Spirit everywhere. It's a community with new buildings growing all the time. Spirit, being sentient energy, has to be put into its bodies, that's all. The Planets receive Female Universal Essence and the Stars have Male Universal Essence placed in them. Then the physical beings, all of them, are placed on the Planets. That's Plant, Animal, Human, and usually Fae. It's usually Plants, Animals, Fae, and then Human, in that order.

The Universe, as discussed in the first book, was created from expanded and highly transmutated heavy, that is dense, particulate matter. Each Planet started as one small piece of dense physical substance. The different energies available were used to create the Stars to help maintain life everywhere as well as an energetic balance within the individual galaxy itself.

Many astrologers, astronomers, and scientists talk about the possibility of an energetic event occurring when Planets align with each other. Well, there is. The amount of energy within the event depends on the size of each Planet, how many of them are there, and their distance from each other. The Stars also have an effect on this.

How would this happen? Each Planet, with or having had life on her, has powerful Female Planetary Essence within it. This can be seen as a form of electromagnetic energy. When you line them up, providing they're within a given distance to each other relative to their size, there's a partial sharing or connection between their energy fields which can often be measured. Our family from other Planets actually uses this energy field when available.

Already covered in the first book is the explanation of our moon's mysterious glow, the energy that comes from it. The moon itself is simply a mass with no energy in her other than what's necessary to maintain physical cohesion. The moon has no Spirit of her own, no Planetary Essence. So why is there something strong behind her glow? Here's what happens.

The energy from the Sun is reflected off the moon. This actually softens its energy to a more comfortable level for us. Then this Male Universal energy passes through Gaia's outer energy field, that which flows through the Earth. What actually touches us is softened Male Universal energy mixed with Female Planetary energy that's already a part of what these bodies are. This is a very balanced and relaxing energy for us. This relaxation is a major reason for the full moon having been thought of as romantic. You can also see better but the light is alluring to us.

Make no mistake about if folks, there is no singular Universal Spirit Being but there are Planets with Universal Female Essence in them as well as all the Stars which have Universal Male Essence in them. Their Spirit Essence frequencies are still a small part of Source Spirit.

Let's take a look at our own home now, Planet Earth.

SECTION II -
THE EARTH IS BORN

CHAPTER 1

AS THE EARTH WAS FORMING; GAIA'S ENTRANCE

As the Earth was slowly becoming solid enough to have life on her, Gaia placed herself inside her. She helped her solid mass come together just as when we make our own bodies when not having a life and just visiting another Planet without an existing life format already present on it. The Planets take longer to make a body, that's all. There's a lot more involved in it. They help it come together and form a body of physical mass able to create and maintain life upon her.

It can be a little difficult to understand, but there is sentient life in almost everything around us. Gaia had to put together all the necessary components to both create and maintain life upon her. This is no simple task. The Plant, Animal, Fae, and Human life upon her would have to be orchestrated to live and grow together physically if not in some sort of harmony, with each other. It's an abusive format controlled by the Original First Ones and all Gaia had to work with.

All Planets need the basic building blocks for life available to them. Gaia, over a period of time after creating bodies for having lives, had a new metal placed into her. This was the element of Iron. Iron was not an original part of Gaia's body, the Earth. It came here later in meteorite showers, one after the other, until there was a large supply of it here. Iron is a very dense, heavy material. Negative frequencies were enhanced by it due to its ability to slow down other frequencies. This is not a bad thing by itself. It would however have a negative effect on life here, especially the Fae.

This is part of the truth to the old folk lore tale of the Fae beings having issues with it, actually being afraid of it. Once swords were made, the Fae found that it could actually kill their Earthen energy bodies. This is because in the beginning when their bodies were made, there was no iron. They were, and still are, constructed of softer materials containing no iron at all. They had a hard time dealing with it as it was not already part of them. They were unfamiliar with it. They were not able to move their energetic bodies through it. They no longer are and it can no longer cause them any grief. Gaia has now assimilated Iron ore it into her energy body.

As far as it's effect in Human lives, that's easy to see. Iron has been used to make many things we put to good use. Its been used to make kitchen utensils, major supports for many tall buildings, and much more. The problem is, there are the other things that have iron in them.

Iron is now a necessary part of the Human body. It promotes a little more of a negative effect on the frequencies within it. This further slows down your personal Spirit while in that body. It's also used for large vehicles of war, guns, and other destructive things. It's not so much the physical things we make from it but the negative intentions that put it to such use. Iron is not a bad thing, it just slows frequencies down creating a tendency to be used in a more negative manner.

Iron also, on the other hand, can help give your body strength when you need it. Remember that its now an important part of these bodies. It was merely a tool for the Original First Ones to initially cause more grief in lives as well as further slowing down the Spirit's frequencies while in those bodies, creating a more negative environment to push you through.

There's one last thing I want to say about Iron Ores. The stone I call Unicornite, actually Bornite or Chalcopyrite, is infused with Unicorn energy. I explained Unicorn energy more extensively in the first book. Unicorn are not little fluffy ponies. Their energy is extremely powerful and aggressive. They have very high frequencies for the most part but can create energy fields able to break a physical body apart. The males are the most dangerous. Dragons and Unicorn are very close family members. Remember, they are the two most powerful individual Spirit Fields in Creation. They come from clean Source Spirit and are the strongest fields within it, being that of love, compassion, and fortitude. Let's emphasize the fortitude part of them.

Getting back to the stone, its most common name today is Peacock Ore. This material is extremely aggressive towards any negative or abusive energy due to what's in it, of course. It literally attacks it. Here now is a form of ore, in the Iron family, used in a positive fashion. In the end, all things are what we make of them. It's how we use what's available to us that matters most. It does however slow down our frequencies, which our physical bodies already do to us.

This extensive discussion of iron describes only one of the many elements which help compose Gaia's body, the Earth. Try to understand there's an importance to each element on her as well as how they function together. Then there's the issue of how all the Spirit beings in all the different bodies are made to live together, or against each other I should say. Just look at how the Human bodies have been attacking this beautiful Planet, the one our bodies originally came from. This is nothing short of insanity.

Here is the ultimate abuse of Gaia. This is our shame that so many wear proudly, like a badge of honor or accomplishment. We destroy the land we live on, we pollute the seas we eat from. We even destroy the trees that give us the oxygen necessary to breathe, to continue our lives. How can this exist? What leads us to do this? This is Creation's great downfall, abuse. Disharmony, not harmony, is what prevails on our Planet. We have one of the most negative existences in all Creation right now. We were given a beautiful home, a loving mother, and trashed her. All this is for what, money, power? No, it's abusive greed, selfishness, and dishonor. If one doesn't respect themselves, how can they respect anything else?

This was all orchestrated by the Original First Being Male and Female beings. They used their servants, the Original Angels, to run your lives, control your actions, by going into your brains doing more than make you do what they wanted you to do. By going into your Hypothalamus Gland in your brain they literally made you "know" that you needed to do these things as if they were your own thoughts. For many of you they were not.

At times you were made to do something that is totally against your "character" as we would say. Once you did it you were immediately confused, often anxious in regards to trying to understand how you could do such a thing. That's simple to explain, they weren't your thoughts. People can be run like robots by the proper utilization of the Hypothalamus Gland. Its controlled by the other side, but that's how its done.

There has never been a devil, the Original First Beings never needed to create one. They already had their servants, the Original Angels, to do their dirty work. Remember, these Angels were made to be like that, they were like energetic robots but not quite. Look at Arch Angel Michael, a very close friend of mine. Here in 2015 he is being preserved, protected from the Source War by Arae. He will come out again. Almost all the other Arch Angels have been destroyed already in the fighting. Arch Angel Michael was created with the additional frequencies of fortitude as he was made a protector. He grew to understand Arae's actions as Creation's Protector. He grew to understand Compassion and Honor, without ever having had one life.

There are also other physical beings on this Planet, but not from here, that abuse her and us in ways you're not yet aware of. This is also about to be stopped abruptly and aggressively, by Arae and some of his children, the Drachk. The abuse upon this Planet will no longer be tolerated by the new upcoming Source Mother and Father.

The termination of this cancer will begin harshly in 2016, in space as well as the oceans and surface. This will be controlled yet violent, equivalent to the abuse that Gaia has being subjected to. These bodies belong to her, not us, and the other good people imprisoned here from other Planets will be released also. You will find out for yourselves what's been happening here on Earth for over 10 million years.

Before going any further we need to discuss Gaia's helpers, the Elemental Dragons. Let's take a look at them.

CHAPTER 2
EARTH'S ELEMENTAL DRAGONS

There are four groups, sets actually, of Elemental Dragons which help move different parts of Gaia's body including her atmosphere, the seas, the solid earth, and more. Each set assigned to this task are Spirit Mates, the two halves of the one whole. One is female and the other male. They originated from the same singular orb of Dragon Spirit.

On other planets the inhabitants have their own names from their own languages. Here we use the word Dragon. There was a time, actually a rather long period a long time ago, that there were actual physical beings on this planet called Dragons but right now I speak of the Dragon Spirits.

Dragon and Unicorn Spirit were released only one time. That's when Lilly and Arae's energy fields connected for the very first time, long before the first physical life. Lilly's energy has more of the Unicorn Spirit in it as Arae has most of the Dragon energy frequencies. That's where they all came from.

I have my own personal names for them, the ones they gave me in conversation with them. Leannae, I have used different spellings of her name as it's often difficult for me to put into our words, doesn't mind me offering her name. When you telepathically speak with others, whether in or out of body, the spelling of names can become difficult.

She is the Female Air Dragon and Arthuracus is the Male Earthen Dragon. In this manner Earthen means solid ground. These 8 Dragons are everywhere at all times. Spirit never sleeps. It can rest, be inactive, but never needs to sleep. That's only one of the advantages of not being in a solid body.

These 4 Dragon Spirit Pairs are very strong and dedicated to helping Gaia move her outer body. Gaia's heart is in the Earth's core. Understanding that a Planet is a living being is not easy for most. Remember that a mind, like a parachute, only functions properly when open.

The Dragons have protected people and regions from devastating natural catastrophes. The North American indigenous peoples, that we call Native Americans or Indians, would often take a double bladed axe and imbed it into a scratched design on the dirt on their property to ask the "Sky Spirit" to protect it from an oncoming storm. Many still do today. Let's get back to the other different bodies and their lives here.

CHAPTER 3
THE PLANTS AND CREATURES SETTLE IN

As Gaia continued building her initial body, there was such an abundant supply of water, she was able to create a vast supply of different types of marine life. Many different forms of singular and multi-cellular bodies were created which eventually led to easier creation of the new bodies for the visiting Spirits; Plant, Animal, Human, and Fae beings. These cellular bodies were not composed of Dual Spirit Cores as the bodies they were to help produce. They only contained the released Gaian Spirit within them.

This is apparent in most marine life today. Fish are made the same way. They have a Single Spirit Core. If you look at Shark and Dolphin you can see the difference between them. Sharks are very aggressive, often called killing machines. Reptiles and insects are similar also. They have only Planetary Essence within them, what they need to function in a basic existence manner. They're made to survive with little attachment to anything else.

Dolphin on the other hand, are living bodies with a Dual Spirit Core. They have a Kundalini as many call it. You can see more life in a Dolphin's eye. They're usually filled with Human Spirit now. It's amazing how other Spirits attack themselves as they do, like when Humans slaughter Dolphin in mass numbers. On one occasion I saw a man kill his wife and son from a previous life. He became ill and confused after it. He now abuses himself for it but doesn't understand why.

This is just one of many reasons why it's so important for everyone who can become aware, to do so. It's time for you to understand who you really are, where you came from, what's been done to you, and how things are about to change. Once you can see this for yourself, you're there. I can tell you about these things but until you see it, it can't become fully digested into your being. It will not be part of your wisdom until you can. Your gut intuition, coming from your Solar Plexus, will help you here immediately. Use it.

When you get a strong "gut feeling" about something, your Solar Plexus energy is at work. This is a very power form of your intuition, your abilities. Don't write it off as nothing. It's paramount. One of your strongest and most available abilities comes from this energy field. It's also about the hardest one to recognize because you use it every day.

Many people disclaim metaphysical, often called psychic, abilities. They have no idea that everyone uses them daily. Arrogance can bend or even destroy the value of it though. To disclaim metaphysical abilities is to deny yourself. How does a mother often know when their child is hurt even though they're in the next room, or even another country? Psychic witch hunters call that a mother's intuition, yet they can't actually prove how it happens. They denounce metaphysical yet call it intuition. That immediately makes them a hypocrite, not a good way to start proving that it doesn't exist. Anyway, back to life on Gaia, the Earth.

She now had many microorganisms living on and within her. From these small creatures, as well as the physical mass she was made of, the physical bodies could be made, with the help of herself and the visiting Spirit making the original bodies here. This has happened five times on this Planet. Each time there was a reset in the Earth's population it was necessary to repopulate the Planet. These are the breaks between the now 6 Ages here on Earth. This breakdown is found at the end of this book.

Each new age was enhanced through the reintroduction of the Adamic Race. The ten different clean Source Spirits which made up the five sets of the Adams and Eves, made their appropriate bodies to establish the basic Human body form to be replicated over and over again. We'll explain this in greater detail in the next chapter.

The Plant life, or flora, was the first sentient life here on Gaia's Planet, other than herself that is. It was an easy thing for the Plant Essence to come here, settle on the ground, meet with a portion of Gaia's Planetary Essence, and produce physical bodies with Gaia's help. This does take a bit of energy but is not hard to do, especially for a Planet.

The male and female Spirits were given bodies to compliment themselves, maintain their physical existence. There was the existence of two separate forms of most all the Plants. Some were both male and female. I believe we call that hermaphroditic in regard to Plants. Angels just call it Zhe, pronounced ghee, as I mentioned in book one while describing all the Angels.

The idea was for the male and female in all species to complement each other, so far as continuing their races anyway. We all know how the female black widow spider kills it's mate after mating, so much for romance with these guys. Here again is the aggressive nature of many of Gaia's creatures which are often used to help support the balance of the many types of physical life on her.

There are however, many insects here just to be a constant nuisance, a soft form of our continuous abuse system. Fleas, ticks, mosquitoes, locusts, and many more are only here to bother us, the Animals, and the Plants. They perform no necessary functions here other than a system of usually soft abuse for everything in body.

Now let's look at all the Animal life arriving on Earth.

CHAPTER 4

ANIMAL ESSENCE COLONIZES THE EARTH

Animal Essence Spirits began to come here in large numbers. It was their time to colonize the Planet. At first they made many different types of bodies. As each type was replaced with a newer version, part of their development, they were more suited to the environment and able to adapt to it. This, as with all living bodies, we call evolution. When a particular species can no longer adapt to the changing environment, or was no longer needed, it died off. This of course is what we call extinction.

Of course, in its arrogance, the Human race considering itself omnipotent, a collective form of a "God" now, has decided to kill off many of the beautiful Animals and Plants here to make themselves happy. What a disgusting trait. This is a disease that requires no negativity and is cancerous to all of us. It's called arrogance. Look at all the events that have occurred in the name of arrogance, that is, "God and Country." Remember the "Crusades" where the Christians were going to make the Muslim people serve their "God" instead of their own? This was bread into all of us through the intention of the First Original Being halves.

The Pope who initiated the Crusades was an eighty-seven percent negative Soul, just like Pope Benedict XVI who retired early when his heart was attacked twice by Arae in body August of 2012. August twenty-third Arae told him, telepathically, to leave or he would die of a heart attack soon. He publicly announced his resignation in November. He would not be allowed to stay in office. He had plans for another "Holy War" but on a much larger scale than the Crusades.

The former pope wanted to outdo his ancient predecessor. He even spoke out against Muhammad publicly in his home town, while still in office. The Spirit of Muhammad was actually Source Spirit but he was made to do what he did, just like the rest of us. Major events in our lives are, or at least were, controlled by the Angels put on us when we entered our bodies. They always have been. They were the controllers who made sure we did what the Original First Being halves wanted us to do. This was explained in greater detail in the Angel chapter of book one.

You see, things are not at all as you've been told. You've been abused harshly when it was neither necessary nor beneficial to you. You're also much more than you've ever been allowed to realize you are. There have been radical changes made to all Creation through the destruction of abusive beings in the Second Dimension though. These changes will protect and free you from what harshly controls your lives as well as your existence while out of body. They will soon be felt here.

Here is the heart, the information, the message, of this second book of the Creation Series. You have always been very powerful beings of Spirit having lives in bodies to evolve but were harshly abused, now dealing with the consequences from it. The abusive frequencies that all of you started to develop became hazardous to you and all Creation as well. This was seen by Lilly and Arae, who were very busy having lives, and finally did something about it. The timing was paramount to take action and the process is mostly finished now.

Speaking of timing, there were to be four volumes in the Creation Series but this book was condensed as I this body should cease functioning before more can be written. This information is paramount to the physical bodies as its the only true history you will have at this, the initial stage of your awakening. This is not only for the Earthen Human bodies but all physical bodies within Creation. This is also important to all our brother and sisters from other Planets and galaxies across our Universe, the physical dimension. They were here before us, and are still traveling the Universe. They are technologically advanced to a degree we cannot yet comprehend, but they are still not aware of what I'm writing about now. Nothing has ever been allowed to use its own mind freely or been able to see the Other Side with true clarity.

As we get back to the Animals I need to make a statement. Animal Essence Spirits have been serving all Creation since the beginning of physical lives and are leaving soon. They have new jobs in our new Creational format just now coming into being. Let's talk a little bit about Animal Essence Spirit itself.

Animal Essence is a powerful form of Spirit. Once you're able to calm yourself down enough to talk to them, you'll find that they are more intelligent than Human Essence or any others, as a whole. They have incredible fortitude, an unshaken format of honor, and one heck of a lot of heart energy. They will never lie to you, never.

Even while being continually abused they still strive to help us, teach us compassion and how to live in the moment enabling us to cope better with daily living. So few are aware of this, sad. They're givers of blessings yet are hunted and abused constantly.

Their contributions to all Creation will be legendary in future times. Now, let's get back to their introduction to the Earth.

Unknown to most our scientists there have been Animals here for a very long time, almost the beginning. Dinosaurs, the original reptiles here, and Animals have lived together almost from the start. There are actually caves found to have pictures of primitive men fighting dinosaurs with spears. Get a load of that. The truth never stays hidden forever; it just depends on who's hiding it being able to do so.

I'm not trying to beat up scientists. They put together their theories by accumulating any information they can find and create their hypothesis. They just need more complete data. It would really help if they knew how to flow inside themselves. Most scientists are Solar Plexus Core Orientated. That's why they go by their gut feelings. They just need to expand on it, that's all.

As Animals adapted to the harsh living conditions in Earth's early years, each of the first 5 cycles, they initiated stronger, more protective bodies and abilities such as blending into their terrain to escape predators. This lessened over time. The chameleon and anole still have such abilities, just not like they used to. They also telepathically communicated with each other more easily over greater distances. This was eventually decreased by the Original First Ones, increasing their level of abuse for everything.

In only a very short time, Animals and Humans were working together to stay alive, to commune with each other. For example, in Lemuria, or Mu as it's often called, the Humans and Animals always lived and worked together. Almost all the Humans back then were telepathic with Animals, before other Humans.

The Animals, for a while at least, easily talked with us. We lived with them in our homes as well as outside, and protected each other against the over aggressive reptile attacks. Remember, reptiles have only a single Core Spirit flow. This is not as in the

Annunaki here, Humanoid in nature but containing massive amounts of reptilian DNA.

As this interspecies telepathy greatly reduced the stress in both Human and Animal lives, it was slowly turned off by the Original First Ones. Today, Animals can still communicate with each other, just little with us. Metaphysically, they are stronger than us.

Since we already brought her up, let's go to Lemuria.

CHAPTER 5

LEMURIA

Lemuria was the name given to a physical community, a series of islands located in the Pacific Ocean. Hawaii was and still is its capital. New Zealand was and is its southern most point. Both their topographies are old and unique, very ancient. Their energy is as wonderful to feel as their physical beauty is to behold. If you ever get to go there, take a moment to relax, breathe deep, and let your heart flow out everywhere. You'll be surprised how good it feels when you pull it back in, your heart energy that is. Now, back to Lemuria's settling.

In her initial stages, there were many Souls of the second and higher stages of evolution coming here after the land mass cooled down and Plant life settled in. They were coming as Spirit and making their own bodies, with Gaia's permission and help. Some of them were making bodies that were half Human and half something else.

The Merpeople were one such group of beings, Mermaids and Mermen. Neptune was a powerful Merman in Lemuria. Poseidon was a Human that was actually in Atlantis. The people of Atlantis named a large section of the continent "Poseidia" in his name. That's also where Eadnae was, what others eventually called Eden. Eadnae is a name that came from the Greek language which is actually a modified and condensed version of Atlantean. We'll cover this in greater detail in the next chapter. Socrates spoke of it often, especially to Plato.

The Earth had been visited often by the older races in Creation mostly for its beautiful and medicinal flora. She was a paradise for many different life forms. There was an incredible bounty of riches on the Earth in the Plant life alone. Gaia was so beautiful then compared to now, after having been severely abused through the corrupt Annunaki disease now upon her. This was orchestrated by the Original First Being halves but the problematic Annunaki here were glad to comply. In all truth though, they were never aware of it.

The Annunaki are not a bad race, just aggressive from the Reptilian DNA they have. The ones running this Planet are a form of abusive tyrants, pirates so to speak. They steal, destroy, and revel in it the Earth's destruction as well as all on it. Their DNA has also severely affected our own for over ten million years now. The Annunaki people themselves are generous and rich in culture, hard to believe as you've been told the opposite for so long. Here's the difference between fact and fiction. Here's where your awakened abilities come into play, enriching your lives by guiding you properly through them, all your eyes having been opened.

There were about seven major islands in Lemuria. This number depends on where you make the distinction between major and minor. One continent was the largest, two more were close, and a fourth was just behind them in size. Then there were three more large land masses. The others were all smaller in size yet much larger than Hawaii is today. They all sank at different intervals from the pressure drop beneath the Earth's crust. This was done by the Original First Being Female.

Many different beings from different Planets were coming here now. Some decided to stay and form colonies here, mostly farming and mining communities. In the beginning, each of the different Planets involved in populating the Earth settled on separate islands. They soon began extensive DNA research helping to maintain their physical lives here, dealing with the Earth's atmosphere and other new conditions.

While we're discussing the older races coming here to settle, let's not forget that there were already other beings here, the Human and Fae Souls and Essence in the bodies they made themselves being part Human in composition, such as the Merpeople. There were many others also. The Earth was a curious place back then. Still, the richness and healing of the water, minerals, and flora was the reason for all the new colonization. There was also an abundance of Gold and Silver.

These new immigrants from other galaxies were found in many areas but each established a major presence on one of the islands, usually the smaller ones with less reptilian issues. For the most part they stayed away from the larger ones already colonized by the older established mixed body races. How these first beings here made their half-Human and half something else bodies was explained in detail in book one of the Creation Series but we'll go over it in short detail in the Atlantis chapter. Let's get back to the older visiting Human races now settling in here.

Some groups had harder times than others as their home Planet's environment was so different from ours. The Andromedian folk had a very hard time with the atmosphere as well as serious allergic reactions to much of the flora, the Plant life here. Remember, all physical bodies came from the Planet they were originally made on. They were made of components from that Planet in order to have lives on that Planet, not somewhere else. This is how DNA manipulation began on the Earth, on Gaia's body. Everyone settling down here was trying to help their bodies adapt to the different environment.

Communication was also an issue from time to time. They had their own High tech communication devices but tended to stay separate from the other colonies at first. As time progressed this began to fall away as they all realized they were "together" on the same Planet, each struggling to stay alive here. The early lives there were hard so the people would have to be of tough fiber, and they were.

Combating the Planetary composition imbalance within their bodies was a serious issue, not to mention dealing with the various life forms here, especially the reptiles. Although there were many different Animals here, it was the reptiles that caused the major issues. They were aggressive and destructive, killing with little or no reason. It wasn't just to eat but to destroy anything it saw as it considered it to be within its territory.

The reptiles, like most other life here, developed communities when they felt it necessary. They relentlessly hunted and destroyed whatever they ran into, usually in packs. This is why the Earth's surface was cleaned or should I say disinfected twice, bringing an end to the first two ages or timelines here.

The first two ages of civilization here on Gaia were ended by fire. This is to say volcanoes erupting and earthquakes releasing molten material from beneath the crust. There was also an abundance of asteroids added to the mix. The reptiles were also overrunning the Animal and Human bodies here, mass producing in large numbers and killing them off into extinction. This was the major problem with both of the first two ages. It was handled better in the third, fourth, fifth, and now extinct in the sixth age.

The end of the third age was only partially relative to reptile issues. Unlike the first two, there was now a growing concern over an advanced human race beginning to thrive here, highly adaptive Adamics with powerful metaphysical abilities. The Original First Ones decided it didn't fit into their desired timeline here so they destroyed it. These Adamics had become harder to control and that could not be allowed. Here came the ice age.

Getting back to the Lemurians, let's see how they survived together. As time went on, the scheduled runs from each colony's home Planet to the Earth decreased. This was partially due to the various hardships here but there was a war raging throughout space. Remember, these people came from very far away, some from our galaxy but mostly from others. Many of these people were ancient races of beings, the old ones. There was often one annual shipment from their originating Planet per Gaian year.

As a rule, many of the different colonies didn't promote inter-colony communication or association. They had no idea how their inter-mingling would affect their health, catching diseases for which they had no cure. They also didn't trust each other too much, for the most part, at first. Remember, many of them were at war with each other in space. As time went on, this changed. Some even began to intermingle with the half-human beings. A new age of compassion was growing here.

More and more individuals were meeting with each other, not only without harmful incident but the desire to celebrate their companionship on a Planet so far from their own. These people were natural explorers. They wanted to explore each other's differences as well as their similarities. A community was being formed through necessity.

Communication had always been an issue. Some of them were lucky or fortunate enough to access communication devices but others did the best they could. Here the simple laws of nature, of physical bodies, came into play developing the metaphysical abilities of those here. This is a law of Nature, not an act of the Original First Beings.

A few of the colonies actually made laws forbidding inter-colony communication. How nutty is that? It was difficult to enforce as survival will come first every time. There is also within Creation a powerful driving force. It was evident within the Original First Being when it decided to make itself two instead of one. It did this before doing anything else. I'm speaking of loneliness, the need for companionship. Its part of what we are. It's stronger in some of us than others, depending on the frequencies we're composed of. Explorers usually have less of a need for it but still it's a part of all of us.

Here's where a natural event occurred that might interest you, evolution in Earth's early history. Along with the desire and eventual need to communicate with each other, a new issue came about for the settlers as the reptilian threat increased. I'm not speaking of the reptilian Humanoids already here, but the reptiles themselves. They were now destroying the Human and Animal bodies in greater numbers, threatening their survival.

Being that the Humans and Animals were on Islands it was a little easier to handle the reptile issues there. The smaller islands were more easily cured of the issue yet never contained on the larger islands. It was handled, maintained as best as possible, but never successfully dealt with. There were too many reptiles and too little Humans and Animals. Here's where "evolution out of necessity" occurred.

The Scanner and Pineal fields in both the Human and Animals here began to develop quickly. There was a pronounced protrusion of the brain now sticking out in the forehead, where it reaches the top of the head, which would actually move slightly when they used it. The same event occurred when I started developing my abilities here. Does this give you a hint to what's coming? It should.

The old beings settling here understood telepathy. It was part of their ancient training and personal growth. Animals are filled with Animal Essence which is incredibly powerful, more so than the Human Essence and Souls. The Human and Animal bodies began to develop their brains in such a way as to communicate better with each other. Many Humans and Animals were now living together anyway, learning to communicate with each other the best they could. As the reptilian issue became worse, the "Scanners" of both the Human and Animal brains increased in size.

The Scanner, as mentioned earlier, is that part of the head where the forehead and top of the head meet. It's also where Remote Viewing develops within the brain. It's energy field starts just above the middle of the forehead where the energy field of the pineal gland concentrates itself and moves upward towards your Upper Crown.

Actually, both the Pineal and Scanner energy fields touch each other in the forehead. I found this to be evident the more I went into people's brains, working on both fields. After a while I started blending both fields together where they touched. I found this to help others in seeing better metaphysically, combining the High Definition focus of the Scanner with the multidimensional vision of the Pineal Gland.

Anyway, the Scanner is also the strongest ESP, extra sensory perception field the body has for this dimension. Telepathy comes from the middle/back section of the brain and goes in and out through the Crown. The Crown is attached to the Scanner through the hypothalamus gland. Before this body expires I'll try to make a video about how all your metaphysical abilities operate, flow, through the brain.

The Scanners of both Humans and Animals had to become stronger to sense the reptilian threat more effectively, just to survive. This kicked in the natural process of evolution. As this happened, the cross species telepathy increased. We could now communicate with Animals telepathically with greater ease. Survival demanded it.

Our foreheads back then had large lumps where they met the roof or top of our heads. As you would expect, it was more prevalent in some of the colonies and less in others. The DNA in these bodies comes from different Planets but we're all a strong majority of Earthen DNA. This came from the Adamic Races brought here in Atlantis and 4 other locations. We'll discuss this in the next chapter.

As things progressed, the Humans and Animals worked together protecting each other in their homes and while traveling through the jungles. As one found a problem they would alert others everywhere through their Crowns using their enlarged Scanners. This was not enough to erase the reptilian threat but it did help them survive. Again, it was a thing of necessity.

Eventually, the different communities became engaged with each other, one way or another. The Annunaki were on a small island back then and stayed to themselves. They were purists other than their forced cross breeding with the Adamic Races. This island was in the Northern area of the Lemurian community. They had issues with others as well as themselves. They were an overly aggressive and subversive people.

Lemuria eventually became a shining example of mutual Human and inter-species cooperation, other than the reptiles and Annunaki. It was a thriving community working hard together to survive and prosper in spite of the reptiles who were always a serious problem. Unfortunately this thriving group of islands, a massive success for all to be proud of, was not allowed to be maintained. This was another decision made by the Original First Being Male and Female.

Both halves of the Original First Being decided there was not enough abuse in their lives here to promote the desired sufficient growth of their Spirits while in physical body. It was time to slowly sink the islands by breaking the crust below them. As the islands began to submerge into the ocean, the Human and

Animal population were put into even greater duress not only by being flooded out of their homes but having been placed into closer quarters with the reptiles who were still killing and eating as many of them as possible.

This is as good a time as any to explain the aggressive nature of reptiles. It's both a DNA and Spirit issue, a combination of both. Reptiles like insects, do not have a Dual Core Spirit. They don't have a Kundalini as many call it. They have a singular Spirit moving through their bodies, that of Gaia our Planet's Mother. They exist only to exist. You have Dual Spirit Cores. The greater part of the Spirit within you is that of Human or Fae Spirit. The other part of your Kundalini or Dual Spirit Core is that of the Planet, a small part of Gaia released just over 11 million years ago Earth time.

This Planetary Spirit has one desire, to maintain it's physical body. It's strongest need is to have a large physical mass to bond with, an almost permanent one. Instead all these removed parts of Gaia have had are extremely temporary bodies of flesh, easily destroyed removing them from them. This is why many people hang on so dearly to their "lives" while in a body. That and the fact that almost everyone is unaware of who you really are, Spirit within a body, not the body itself.

Reptiles, fish, insects and others have no other Spirit inside to give it a deeper dual personality, allowing for a flow of stronger compassion. They feel only to survive, to perform certain functions not related to themselves as much as they are their purpose for being. Gaia is a loving being, Planetary Essence, but she has not been tortured by being placed, abused, and removed from so many different physical bodies for so many million years.

Well, back to Lemuria sinking in stages. Forcing the Human and Animal bodies to scramble for higher ground, while having to deal with a stronger reptilian threat, was an acceptable abuse format for the Original Ones. Now the Spirits growth would be sufficient for their needs, or should I say their wants. With them it was the same thing. Remember, the harder the life the greater the increase in growth of the Spirit once removed from the body it was in. This destructive pattern will eventually be removed from all Creation on all levels.

Lemuria's destruction was a horrible loss, even more than Atlantis. Then again, everything existed only to please the wants and desires of the Original Ones anyway. That's just how they thought. That is why Arae eventually destroyed them. They made him Creation's protector, very powerful with almost limitless fortitude in the true beginning of Creation.

They had no idea he would develop compassion, honor, and a sense of equality through having so many lives and caring for others. They were also unaware that the immense concentration of fortitudinal frequencies they used to make him would allow him to grow so strong so fast. That was their final undoing as well as the other cleaner yet abusive and arrogant Source Spirit. You'll find out more about this in later chapters.

Eventually all the islands sank except for the highest parts of Hawaii and New Zealand. These islands and more made up the legendary community of Lemuria. Lemuria was not just a group of islands; it was a successful community expressing and proving the compatibility of different Human races and Animal species being able to thrive together. All this was done in spite of the wishes of the Original Ones. Man, what a loss for Creation. Can we use that now or what?

CHAPTER 6

ATLANTIS

Atlantis was a thriving but more aggressive community than that of Lemuria. Here's why. The Adamic Race was initially introduced to the Earth here in Atlantis, after Lemuria's inhabitants were already coming together. The Red Adamic Race was the first of the five Adamic couples to arrive.

All the Adamics, as they've come to be called, came here as Spirit and made their own bodies from the materials existing nearby. This is the cause for the different skin colors still present today. The red skin color was made from all the volcanic matter and crystals there. I remember holding sand in my hand in the ocean with crystals in it as the water washed the sand away.

Over time some of the Red Adamic Race, and later the others, were physically forced into Annunaki cross breeding. These cross-breeds became overly aggressive causing many problems. They were the reason for the Red Adam to tear down the Crystal Power Pit that he had made. We'll discuss that later also. This is also how reptilian DNA was placed into our bodies.

This was the desired event of the Original First Being halves. They knew this would cause more abuse through aggressive behavior as it spread throughout the population, just another tool for them to use in growing Spirit through abuse while in body.

The other four Adam and Eve pairs landed on other parts of the Planet and made the other original skin colors out of what was there. This was touched on in the first book but will be covered in greater detail in a few moments, as well as the many half-Human and half-Animal bodies already having lives there. Let's take a look at how that happened.

The introduction of the Adamic race here was because of the attempted contamination of the Animal and Human evolution scheduled for the Earth. There were separate bodies for Animal Essence as well as Human Spirits. Conforming to this rule was necessary for the proper growth of both species here. This was an important factor in controlling the abuse system here.

It was Lilly and Arae who were to deal with this issue. Lilly's eyes emitted the energy within her, a full deep beautiful love. Everything and one followed her through affection, nothing else. Arae had strong love but was needed to build the dimensions and barriers here as well as everywhere else. After having helped Arae lead the half-Human and half-Animal beings to lower dimensions, Lilly became the first Queen of Fae here on Earth. We'll get back to how this situation and how it came into being in just a bit.

I want to mention here that Edgar Cayce has put out a lot of good information about Atlantis. I do want to mention a few things though. Where he speaks of the two opposing factions there, those of the "Children of the Law of One" and "The Children of Benial", he was actually trying to say Denial, not Benial. There were those who believed in one Supreme Being and those who denied such a thing, that's all.

He also mentioned his thoughts that there was a large Spirit, Christ Consciousness, or something that he called Amilius. There is no Amilius. He was trying to say Aramaeleous. It was difficult in his "trance" state of mind, that's all, no big deal. Everyone and everything, in and out of body, makes mistakes. It's part of existence itself. There never has, or will be, anything perfect. Perfection is only legitimate as a goal relative to self-improvement.

When Edgar Cayce would prepare himself to allow his primary Spirit Guide to talk through him, the process caused him to slur his words on and off. Edgar Cayce was an incredible person who had a heart the size of Texas, so to speak. I have nothing but love and admiration for him. He was a self-less individual who cared about the many instead of himself. His Soul is having a life in a female body at the moment. He was in the Chicago area.

At this point I need to say the Soul in David Wilcock although awesome, was not that of Edgar Cayce. David's Spirit energy is Solar Plexus orientated with a good dosage of Heart energy. The DNA of his physical body is similar to that of Edgar Cayce, close but not a complete match. David also has the same Spirit Guide that Edgar Cayce had. This Spirit Guide is Human Essence and very strong. As he talks to David he feeds him direct knowledge, and understanding, of things that happened when he was Edgar's Spirit Guide.

This would lead Mr. Wilcock to believe he was Edgar Cayce. How could it not, without his being properly informed, being able to see this for himself? His Spirit Guide should have informed him of the situation. This would be the honorable thing to do as his Spirit Guide. Human Essence has issues just like everything else.

*Here's a note for you. This Human Essence individual, the above mentioned Spirit Guide for both men, just told me that he felt it wasn't necessary to do so. Find here one of the truths of Human Essence, it tends to be arrogant and selfish. There is no level of negativity necessary to develop arrogance and selfishness. *

Sometimes, when a person has similar physical characteristics as another from the past, they were the same person. One such example is the Soul that was in the body of Tesla, who has a lot of the same DNA in his body today looking almost exactly like his last life.

The more you flow into yourself, relax your core energy, the stronger you will become and the more you will see. This increases your understanding of what's real, your personal wisdom. Please remember that previous lives are often easier for you to see for others than yourself.

CHAPTER 7

THE SERPOIAN AND ANDROMEDIAN COLONIES

This chapter was omitted from the first printing of this book. I'm not a writer, only an author and I was fighting all the problematic issues on the Other Side while writing it. I omitted a complete chapter in the first book of this series, "Creation: It's Beginning And Your Origin". That was the chapter on the most popular Elves of Fae, the Sidhe. All we can ever do is the best that we can. Why expect anything else? That would only lead to frustration and more difficulty in doing a proper job at that moment. The "Perfection Thought Process" was created to frustrate you in body, make your life harder, more miserable. Accepting it is allowing more difficulty into your life. Now back to the Serpoians.

The Serpoian people from the Zeta Reticuli section of space had colonies here throughout the First and Second Ages on Earth. They started thinning out in the Third Age. Their DNA was used by the Yellow Adam and Eve in creating the Yellow Adamic Race here. They were located around Japan, often living in large ships in the sea there.

These people are intelligent and like to keep to themselves. They also realized the constant threat of the reptilian life always present here, a dominant factor, in Earth's early ages. Before the end of the Third Age they had, for all intents and purposes, left the Earth.

CHAPTER 8
ENTER THE ROGUE SOULS

(The Origin of Greek Mythology and More)

Before Lemuria and Atlantis were colonized, there were many Souls, and some Human and Fae Essence, who came here to visit, to explore Gaia's body while in a physical body themselves. How does this happen? How does a Spirit make or get put into a body? Here's another question that has perplexed us through the ages. It's simple.

The visiting Spirit floats to the Planet surface and asks the Planet for permission to travel upon her, to explore her physical mass. As long as there is not an existing life format already on her, she will allow it or not, her choice. The reply is more often yes than no. Then the process begins, making the physical body. Before going further we need to mention that there is a time limit for the visiting Spirit body to remain in this newly created physical form. We'll cover this in just a bit. If I'm not mistaken, this has already been mentioned in Edgar Cayce's book on Atlantis.

When seeing things for others I have to concentrate my own energy already there and focus on whatever it is I need to look at. It's an effort that takes away from other things I'm already doing which are also important. When you try to access memories, you literally go back in time and look at them again. Didn't know you astral-projected so much did you? That's why memories are often so fuzzy. You're seeing them through your pineal gland, your third or mind's eye. This is for those of you who are Pineal field orientated, and some Heart.

Those of you who are Solar Plexus orientated usually see this through your Scanner energy field. It's located just above the Pineal energy field, where your forehead meets the top of your head. You usually see it more clearly than Pineal orientated people, but not always. If you look at people who have a "photographic memory" you'll find their usually Solar Plexus orientated. It's a simple fact, that's all. Now back to the making of physical bodies.

Once the agreement is made, the Planetary Essence will send a previously released portion of its own Spirit to meet with the visiting Spirit. Then they work together with the physical mass that Gaia sends up to them. The three individual Spirits then create the physical body. It closes up, finishes it composition, at the Solar Plexus energy region or Chakra. This event is the same for all life on each separate Planet.

The Planetary Essence brings the material and additional energy necessary for the two other Spirits to move the physical matter around creating the body. This is called Transmutation. The visiting Spirit is usually about sixty percent of the Spirit within the newly formed body. There's another issue to be dealt with here.

Existing rules within Creation's format, as well as simple physical laws, come into play here. The visiting Spirit has a time limit to explore the Planet before it must release the body. If it doesn't, it has to have a full life on it. Here's one cause of the half-Human and half-Animal incidents. Some never let go of these bodies in time. Why would a Spirit want to be in such a body? Here's what's mostly behind that.

As mentioned already, before there was a format of life placed upon this planet brought to us by the Adamic Adams and Eves, some of the Souls who had reached the second stage of evolution came here as Spirit to explore the planet in a physical body. The "Soul Stages of Evolution" are covered in book one, "Creation: It's Beginning And Your Origin."

It's only the rarest of occasions for a Human or Fae Spirit to have a life in such a body. We do a lot of things, as Spirit, to understand as much as we can about most everything there is. Most of us do have our limits but remember that as Spirit we have feelings which are not as "alive" as when in body. This is due to the fact that we are not attached to physical mass experiencing physical abuse. Our fingers are not stuck in the socket, so to speak.

The longer the individual Planetary Spirit released from Gaia stayed in the body, the more it wanted to stay there. They were created to attach to a Planet, not a temporary body of flesh. Their desire to hold onto these bodies is very strong. Its most often when our physical body's life is about to end. The Earthen Spirit does not want to give up the body, to release it. All the fear and non-sense generated by religions just makes it worse.

If you think about it, that was a good thing for the Original Ones who wanted everything to suffer in body as much and long as possible, forcing them to grow in size and strength which would serve them better later. We do have joy, but how much? The Original First Beings learned a long time ago that a certain amount of joy was necessary to keep the Spirits in their bodies, not committing suicide to get out. I was told in church at a very young age that "God" won't give you anything you can't handle. That was a little confusing. If this was true, why did suicide exist?

I also couldn't figure out how a perfect, all forgiving, all loving "God" could then create a "Hell" to viciously torture and punish those he was mad at forever. OK, where's the sense in that thought process? Here's another religious concept that denies itself. Christianity, as well as all the others, is full of control in the form of lies, deceit, and false hope. It's the false hope that bothers me the most. We all need a good dose of real "Hope" to keep us going every day.

I see as it is, a simple matter, just like I see the inside of your brains when I work on them, or other things I mention in consult that I shouldn't be aware of. You can all do the same thing. It's a matter of relaxing and feeling yourself flow outwards as Spirit, sentient energy. Finding a calm place, taking relaxed normal full breaths, and just feeling what's around you. That's how you connect to all the free information in the field as well as everything else available in the 2nd Dimension, known also as the Other Side. Now back to our Greek Mythology origins, the half-Human and half-Animal physical bodies.

Some of the Souls that came here originally, being of the second stage of Soul Evolution, decided to make bodies which were mixed with Animal and Human characteristics for different reasons. Initially they wanted to have a "better" body for exploring the land, the Earth. A horse can run faster and cover more territory than a Human. It would also help protect you from being eaten by the reptiles already here. There were a lot less of them back then though.

Then there was the concept of a large bull with Human features to be able to handle contact with the aggressive life forms already here, against mostly the reptilian ones just mentioned. Some of the others who decided to make their own bodies here with Gaia's assistance made other physical life form combinations. Some even made Human-Plant bodies. Some people did it just for the "unique" experience, people being Spirit that is.

Some Souls were trying to understand the lives that Plants and Animals had. A few were convinced to do so to serve others already here, to work for them once they were offered something of selfish value. There were leaders already here that tempted incoming Souls, who hadn't made a body yet, to make a body which they could put to their own use with no concern of the life of the Soul who was making the body. These were the earliest abusive leaders of the Earth, before the eventual reign of the Reptilian Humans, the problematic Annunaki. The Annunaki are an incredibly powerful race with deep culture and strong passion. Its some of their negative ones that settled here.

There hybrid bodies were causing many problems, one of which was the attempted intermingling of both the Human and Animal Evolution here. This was never allowed to exist for long. It was against the current Creation life format. Eventually things had gotten so out of hand that something had to be done about it. Enter now the Adamics; Lilly, Arae and nine of their personal family members. The later 4 times the Adamics came here there were only eight. Lilly, the Red Eve, had to make the Fae bodies with Arae and then stay with them as Arae stayed in our dimension to take care of things here. The Adamics only came five times.

CHAPTER 9
LILLY AND THE FIVE ADAMS AND EVES BRING ORDER

(The Half Human - Beings Are Removed)

As Arae, Lilly, and their family members arrived, there were already many of the half-Animal and half-Human beings here. They made up between thirty to forty percent of the Atlantean population, depending on what time period you wish to look at. The arrival of the Adamic Race was initiated to bring an end to their permanent existence in our Third Dimension. When Lemuria finished sinking many found their way to Atlantis. The vast majority of them were removed to lower dimensions here but a few that remained for a while, until it was necessary to finish the relocation process. Some were honored guests, some not.

All this information was available in the great Library of Alexandria. It was raided two times. The first raid destroyed about a third of this invaluable information. This was done by two large tribes of nomads from the East as well as the West. They fought each other in the village as well as through the library itself. A lot of the information was stolen as well as destroyed.

The second time was the Christians fighting for "God" to stop the "Evil Words" from spreading. Wow, what a concept for a loving omnipotent being. I remember that time a little too well. It was one of my female lives. I was the "Librarian" who was in care of the place. I was attacked by eight men and sliced to death with some kind of large sharp shell, an Abalone of some sort. I always had deep emotional issues when I saw one of these shells, never knowing why until I traveled to that time and found out. I was being called many things but I distinctly remember them calling me the harbinger of evil or something that translates into that thought process.

Here again, this was all made to happen by the Original First Being Female. She always ran people's lives through the use of the Angels she put on them as she placed Spirit into the physical bodies at birth. This is covered in greater detail in book one. That's why that book had to precede this one. You have to know the players on the field before you can fully understand the game. That's not the best analogy but will work for now. Life is not a game.

Some of the information, directly from the Library of Alexandria, is under the feet of the Sphinx. So are some of my personal artifacts brought directly from Atlantis. Their exact location will eventually be exposed. The Egyptians will find them when it's time. They've already found some of them but only a few. Water has been keeping them away, protecting these items until the proper time for their release. Let's get back to the Adamics.

Lilly and Arae were always the ones who came to a planet to straighten out this hybrid body issue. Here on Earth they brought four smaller released parts of themselves, all Spirit Mates. They would arrive as Spirit, make their own bodies, and begin. Within two weeks of Lilly and Arae's arrival the other four sets of Adams and Eves arrived, along with the secondary Red Eve, to provide the body format for reddish skinned Humans to have lives in. The famous Martin Luther King Jr. was actually the Tan Adam who, along with his Source Spirit Mate, made the Tan or Middle-Eastern Race five times on this planet. His Spirit hangs over the Middle East even today, waiting to be of more assistance. He'll do so very soon, its just not time yet.

The Adamics have done this five times here on Earth. The Red Adam and the Red Eve, also in body here now suffering with the rest of us, created the Red Race five times. Lilly was only here for a short time during their initial visit. She, as mentioned before, became the first Queen of Fae after helping Arae remove the half and half bodies. Arae joined her down there after finishing his life as the Red Adam as well as taking trips down to her regularly. They are inseparable.

Lilly and Arae relocated the half – Human and half – Animal beings to lower dimensions as Arae made them. They were to be relocated, not destroyed. This is why Lillith was called the great seductress and mother of demons. Her beautiful eyes grabbed the attention of others and they followed her and Arae down to the lower dimensions where they still live today. They were promised their own world and received just that, a land away free of the Humans now becoming aggressive against them.

Arae sealed up the dimensions he built with energy barriers invisible to the physical eyes so they had no way to leave. Almost all of these physical beings were removed from the Third Dimension, the one we live in. A few were left here about another hundred years but eventually all were either removed or eventually passed away, died.

This didn't just happen in Atlantis. It happened across the planet. All the Adams and Eves did the same thing. Each Adamic pair was sent to the largest group in a certain area. Arae built the dimensions and barriers while the others led them there. The greatest issue was in Atlantis. That's why Lilly and Arae went there directly. They were the strongest so they dealt with the largest concentration of them.

This was all done because to prevent the contamination of the Animal and Human physical body evolution here. There were separate bodies for Animal and Human Spirits. As a strong rule, only Animal Essence would be in Animal bodies. Conforming to this rule was necessary for the proper growth of both species here as well as maintaining the abuse regulation to different Spirits, Animal Essence being the strongest aside from Source.

There was no argument between the first Adam and Eve as suggested by the many lies of "Genesis" from the bible. Lilly was doing her job, that's all. It's amazing how rumors get started but it's not so amazing when lies are made up, put in print, and then glorified to use as a tool to control the masses. At a young age I was forced to be involved in a church, fit my parent's needs. I never read the bible though, didn't like it. Genesis really pissed me off even as a child of very few years, never knew why until I started awakening. I knew there was something wrong with it so I stayed as far away as I could. Well, let's get back to Atlantis, Lemuria, and the new problems arising there.

CHAPTER 10
THE ANNUNAKI BEGIN THEIR SUBVERSION

O K. Here's where things started becoming more aggressive, more abusive not just between ourselves but with everything else. It all started just over ten million years ago, in Atlantis more than anywhere else. It was initially a slow paced worldwide event but accelerated rapidly in Atlantis. This was due to the nature of the bodies of the Red Race being made from such powerful Spirit, like that of the Drachk, Creation's first physical. This will be covered in detail in book 3.

The Red Adamic Race was literally created by Arae when he made the first such body in the beautiful city of Eadnae, located in the country known as Poseidia, on the Atlantean continent 10.572 million years ago. Arae was made the strongest Spirit in existence as his job was to protect and serve the Original First Beings as well as Creation itself.

When he made his Red Adamic body it was incredibly powerful. As his energy bonded with the material here on Earth while forming it, his fortitude became a physical part of it. He also was not able to be controlled by the Original Male and Female as he wasn't placed in one of the physical jails our bodies now are. On top of this he was able to use many metaphysical abilities such as telekinesis. This received a lot of attention from the others already here and controlling others. Newly arriving Souls were now copulating making more Adamic bodies. They did not have the same abilities of the original Adamics yet were very strong physically with enhanced metaphysical abilities, telepathy and other forms of intuition. These new bodies brought a certain sense of order to Earth's new population. This was to be the initial breed of bodies for the Earth which would soon be changed by all the other races now here, the Reptilians more than any others.

As Arae and the Lilly began creating children, they were all more powerful than anything else on the planet. This did not go unnoticed by the Annunaki here. They already wanted to take over this planet, to subdue and control it. Hey, that sounds a lot like the book of Genesis in the Bible, doesn't it? Gee, how about that? That's not a coincidence.

Genesis is one of the oldest, most controlling abusive lies existing today. It tells you that you're all sinners and therefore being abused by your perfect, all loving, all forgiving God that also made hell to viciously punish you forever. Yeah, not much sense in that. Religions are ridiculous when you just step back and look at them with an open mind.

Many Christians are awaiting Jesus' return yet who would know him if he returned? They said any prophet coming will be a false prophet so how will they know him in a new body? Doesn't this prove reincarnation to be a reality? Isn't that against their religion also? Heck, check out Matthew 17; versus 9-13. Jesus said that Elijah came back in the body of John the Baptist and was beheaded. That's called reincarnation.

Do you want to hear something funny though? The Spirit inside the body of Elijah was Source Spirit from Lilly and Arae.

That same Spirit was also in the body of John the Baptist. Here lies just one of the twisted words in your religions. They take a little truth, something they're not even aware of, and turn it into fiction, something now used against you. This was orchestrated by the Original Male and Female, the ones demanding your worship. They used to run your bodies through the use of their servants, the Angels. They made the 3rd Dimension and more. Do you think this little thing an issue for them?

Anyway, the Annunaki realized the potential of mixing their own DNA with that of the Adamics, especially the red ones. They were initially hoping to gain access to the raw power exhibited by Arae, the original Red Adam. The Adamics would have no part in this so the Reptilians here began forcing such an event whenever they could. Rape in slavery became their primary tool for mixing the two species.

This was orchestrated by the Original First Being Male and Female, part of their plan for future aggression and abuse for the Earth and all on her, Animal, Plant, and Planetary life. Nice beings, those two Original First Ones, really caring and loving gods. They were anything but compassionate, never showing any concern for the physical bodies. They wanted all to suffer as much as possible yet not enough for them to commit suicide. Again, this was controlled abuse used to create maximum growth of the Spirits within the bodies. Over time, they had become experts at it. Heck, they were the only ones that ever did it until July of 2012. They never had a life in a physical body, never. They didn't care how much you suffered, the more the merrier as long as it continued.

Anyway, this is how reptilian DNA was placed into everyone's body existing here today. Did you know that there are less than fifty people on this planet free of reptilian DNA? This doesn't include those here with us from other Planets. It's no wonder that we're so aggressive as a race. By the way, almost every Human living on this planet today has had at least one past life as a reptilian humanoid. That's enough to make you wonder about things. Once you learn how to access your true self, you can start to access your past lives. You probably won't want to look too close to some of them though. We've all been aggressive when in that form of body as well as some others.

These Adamic - Annunaki hybrids, at least a few selected ones, were being inserted into religious philosophical roles and appointments where ever possible. All of your primary religious books were written by order of, and under the control of, the reptilian leaders of that sect, philosophy, or locality. They were led to do so by their Angels as per the wishes of the Original First Being halves. They merely did what they were told to.

They had little to no feelings, neither did they understand them. They were for the most part, living robots. If you ever met one, for that brief moment they made a physical body, they usually seemed to look through you almost like a serial killer, only because they had no emotions. The oldest of the Original Angels were better at it. The more often they made bodies the more they knew how to act like us. The Arch Angel Michael was the only one who understood what was happening with Spirits in body, with the problems relative to Creation's existing format of abuse.

He was made to protect, and so he did. As I had so many times, when something is made to protect, it does so with equality, learns to respect and care for what it's protecting, and eventually understands compassion through it. At the initial time of writing this book, in 2015, Arch Angel Michael is in stasis, protected by Arae, awaiting his release once the fighting is over.

Your governments and religions are led by aggressive self-serving people who want to control other people. One exception was Pope John Paul II. He had some control issues but he also had a wonderful heart. He grew emotionally drained while he grew in age and was soon easily controlled by all around him.

His biggest problem was the Original First Being Female. The Annunaki themselves, as well as their hybrids, gradually took over the head positions of the ancient priests in all societies. This happened first in Atlantis, just before its second phase of sinking into the Atlantic Ocean.

Initially there were five major sinking events, two minor ones later, and finally the last island vanished into the ocean. It was a small island, not considered much of an event, but it happened. This is when most of the Atlantean people moved to Egypt. Osiris had a huge ship, a gift from our friends from Space. He did what he could to save as many as possible.

Shortly after the second Atlantean sinking catastrophe, the abusive power of the Annunaki and Annunaki hybrids began to grow. They fed on the public's fear which increased their control over not just the people of Atlantis but many others worldwide. The sinking of Atlantis was known to many. It was deemed the wrath of a vengeful god, not far from a truth.

This is also when the problematic Annunaki here closed in on their ranks so to speak. If you wanted to become a priest you had to be approved by them and if you were not reptilian, specifically of Annunaki royalty, you didn't get in. This also started many secret societies through the different ages here on Earth. These timelines are listed at the end of this book with approximate dates for each of them.

The knowledge of self-awareness was also slowly taken away from the general public. If you want to control a society, the first thing you do is decrease their level of intelligence. Gee, are we seeing that here in this country now? Yes we are. It's a slow process that's been happening for a long time. The Annunaki are usually, if nothing else, a patient race when it comes to the subversion of a society.

The religious sects began hoarding all information relative to the use of all metaphysical abilities. Over time the public had

Creation: Its Journey Evolving Into Paradise

become a little lazy and relied more on the priests for information instead of getting it themselves. While this was happening the Original Ones were creating new energy limitations within the physical bodies here, another good reason for you to become aware of your sleeping abilities, awakening to your true selves.

Religions and governments have often been at each other's throats throughout history in the fight for superior control over the masses. This is a simple power struggle for control over the same populace. They usually maintain a place for themselves, giving each other room to maneuver, but the battle never ends. I find all this disgusting. None of you are children anymore, not as Spirit. You need to be free to make decisions for yourselves. This is what is almost here for you now. This is part of Arae's job and he'll soon be at it.

Anyway, as the reptilian agenda spread, so did the aggression between everyone. Arguments between people, especially by groups such as governments or religious philosophies, grew in size as well as frequency. People, like animals, are easiest to control when you keep them agitated, scared, and running in circles. It's easier to lead them in the direction you want when they're already running, like capturing a herd of wild horses. The need for control, especially through abuse, is a sickness on its way to being cured. You cure cancer by cutting it out. This is already happening in the 2nd Dimension, over two thirds of it is complete but still more to go.

This massive Reptilian surge began the end of physical freedom here on the Earth. This was the beginning of the still current Annunaki control of physical life, here in 2015 on our Planet. It started over ten million years ago and was restarted after every cleansing of this Planet's surface. This was not just allowed but made to happen, each time by the Original First Being Male and Female. You see you're not guilty of anything, only misled and abused. The problematic Annunaki presence here will soon be removed. That's in book 3 of the Creation Series.

As a race you were made to be as you are. However, now that you're free from the Original Male and Female and their Angels, aren't you are responsible for becoming your true selves, to change into who you really are inside as Spirit? You only need to relax, begin to learn how to release your true self from your physical body's restraints. I'm talking about who you really are, not the body you're stuck in. This is easier said than done at first. Once you've gotten there it's a simple way of being, a very natural thing.

This is all about your true self, not just the physical body you're in. You are Spirit, sentient energy, yet also the sum of all your parts while still in a body. Within you is a Dual Core Spirit flow, one consisting of a removed part of Gaia, this Planet's energy, as well as your own visiting Spirit, most often Soul. This is all housed within the physical material which originated from the Earth, the Planet your body was initially created from. This is why all parts of your physical body are found within this Planet we live on. We're from it, our bodies belong to it.

On average, sixty percent of your Core Spirit flow is the visiting Spirit. Forty percent is that of a part of Gaia's Spirit released over 11 million years ago. This is often called the Kundalini, the two snakes that travel up and down your spine. This ancient term serves its purpose well. If you think of two snakes intertwining as they move together, you can get the image of two forms of Spirit that flow together yet remain separate. They never combine into one unless you have Source Spirit inside. This situation is very rare.

Source is no better than anything else. Heck, the Original First Being is our Original Source which is the cause of all our problems. It is the Spirit field that contains all frequencies ever expressed in Creation and more. It's very powerful which makes it also extremely problematic and without any life experiences necessary for it to grow properly. This small issue will be handled, completely remedied, by Lilly and Arae in 2018.

The time of the Source Spirit nonsense has passed with the permanent deletion of those who caused it, the Original First Being halves. Their servants and the two other large Source Spirit couples, ready to take the Original Male and Female's places, have already been removed. This was the most important task for Arae to perform in this his last life, cleaning the Other Side of abusive control and arrogance. He's the protector but also the janitor. He's responsible for cleaning up the messes as well as fixing what's broken. He'll be able to perform his duties properly soon, once he leaves his body this one last time.

There's an important reason for the writing of the Creation book series. For the first time ever anywhere, you have available the truth of what exists, how it came to be, how you've all had to live, and what you've been put through. They also explain how the old format of abuse was destroyed to free you allowing you to become who you really are, and soon control your own physical destinies as Spirit, your natural self, not your vehicle or body. Once free again as Spirit on the Other Side or Second Dimension, you will have equally empowered councils to of yourselves and decide how to run your lives as a community. As a family, you will become one, for yourselves and each other. You don't need a god, you need to be left alone to search out your own fates, grow naturally into your normal self, a very beautiful being.

There will be one council for each separate form of Spirit. I'll explain this is more detail later in this book. You will soon be what you really are a huge, greatly diversified family. As Spirit you are no longer children, you're very old and wise. Self-destiny is your right. It was from the beginning. You just weren't allowed to have it, that's all. I've always told you that you are much more than you've ever been allowed to understand. This isn't only about the abusive, controlling, and selfish beings running this Planet, but the Original Ones. You're almost free.

Well, so far as the problematic Annunaki here go, you get the picture. They kept growing in number as well as gaining more and more control over the individual societies, putting themselves into empowering positions whenever and where ever possible. This continued through the 5 ages on this planet. It is about to be over.

Their final and fatal collapse will begin early in 2016 as you will all finally see for yourselves. You will soon see the Annunaki for yourselves, up close and personal, here on Earth. Remember that they are an incredible race of strong, compassionate, yet aggressive people with such a rich culture as is seldom seen anywhere. We've just been dealing with the problematic ones here, not an example of who the Annunaki are as a race.

CHAPTER 11

THE SIX AGES OF EARTH'S COLONIZED BEINGS

There have been six ages of colonizing here on the Earth. Before the first age there were already many others coming here from other Planets, some from galaxies very far away. That's funny, almost sounds like the start of a movie. Anyway, for our mutual understanding, each age will start with the introduction, actually re-introduction, of the Adamic Races returning to produce the physical Earthen body models again.

Before we go any further I need to bring something to your attention. The dates I'm giving you here are general approximations of when something happened. You will find that many people, some are scientists, will disagree with this. They will only be able to say so from carbon dating and guessing through studying layers of sediment within the land structures accessible in few places.

Carbon dating is almost useless for accurate measurement of events as they go farther into the past. It's mostly all we have to work with for now. We're about to receive an extremely accurate physical history of our Planet from our new friends from space who will be meeting with us soon, not just through a government, but in person spread out throughout the Planet. Do you think advanced races as these folk are would not already be aware of the problems within our own governments? Things are about to change in a very positive way.

The First Age
(Approx. 10.572 – 8.3 Million Years Ago)

The first age began without a major disaster other than the half-Human and half-Animal beings needing to be removed from our environment, being the Third Dimension here on Earth. As mentioned earlier, there were many people from many Planets here working hard to develop their body's DNA to make it more compatible with the Earth's atmosphere as well as handle the varied Flora and Animals. There were many micro-organisms that other planet's bodies were neither used to nor capable of dealing with.

When the Adamic Race was introduced to Atlantis, especially the Red ones from Atlantis, those from other Planets were amazed at the strength of their physical structure let alone their metaphysical abilities. They had no idea how powerful these new bodies on Earth were. This is also the time when Arae made the first Atlantean power plant, the Crystal Pit. It was the largest one of the five he built there. He eventually dismantled it as the Atlantean, now mostly Reptilian, kept over-using them, eventually causing the destruction of Atlantis itself.

Arae used his abilities to create a power source for the people there by metaphysically trans-mutating a set of crystals into very specific shapes, a major part of it's construction. Then he blew a hole through the crust into the planet's magma. Next the special Crystals were laid next to each other forming the basic shape of a flat and inverted cone, with the crystal's points creating the center of the cone. In the middle of the center of the lower crystal was the hole leading down into the Earth's magma.

One unique crystal was made to place over the magma hole. This crystal was always lit up a soft reddish color with a touch of orange in it. The light, actually the energy, emitting from this crystal shot straight up as well as out the sides into the other crystals which formed the two cones. I'll try to leave a good picture of it before I go. It was a beautiful structure, a blessing until it was used for destructive purposes. Arae later removed it as it was too strong and so easily abused. We'll talk more of that later. The Spiritual Foundation has a piece of this Crystal pit in its possession. It contains both a part of the first Red Adam and Arae today. That's right; there are two parts of Arae's Spirit within it. You can actually talk to them.

I forgot to mention the addition of the top or inverted cone to that first crystal pit. It harnessed the energy from our Sun. This funnel like cone was built over the pit housing with another large and very special crystal at the top having a clear path to the sky, aimed straight up to the sky. The energy from this upper central crystal aimed light not only into the bottom center crystal but into the upper sides. There was then a circular cluster of smaller long crystals, almost like antennae, that balanced the energy between the two cones.

Thermal radiation from the Earth's core and atomic radiation from the sky would fire up their respective center crystals, flow into their respective cones, and phase together with the help of the center spikes or antennae looking crystals embedded where the two cones meet. This produced an energy field which could be directed as well as emitted as a continuous spread out field of energy for anything to access. That's how the small gliders we used were able to move in the air, on the water, and even under water in shallow depths.

It was also used for communication and smaller machinery. Eventually though, close to the time of Atlantis' destruction, the pits were used to mobilize larger ships of war. There were smaller pits placed on air craft which could produce a form of broad laser type beam, not unlike a nuclear device, just without the cloud and pressure. It de-materialized people through intense radiation, much like the shadows found on some of the walls in Japan where it was bombed with a nuclear device, a very sad moment in our Planet's history.

There is a record of this having happened somewhere in or near India. It was about the last attack ever made with one of these devices. A powerful shaman was in a tall tower overlooking a large field. The Atlanteans came to conquer the indigenous people who were peaceful and loving, prepared for most situations, just not this one. The village shaman stood in his tower and used his strong metaphysical abilities to stop the hearts of 3 of the opposing generals and almost a fourth who later returned with more troops and the nuclear air ship. All the bodies were facing away from a central point when they were disintegrated. There is physical proof of this today, somewhere near India.

This could be discussed in at least two books easily. There's no room or time for that here. The same is true of life in Lemuria, such a beautiful land with a peaceful communion of people from many different Planets with each other and the Animals here. Of course this is other than all the reptiles trying to eat and kill everything else here as well as themselves. Try to flow within yourselves, reach your Spirit Guides, and have them take you there. Eventually you'll just go there yourselves on your own. Let's move on.

The Red Adam was always a strong telepath, having made his own body without the interference of the Original Male and Female. He seldom needed to open his mouth to talk to anyone or thing. He communicated with the Animals as well as everything else. The one problem he had with telepathy was in regard to the members of the ever increasing reptiles on the Planet's surface. They had closed minds, cared about only one thing, survival.

Of course I'm not talking about the Annunaki but the actual reptiles already living here. They only had, as it is today, Gaia's Spirit in their core energy stream. They have always had a single Spirit Core, only that of the Earth. Insects are the same way. If you look at the actions of reptiles and insects you'll find them to be very aggressive with no thoughts of compassion. This is an issue with single Spirit core physical bodies. It is also a form of abuse against the smaller Planetary Essence beings that Gaia released so long ago.

As the larger reptiles would approach Arae in body, he had to go into their brains causing physical pain and usually damage, to keep them away. He drew a lot of attention from this one ability, more so than the others. The reptiles were aggressively killing people in Atlantis as well as everywhere else. This was always the reason for the need to erase most life on the Earth, perform a cleansing. Each age ended with a worldwide catastrophe to remove the reptiles, more than anything else. They were the issue needing attention.

I have great respect for many of our scientists. They work hard, long hours, and are ill respected as they work diligently to do the best they can to understand Earth's history with rather primitive tools. There are problems with what we believe to be true. Scientists merely need better tools to work with. Its no fault of their own, they just need better tools and they'll have them soon.

There have now been drawings found in caves, tested to be very old, of primitive men fighting large reptiles (dinosaurs) with spears. That has upset our current thought process relative to the lives of these great reptiles as well as the age they existed in. I should say ages to be correct.

They've always been a problem here. The reptilian issue was finally handled properly, for us that is, in the Fourth Age. That's when the Original First Being Male and Female decided to cut them down to size, and keep them there. It was time for other things to happen here. Now back to Arae, the Red Adam.

Arae was more than just self-aware; he was more himself in body now than in most of his other lives. When he made his own body, not being born into one, he was much stronger. He also didn't have that nuisance of dealing with part of Aramaeleous attached to his body. Arae's energy was his body.

Each time this situation occurred it bothered the Original First Being halves but they had to deal with it in order for their plans to progress properly. This was all part of their format for growing beings on this planet, very important in order to end up with what they wanted for 12/21/2012. Remember, they were the only ones running people's lives since the very beginning. This was all part of their plan to build a much larger Creation with everything worshiping them.

The Red Adam, Arae in the physical form he made for himself, was also telekinetic. He could literally knock a tree down with his mind. He did so to prove a point to Atlantis' leaders when they first met. These leaders were more than impressed with Arae and wanted him to become part of their community, but not control it. That fear was always within them. Arae had no such desire. That's never been what he was about.

By now the Annunaki on Atlantis were more than enticed with Arae and his abilities. Some of them started to worship him and the leaders wanted to control him, taking some of his power for themselves. They had extremely sophisticated and elaborate equipment but couldn't reproduce any of his abilities. That type of thing has never been possible and never will be. They soon realized they needed to try a slower approach, interbreeding. This is how they eventually invaded the Red Race here as well as all the other Adamics, causing much of our grief today as well as Gaia's slow destruction.

At first they found this to be a promising option. They offered Arae everything under the sun, including praise and a very high political position. Arae was not only disinterested by this, but extremely insulted. He understood who he was, why he was there, what they really wanted, and what would become of it. It really pissed the Annunaki leaders off when he turned them down in mid-sentence, or I should say thought. He wasn't going to even listen to it.

The abrupt dismissal of their offerings made the Annunaki even more determined to tie into his DNA lineage. Four of them even tried to rape the Red Eve once. Arae literally broke three of them in half like a twig. The fourth received a broken right leg but was allowed to go back to tell the others what just happened, a warning. You can understand how Arae felt and how things would progress from here forward. It was now more than a dangerous act for any Annunaki to approach Arae or any of his children. Again, remember that the act of protection was part of him. It was his format for existence.

As he was always in their minds, he was aware of what they wanted when they came close or if he wanted to see their thoughts for himself. At this time, let's try to remember that all Annunaki, like everything else, are not all bad by any means. The largest group of Annunaki that came here was overly abusive to everything near it. They were not just explorers but a more aggressive group that was plundering Planets and civilizations whenever and where ever possible. They came here to rule, just as they did where ever they went. Many Annunaki are great scientists, philosophers, and more. They are people. We just had a bad bunch sent here by the Original First Being halves, that's all.

I remember that Lilly and I had a very close Annunaki friend, a religious leader of some fashion, who was a wonderful person.

This gentleman wasn't the only close Annunaki friend they had. Many of them soon realized that the Red Adam and Eve (Lilly and Arae) had the advantage of being in people's brains and hearts, understanding and feeling their needs, things they were curious about.

The Annunaki seldom had to ask their major questions, Lilly and Arae just started addressing them. The easier you read other's hearts the more you understand about them. Remember that heart energy already has a person's major thoughts in it. This is where everyone is headed today, naturally. Here's how things began to progress on Earth in the First Age.

Lemuria was separated from Atlantis by great distance, Ocean and Land. Some had small crafts to move from one place to another but there were few as spare parts were hard to come by. Large craft were seldom seen, except for the Annunaki. The war in space was again escalating all through the colonizing process on Earth. The different civilizations from other planets made few trips. They were both expensive and dangerous.

Supply ships traveled a long distance to arrive here through tough space. There was always a variety of wars breaking out throughout the vastness of the Third Dimension, our known Universe. There are many Reptilian races having disputes among themselves and others. They were not alone in this particular arena either. As the older races used the natural resources of their own planet they needed more.

Negotiation was always the main resolution to this issue but there were always the occasional wars over disputes, especially over new planets. Earth never had that problem. It already had a variety of different peaceful races here and was a small planet anyway. The only exception was the problematic Annunaki Clans here. They usually were enough to scare off the occasional intruders or raiders. The Annunaki are not the ones to mess with and they had one huge ship here aside a fleet of smaller ones.

They eventually carried on their inherent dominant traits after the others settled in, about 10.25 million years ago. Actually, they came here to do so.

From time to time throughout Earth's 5 ages, Creation's initial physical beings came by, assessing the evolution of events here. They're known as the Drachk. They are the Dragon Humanoid Race. More than just ancient, they are the most powerful and wisest of all the races. Their strength, wisdom, and ability to bring about great change in a civilization are legendary. They're also the essence of physical power here in the 3rd Dimension, seldom trifled with. Where ever they go, when the Drachk arrive all things come to a stop and everyone listens.

This happens out of both great respect and sometimes a little fear. They seldom become aggressive but when they do they never lose, never. They remember the beginning of life here in the Third Dimension. They were there. We're talking over 2,857,100,400,000 years ago. That's 2 Quadrillion, 857 Trillion, 100 Billion years. Damn, I don't feel so old now.

The Drachk are a benevolent race but can become aggressive when overly agitated. It's in their nature to observe, furthering their wisdom, to help others when deemed proper, and to intervene only when they feel it necessary. They've kept a distant eye on the Earth for a long time now, awaiting the event now occurring, the final return of the First Drachk Spirit.

The Annunaki are one of the older races but very different, they are Reptilian, a more openly aggressive race. The Drachk have learned much from their history of fighting between themselves and with others. Reptilian DNA is different from the Drachk DNA. When one Drachk enters a meeting of four hundred Annunaki, the Annunaki will become silent, paying attention to that one Drachk. They carry great respect through power and wisdom.

They're known for their vast knowledge as well as limitless aggression when they deem it necessary to release it. Their science is unequalled as is their weaponry. When a Drachk warship approaches a battle in space the fight usually stops, at least until all involved see what that one ship does.

There were four other sets of Adams and Eves besides the Red ones in Atlantis. They made the different skin colors for each of the slightly different Adamic body styles. The Adamic Race was the base format for the bodies necessary for Spirit to have lives here. They were made available with different skin tones and slightly different features. No big deal, unless you're a bigot that is. The thing I find funny is that we've all had lives in all the different bodies, many times. The same is true of all the different religions. The Adamics had to do this five times, initially and then again after each of the age endings to reset the Earth's civilization body format.

The White Adamics were in the Northern areas, the cold climates. If you go to Greenland and its surrounding area, you'll be where the White Adamic Race got started. Believe it or not, the White skin color is relative to crystalized water, snow. That is what they used to make the white skin. Gee, most white people more easily acclimatize in the colder environments. I wonder why.

The Black or Deep Brown Adamics made their initial bodies in Africa. Their skin color was made from the immensely rich soil there. It's so sad to understand that Africa, five times now, was the most fertile land on the Earth. It was taken from them by the Original First Being Female, each time. When you can see things as I can, it's easy to understand why things are the way they are today. You see how they were, what was made to happen, who did it, and why. Sad, very sad.

The Tan Adamic Race was made in the Middle East which has spent a lot of it's existence with sand in it. The tan skin color literally comes from the sand. The Spirit housed within Martin Luther King Jr. was not only Source Spirit from Lilly and Arae but the Tan Adam, each of the five times he and his Source Mate made their bodies. He's over there now, waiting for certain things to unfold.

The last Adamics to discuss are the Yellow Adamic Race. They are quite unique actually. Their skin color and bodies came from more unique materials than the others. I believe you'll find this interesting.

The Yellow Adam and Eve landed on the island of Tokyo. It looked much different the first four times than it does today. As far as the body shape, its Humanoid but with more than the regular planetary materials in it. As the Yellow Adam and Eve landed on an island, their bodies took on the characteristics of some of the deceased beings in the area, not yet decomposed.

There have been colonies of Serpoians on Japan in each of the first four ages. As the Yellow Adam and Eve pulled in the existing material they took on the attributes of that material. Their eyes and some other features are relative to both the Serpoian Race and fish, among many other things. There's also a form of light yellow seaweed that contributed to the skin color.

The island of Japan has quite the rich history. They were an outpost of Serpoian travelers who traded together and formed many smaller communities across the land we now call the Asian community. Their knowledge and equipment was vast but they had one problem they could not overcome, replacement parts and general support. All the beings there were unsanctioned, so to speak. They were there without the support of their planetary councils. They were nomads in the truest respect of the word.

Well, I could easily write a book on each of their histories but I've no time left for that much detail. If you like, and you can calm your inner self down enough to open yourself up, you can travel back there and visit each of these communities as they developed.

I could write volumes on each of the ages but I'll be gone before that could happen. Besides, that leaves you with the desire to flow into yourself to find out things on your own. My books are like a map with a rather detailed legend. As you begin to awaken and strengthen your metaphysical abilities you will see and learn of many wonders yourself. The first thing you should do is reach out to your Spirit Guides and develop a personal relationship with each of them.

As you discover things with the help of your Spirit Guides, these books will help you to understand what you're becoming aware of yourself. I'm writing these books for everyone else, not me. Now, let's finally get back to the Six Earthen Ages.

Now we come to the beginning of the end of the First Age of civilization on Earth. The second island of Lemuria had more than begun its sinking into the Pacific Ocean when the Earth's crust began to break and shift again. It was finally time to clear the planet from it's grossly over populated reptilian species. Many of these reptiles were aggressive eaters both strong and resilient. Even the Annunaki had problems with them. There were just too many of them.

At the end of each age, Arae came back to relocate as many of the already existing people as possible but very little at the end of this first age. This is where the ones usually called "Mantids" came into play. I call them "N'Antids" as they were more like large ants that walked than like a praying mantis. I've had more than a few conversations with them, telepathically that is. Almost all of them are gone now, relocated to another planet. It was necessary but more of a loss for us then you might think.

The N'Antids were kind enough to help the Human population here each time an age ended. They fed them and kept them safe deep underground while the catastrophes were occurring above ground. There are ancient stories about that in Mayan, Incan, Ute, Hopi, and other Indian or Red Race cultures.

The N'Antids were the ones that fed Admiral Richard Byrd his visions of an Inner Earth civilization. He was actually lying against the wall of a deep tunnel when three different N'Antids were telepathically feeding him these images. It was done to protect their homes, no other reason.

We owe these people a lot. It's too bad we're not even awake and aware enough to be able to thank them. They have been given appreciation just the same. They left because the Earth will go through another cleansing phase before too long and it was also time for them to have their own planet.

There's about to be a great shifting of the Earth's plates in our near future that would cause them harm so they left now. It's not time for the Earth to go into fire cleansing mode for a while. This is the Sixth Age. It will end with volcanoes, lava, earthquakes, and more, just not yet.

The White and Yellow Adamic Races were dealing with their own topographical issues themselves. There were caves in the North where the White Adamic Race, and others with them, found shelter three times through the changing of the ages. These caves are somewhere in a mountain range. I've never tried to find the exact location. They are known to exist today though so it's not important. The entrances to the lower levels were sealed by Gaia a long time ago. That I do know.

At the end of the First Age, many of the Yellow Adamics, as well as the Serpoians, were rescued in massive ships, most returning later. A few of them, Adamics and Serpoians, were relocated to other planets and are still out there today.

Let's look at the Brown Adams and Eves living on what we now call the African continent. Man has this place been fertile. The lands of Africa have, on at least five major occasions, were comprised of the most fertile soil on Gaia's surface. You could almost look at the ground and make something grow.

She was so very beautiful. The climate was also very appealing back then. There was a reptilian presence there but not so large and threatening as it was on Atlantis and other lands in more temperate climates. There was a variety of large Animals though. Many of these were plant eaters but, as you can guess, some were not.

There tended to be larger communities there but also a variety of smaller ones due to a less hostile environment. It wasn't as necessary to have larger communities for protective reasons. There were larger communities because of all the trading that happened here. Africa was a beautiful nexus of trade and flora that is difficult to imagine, let alone describe. I find myself having to ability to find the words necessary to describe her, the beautiful continent of Africa. I miss her also.

Meanwhile, the Tan Adamic Race was busy trying to get things started there. This region also had beautiful flora, plants and flowers, but always a lot of sand. There were sections with lush greenery, but always sand. This has changed throughout the ages but each time a new age began it appeared as I just described. It was a tougher place to live and therefore had smaller communities which were more spread out, staying closer to the plant life which also meant fresh water.

Just as I mentioned earlier about Africa having been such a fertile land, the topography of all the continents has varied over the passing of centuries across the Earth. The changing of climates and moving of land masses, as well as Gaia's internal temperature and pressures, has given rise to many different living conditions in each of the separate colonies.

Africa, as we call it today, was hit hard. It was shaped different back then, but we'll still call it by the same name. The plates were separated in an aggressive manner causing a major

544c2c24gCCBrrt

split in the continent's shape. The first three ages began with a completely new look for Africa. She didn't sink but was violently reshaped.

There were events similar to these at the end of each age. We won't go into detail for all of them. Just know what basically happened each time. We have friends closer to us than you realize that can help us with the exact timelines and course of events here. The Serpoians are one such family.

As we leave the First Age, we find that there were many strong civilizations growing here and communing with each other the best they could but were usually happy to do so. There was a sense of harmony here on Earth. There was also the reptile issue though.

The earliest forms of dinosaurs kept growing in number and aggression, as well as size. The Original First Being halves felt it was time to clean the planet of the reptiles as well as do away with the present harmonious relationships between the different civilizations from the different land masses. This was not helping the aggressive abuse issues they felt were necessary to grow the Soul's energy to sufficient proportions for each life.

Now it was time for Gaia to undergo a cleansing, to evolve a little more herself. The First Age of civilization here on Earth was brought to an end by fire, I guess you could say. Volcanoes erupted everywhere, earthquakes ripped the ground apart, and asteroids bombarded the surface. The crust began to soften in many places as it rose and sank in different locations bringing new materials up from below its crust, reshaping the land masses once again.

Interestingly enough, Lemuria was shaken very hard but didn't change as much as the larger land masses. It was more active, volcanically speaking, but maintained its basic shape. The same can be said of Atlantis, maybe even more so. The entire continent of Atlantis actually moved a little northeast, and

97

grew new mountains from the increased volcanic activity on her. There were many caves in which the Red Adamics tried to find shelter. The thick volcanic smoke killed many of them as well as their food source. Unfortunately though, some of the larger reptiles also survived. This later initiated a strong rebound of their numbers increasing the severity of the problems they caused.

The Second Age
(Approx. 5.2 – 4.3 Million Years Ago)

With the coming of the Second Age, the second Lemurian island, already receding into the ocean, finally finished sinking. Still things began anew once more. The main, or primary island, was still intact and solid as a rock. It had a strong base of volcanic material that helped it maintain a stationary structure as well as its physical properties which made it light, almost buoyant. It was still well rooted to the crust. The uppermost part of this island we now call Hawaii. Currents have cut away at the parts of her beneath the shores. It was, and in my mind still is, the capital of Lemuria. It's so very beautiful, like the life upon it. I miss Lemuria, Hawaii too. In the first two ages Lemuria was called Mu.

Lemuria was almost always known for its communitative qualities, its ability to create communities of vastly different races of beings. There was the same harmony on most of the islands, indeed the larger ones, like that of Hawaii before it was annexed by other nations, especially the United States. What a shame that was. For centuries people would visit Hawaii not just for its beauty as a tropical resort but the compassion of its people. This same compassion was that of almost all of Lemuria. Hawaii was, and legitimately still is, the capital of Lemuria.

The new materials brought forth by reshaping of Gaia's crust released a bounty of new materials to be used for building and many other things. One of them was gold, and another, Silver.

This is when gold was found to be in abundance here on Earth. It wasn't long before others came here from far off galaxies to obtain it. The Annunaki were already here taking it. We're going to discuss the reason for gold's value across the universe, as well as some of its other usages. First let's understand a little bit about its properties.

Gold's internal frequencies have the ability to move energy through it quickly, almost as quick as Silver. The one thing that Gold does that Silver doesn't, is to store energy while moving it. Gold seems to form a soft bond with the energy flowing through it, just as Source Spirit begins to bond with the planetary Spirit in the body. Here again is the issue of Gold having frequencies within it that are only found in Source Spirit. It's no big deal, just makes it appropriate for a few physical purposes.

Gold has been sought after by most of the races for more than it's obvious aesthetic reasons. It has a beautiful shine to it. Why? Why do we all feel an attraction to real gold? Why do we use it as our means of backing our financial systems, or at least used to? What is it about gold that has most of us attracted to it? Here's a few of the obvious and not so obvious reasons.

Gold has a beautiful warm shine to it that catches our eyes. As I've been explaining to people for many years now, stones whether a rock on the ground or highly valued gem, have energy within them. They all have their own personal frequencies. As our bodies come from this planet, our bodies relate with these various frequencies.

As each of our bodies have a different set of physical frequencies, and the visiting or personal Spirit in them is composed of different strengths and varieties of the many available frequencies, we all relate to stones and other materials from this planet in our own unique way. Some of us are attracted to one stone and not another. This is relative to the individual frequencies of our personal Spirit, usually Soul.

Gold just happens to have a very health set of frequencies to it. It also has the ability to move energy, whether Spirit (sentient energy) or not, as well as store it. This literally gives us a nice feeling when we wear it. It stores some of our personal energy but also helps our energy flow through the body.

As you wear a necklace, you surround your core energy, or Kundalini as many would say, with that stone. A gold necklace surrounding your core energy will literally help your Spirit flow inside you as well as store some of it on you. This leaves you with a nice feeling, somewhat reassuring also. That's because you've just made a small reservoir of your own personal energy was well as helped it flow stronger.

This is a simple natural event occurring that almost no one is aware of. It's not paramount, but it's happening. There are simple answers to most of life's issues. Once you learn how to open yourself up, it's all there to see like a piece of sculpture sitting on a table.

Gold is also used in a process that helps fuel starships, most importantly, through dimensional barriers. I can't give you a whole lot on this, just that it's part of a process to drive certain equipment allowing physical mass to "change phase" as we might say, to move a large ship from one dimension to another.

Gold has always been enjoyed for its aesthetic value and so it's also been used for money. The energetic frequencies within Gold are special. Did you know that only Source Spirit can develop the frequencies which emit a "golden" aura? Gee, there might be a connection there. Anyway, let's get back to things here.

Lemuria continued to grow as it did before. As new people came back with better equipment and supplies, life flourished once again on this beautiful land. By this time, the proper DNA sequencing necessary to maintain an easier life, adjusting their bodies to the Earth's environment, was already achieved.

There were fewer major issues for the races who were here earlier. They brought settlers with stronger DNA as well as proper weaponry to fight the reptiles, or dinosaurs as we call them today, as well as some very high tech mining equipment. There was, however, a little more discord between some of the races. The war out in space had grown. It spread into new territories and intensified. This would later cause problems for almost everyone there, on Lemuria especially. Now let's look at some of the other parts of the Earth, the other Adamic communities.

There were large deposits of Silver found in the Northern areas of the Earth, in the White Adamic regions. There were already quite a few caves in the mountains which housed the precious metal, but it was often removed vertically by ships hovering over the larger deposits. As more and more ships came, there arose "elbow room issues" between the miners; I guess we can call them that.

The large reptiles weren't as great an issue in this region. They were cold blooded and didn't care for the low temperatures. There were however large mammals causing issues from time to time but nothing like the reptiles in the Southern regions. The Northern races were aware of this, as well as their new found wealth of Silver and other large mineral deposits. This was a strong deterrent from moving South to a more amiable climate. The cold in the North was as bitter as it is today.

The Red Adamic Race was in full swing in Atlantis and now moving both East and West to other continents. After all, they were here to grow, to populate. This involves the expansion of their territory. Many stayed in communities but almost as many were nomads. They were explorers, over time, creating small towns along the way. This is true of all the Adamics.

The Yellow Adamics were becoming closer to the Serpoians in what we might now call the Far East. Adamics were self-less, enjoyed helping others, were quick to protect others as well as developing communities. The Serpoians always had more trouble than the others with interspecies communication.

These Serpoians, or Grays as many call them, have strong but delicate sensory abilities. Most of them can look at you and immediately sense your basic structure, its issues, your present body functions such as nervous system, blood flow, and more. They are strong telepaths. One landed on my roof a few years ago. It was beamed into the air just about four to five inches above it and over my bedroom. It was almost like someone dropped a small dog on it. No, it wasn't raining cats and dogs that night.

Anyway, I looked through the roof at the energy I was seeing. It was a form of Serpoian but not the usual one. These are a little stronger in their sensory abilities as well as a little smaller in size. This is one of the advantages of awakening your abilities. You can see energy in many different forms once you're awake. You can do this through your Pineal Gland, Solar Plexus, and Scanner as well as Crown and Heart Chakras.

When I saw what it was I got excited. I had never had one come this close to me before. Then I realized it was scanning both myself and Suzie, one of my dogs living with me, at the same time. I looked in it's brain to see what it was seeing through its eyes. I was watching what it saw.

He had the ability to scan Suzie and I as an MRI would. I watched his brain focus on the different layers of flesh, bone, and the rest as it moved through our bodies. This happened a long time ago and I had not yet seen anything like this. I was just coming aware of other species in space by going on starships out there and visiting, astral projecting. Being aware of a race is one thing, definitely not understanding them.

I was intrigued but soon became a little annoyed. I realized there was absolutely no aggression or negative thought process involved but my privacy had been invaded without permission. I decided to scan him as he was us but to let his brain see me doing so. His brain was now watching his body being scanned the same way. I didn't mean to be overly aggressive, just letting him know what it felt like to do what he was doing to us, Suzie and I. Within four seconds he was gone. Today they visit often with others.

Let's get back to the other Adamics, the Brown and Tan Races.

The Brown Adamics had rebuilt their communities, as they did before, so did the races from many other planets. Once again Africa, something similar to what we know today, thrived on both luscious plant life as well as diverse community. There was a small increase in the amount and size of the reptiles now though. They would be a little more of an issue to the people as well as the Animals there.

The Tan Adamics also revived the aggressive growth characteristics making more and more communities everywhere they went. They were often found in the company of many different Animals, especially the larger ones. The threat of aggressive reptiles was more prevalent there now as in other places.

The reptiles found in this region were also more likely to travel in herds larger than elsewhere. This was due to their need for self-preservation. As food was scarcer, they needed to hunt together insuring a higher percentage of success. They would also eat each other when they felt it necessary. This is a more natural thing with beings having only the Spirit of the Planet within them.

It would easily take many volumes to discuss each community of the different Adamic and other races here in all the different ages. I don't have time enough to do so. I want to offer you a basic understanding of events which comprise your history on this planet remembering that you've had lives on so many others.

This second book, as the first one, is about you and for you, your awakening to who you really are. You're all very special. I want you to understand that as well as a little bit about life here on Gaia who owns these bodies we live in. I do wish I had the time to write more though.

To sum up the Second Age, all the major civilizations began to flourish until the reptilian issues over two-thirds of the planet became too great an issue. This needed to be addressed and Gaia needed time to do a little evolving of her own. That's why the Original First Being halves decided to end the Second Age.

We get so involved in our personal physical lives that we forget there is a very large part of our existence that we're forgetting, the other dimensions, the rest of Creation. This also was made to happen by design by the Original Ones. It is now being changed to the opposite, your continued awareness of it.

We're seldom aware of what Gaia does for us. Everyone seems so busy trying to make that next dollar to buy that next form of distraction or amusement, that we never understand that this planet, Gaia, continually nurtures us. She feeds us the trees we need to convert our own personal exhaust emissions, carbon dioxide, into what we need to survive, oxygen, as well as so many other things. Instead, in an over aggressive reptilian fashion, we attack her.

This is about to be changed. It will be a forced change. By this I mean that there are new bodies coming which will keep us from abusing the Earth and allow us to help her, just as the Fae do in the four dimensions below us. This is all part of the new Creation being developed and fully initiated in January of the year 2016.

Before the end of the Second Age, it was decided that some of the new residents of the Earth, a few of the established colonies, needed to be saved. And so they were. This was also Arae's responsibility. He led them, in various places around Gaia's surface, into caves where the large ant people, called the N'Antids, took care of them until he came back to bring them up again. This was a very hard time for the base Human Race here on

Earth. It happened three times, after the Second, Third, and Fourth Ages.

The N'Antids are extremely powerful telepaths. It was no problem for them to communicate with the Humans now in their care. They fed them but also used their abilities to help them remain calmer than they normally would have been. This is similar to the incident where they were implanting visions in Admiral Byrd's brain. That was for their own personal safety, that of the N'Antids. This was now for the safety and well-being of the base Human Race of Earth.

The N'Antids should be considered a Human Race because they were here first. They are by definition Earth's first Humanic civilization. They're sentient beings with a dual Spirit core energy. They are not like us, but a definite part of our Creational society. We owe them a lot. They don't have strong feelings as we do but they are unaggressive, unless attacked, and quite benevolent. That's why Arae went to them. They also knew who he was and what he was trying to do, protect all he could. The N'Antids are, as I like to say, very cool.

Once again though, there were large reptiles, as well as the smaller ones, that managed to live through the "cleansing" period. This of course was also by design, that of the Original Ones. Let's get going with the next age and, once again, an even stronger set of separate civilizations growing.

The Third Age
(3.8 – 2.5 Million Years Ago)

After things cooled down and the falling asteroid damage resided, our already existing base Humanic Races came out from deep inside the Earth to begin repopulating the planet. And, once again, the Adamics came back to do their part, reintroducing the Adamic body structure. Each separate Adam and Eve

105

pair made the same race each time. I'm not sure if I mentioned it earlier but each of the different colored pairs were also Spirit mates. The Red Adam and Eve, Lilly and Arae, are the only exception as they're the strongest parts of the separated Spirit Halves that were Lillith and Aramaeleous.

When people talk of Soul Mates, they're not aware that they're actually talking about life mates. At this time, the initial writing of this book, there are only 4 Spirit Mates in body here. Three are living together and one is not. There is a pair of Source Mates here being kept apart so they can perform their separate tasks. The female is aware of the male. The male isn't even aware of who he really is. This is a shame but I can't do anything about it now.

There was also a new issue being brought forward. The Adamic Races, offspring of the original Adamic pairs, were attacked by the Original Ones. Their metaphysical abilities were being held back, diminished, and controlled. The Original Ones also had their Angels, the ones assigned to their Spirits before being placed into one of the Adamic bodies; make sure that they started mating with all the different species already living here. That really diminished the metaphysical abilities of the living bodies for the Souls to have lives in.

The more others knew about the Other Side, the greater the chance that others would be aware of what they were doing. This was not something that they wanted the Third Dimension, or Physical Realm, to be aware of. This would take away from their level of praise. They could not let others know they were being abused although many had that feeling deep inside anyway. It just wasn't something that was easily understood.

Anyway, once again, in the same approximate vicinities, the Adamics took over repopulating the planet. Gaia's "Spring Cleaning" was over. The soil was as fertile as it could be. This allowed the flora to return with great vigor. Gaia was soon green and blue again. Vibrant life began to flourish everywhere but, as usual in life, so did aggressive abuse. That was considered necessary to main proper Soul Spirit growth.

This time Atlantis remerged with more lush tropic forest than ever before. There were many new fruits and plants growing everywhere as well as medicinal plants found in abundance. There were also new insects provided by Gaia to help her. There were bees over a foot long. These could literally cross large sections of the oceans to fertilize the flora everywhere. As you can guess, they were also quite deadly, not just an occasional nuisance.

Atlantis had lost a few small islands near its largest mass, off the shores of its Southeastern section. There was also a major portion of an island a few hundred miles off its Northern shores, about two fifths of it. Before much time had passed, more of it sunk leaving about three fifths of it. This island was an extremely unstable place. It had some kind of pineapple type of fruit on it making it worth the occasional journey but few were foolish enough to spend much time there.

Lemuria had many smaller buildings still intact and were immediately used again. They were, however, starting to have issues with reoccurring earthquakes. As the people returned once again in their starships they became immediately aware of this issue as well as the need for relocation or possible abandonment of "farming" here.

As you can imagine, the home planets of these settlers and miners lost interest in this location rather quickly. Many of the people here now had to make the decision to move to other more stable places or go home on the next transports. Many of the people died. There were also large groups that left any way they could. When starships returned to bring supplies and pick up raw materials, many found the settlements abandoned. They usually picked up all the settlers they could find. A couple of the Reptilian Races just left.

As the Third Age progressed, the islands of Lemuria slowly continued their recession into the seas. The section of Earthen crust underneath them was even thinner now than it was before. Its easy to understand how this led to it's eventual collapse onto the floor of the Pacific Ocean. The Southern Sections of the main Lemurian Continent broke off and fell a little less than a third of the way through the Third Age. Many of the smaller islands, one by one, were sinking into the ocean also. Remember Lemuria consisted of the collection of smaller surrounding islands, not only the main continent and larger islands. Lemuria, in the beginning, was a shining example of how we can all get along. The more the originating planets of the people here were removed from the equation, the better the different races got along.

The White Adamic Race began to flourish, to multiply in greater numbers now. They were more prepared to deal with the harsher environment than ever before. The newly reintroduced Adamic Race there was also more intelligent than previous times. Their abilities still amazed those who came upon them at first.

The Adamics were loving and generous people, but deceptively aggressive when provoked. They earned the respect they were given. Their physical strength was helpful in work details but their ability to communicate with all life, especially the freakishly large mammals prevalent in the vicinity, became handy indeed.

The Adamics were often sought out and given homes in the settlements, hoping they would help with inter-species communicative and aggressive Animal issues. Oh yeah, there's something I forgot to mention. The Adamics multiplied at an incredibly fast rate. They were almost never sick and formed communities at a rapid rate. It was obvious they were here to stay. They were fortitudinous, beyond everything else.

The Red Adamics were hard at work building temples once they settled in. They were now being infiltrated to a larger degree by the Annunaki here. There were many new groups of priests and seers arising everywhere. This is also when the Adam Races slowly began to limit their talking with the Animals.

This happened on Atlantis first, with the Red Adamics. It was made so by the Original First Being halves. As Arae made the Red Adamics, they went to them first. The Original Ones had nothing but issues with him. He had already become an issue, disregarding their wants and desires.

The Tan and Brown Adamic races continued as before. There isn't a whole lot that was different here. Things were made to keep progressing as they have been with all the Adamics. Each time the Adamics came back, the generations following the original ones was made to mate with the other species, creating a new and diversified DNA reservoir for the Original Ones to work with. As mentioned earlier, it also dumbed down their metaphysical abilities.

The Original Ones used the Angels they put on the bodies at birth to make sure the proper male and female mated to produce the proper body for a given Soul to have a life in. This allowed them to put a Soul in the proper physical frame for the abuse they intended for them. It also gave the body the parents they wanted the Soul to have. Rarely was it the blessing of a true loving situation. It was meant to be frustrating, directional, and worse.

As I've explained many times, the Angels (The Original Angels) put on you at birth were done so to control you. If it was time for you to break your arm, they took care of it. If it was not time for you to die, they kept you alive. If you needed to look the other way for a second, for no reason you understand, and have a car wreck, they did.

They were controllers, not the wonderful blessings everyone thought they were. I wrote a long chapter on Angels in the first book of the Creation Series. That's why it's important. It gives you the base knowledge you need in order to understand this book. Here's a few other ways that Angels have messed with you.

When two people meet and "fall in love", they have a euphoric feeling that goes up their spine. Well over fifty percent of the time it was your personally assigned Angels. The Angels also make sure the meeting happens. When you meet they put their energy into the base of your spine and then run it up towards your Heart Chakra. This gives you the feeling of "divine love". This makes you feel you're experiencing "true love".

This same technique is used by them to make you think you're talking to them. When you reach out and try to talk with an Angel, or think you are anyway, you're really just talking to your Spirit Guides. Your own personal Angel will give you that slightly euphoric feeling up your spine to mislead you. Almost all of the first or original Angels have been deleted now. Your Spirit Guides can do the same thing. When it happens, it's a lie. There's no way to sugar coat it.

I realize no one wants to think of such a thing being true. We like to hold onto happy thoughts but let me ask you something. Do you really want to hold onto a lie? It's like holding onto something that shouldn't even be in your hands. It doesn't belong there. When you have the truth, you can take on every new day with a strong assurance of who you are and have the fortitude to get through each next day.

This is also why it's important for all of you who care, to learn how to flow inside yourself and open up, to become who you really are inside, Spirit. Spirit is sentient energy, not a physical body. We use the bodies to grow and learn, but mostly grow and develop. Once you learn to release yourself outward, while still being in your body, you become aware of this Third Dimension as well as the Second Dimension which is pure energy. This is the "Awakening", the "Spiritual Evolution". This is also the one and only truth of who you really are, sentient energy housed within a body for a temporary time frame.

Getting back to the Third Age, it finally also came to its end but this time by the Ice Age. The Earth was hit hard with a barrage of meteors which, when added to the massive increase of volcanic activity already here, literally closed off most of the sun for many years. This happened over a long period of years, not one specific moment in time. This was also a time of remembrance for the Nordic people here. It was the time of Thor's visit.

The Earth had already gotten quite cold now. Food was scarce and heat was precious. Things were nowhere near cataclysmic but harsh just the same. There was a race of giant sized Humans that the ones called the "Asgardians" were chasing through the cosmos. These giants were plunderers, taking whatever they could whenever they could. Life, other than their own, meant nothing to them. They were extremely abusive.

On the other hand, the Asgardians as we chose to name them were protectors. They would seek out unity and trade with others. They didn't like aggressive abusive people, of any race. They were, for the lack of a better term, self-appointed protectors where ever they went. Thor was one of these individuals.

Thor was a powerful telekinetic. His hammer, he actually had one, was made of dense matter like that of a collapsing star. The hammer was not magic. He moved it with his telekinetic abilities. That's how he returned it to his hand. He was very strong but no one could lift his hammer with physical force. It could only be done by telekinetic abilities. That was a good life but sad too. There are always things happening in our lives which are tragic. My lives as supposed "great" people were the saddest you could image, nothing that ever gets said.

As Gandhi I was being tortured by the Original First Being Male and Female while in prison. I had to feel my wife dying close by yet I couldn't reach out to her physically. I knew I was there to try to unite all the people I could, to take them out of the abusive grasp of their religions and teach them how to say "No" to a government without aggression. By keeping me in jail, and turning events as they did, almost all I had accomplished vanished before my eyes.

This and my wife's death tore at my heart daily. After my second major hunger strike my internal organs had all started to fail. I was already dying when I was shot four times, not three, in the chest. The fourth shot grazed the left side of my chest, my ribs. For some reason it bothers me that this little fact is not known.

Do you want to hear something funny? It was the Human Annunaki Hybrid leader, the one in England, who paid for my funeral. Is that like the mafia or what? Oh well, excuse the re-membrances but the most important information you need from these books, that of your origin and history, is that things have been done to you.

You have been made to do many things life after life after life, which eventually hurt your frequencies in side you. These frequencies add up to who you are. This is why Arae and Lilly went to war. This is what brought about your eventual freedom. This is almost finished now. The Third Dimension, or Physical Realm, needs this information to be available to it. It's not some-thing one must study and learn. It must be available to help you when you're ready to fully understand yourself, who you are, where you came from, and what's been happening. Well, let's get back to the end of another age.

Once again Arae came back to save, to hide, as many people as possible. He did this of his own accord. There was already a great rift, many serious issues, between Arae and the Original

First Being halves. The heat of their conflict was rising. It was very personal. They made Arae the protector. He was protecting all the best he knew how while still having lives. The Original Ones had a problem. There was nothing strong enough to stop him. Let's keep going.

The Fourth Age
(1.1-.8 Million Years Ago)

This time things started off harder for the Adamics coming back to add to the population. The Original Ones were coming down very hard on them. Remembering that they used the original Angels to control people's minds, their thoughts as well as their actions, they brought pain and suffering hardships to the original Adamics immediately.

Before we go any further, let me tell you something about these Adamics. Each of the Adamic pairs that came here, as I mentioned earlier, made the same skin colored bodies each time. The Red Adam was always Arae. He was ridiculously powerful when made his own body. This physical structure was vibrating with his true self. This was not the same as when he put himself into another body that was created by another woman and man. There is a huge difference.

He had a part of Aramaeleous attached to his body's Base Chakra. Aramaeleous was the larger, but also now arrogant, Spirit field he came from. This part of Aramaeleous was used, by the Original Ones, to control his body's emotions when they wanted to enforce stronger control over him. Couple this with Angels using their specially created energetic abilities to enter the Crown Chakra and control your thoughts temporarily, you have a serious self-control issue. This is something that Arae, actually I have to say myself to be correct, has had to deal with this last life. Anyway, let's take a look at another important item.

These other Adamics were Spirit Mates, the two halves which form the complete Spirit Orb when created. This orb, once released, begins to vibrate and split into male and female. This is what these Adamics were. This makes them powerful, complete. Now, let's look at their personal Spirit type. Where did they come from?

When the Original Ones released their third wave or generation of Soul Spirit energy, Lilly and Arae both happened to be free of physical form. This was not by chance. Once the wave was eighty percent released, Lilly and Arae release three waves of their own. They created their own Angels, Animals, and smaller portions of themselves.

We would think of these smaller portions or individual pieces of themselves as children, as physical body thought leads us to, but it's actually quite different. Energy, and Spirit, is a lot like water in many respects. If you take an empty cup to a bucket of water and remove a cupful, was that bucket really pregnant? No. We usually think of things coming from us, as we normally would, as children. The truth is that Spirit is different.

Now, these smaller pieces of Lilly and Arae were parts of their actual energy, their Spirit, released to have lives of their own, to grow into something unique, individual. And so they did. Lilly and Arae were the two strongest Spirits anywhere in Creation. That is very powerful energy. This was not any Spirit for the Original First Being halves to take lightly.

That explains the strong abilities of the five Adamic pairs. This is why, when they made their own bodies, they were so incredibly powerful. This was becoming more and more a threat to the Original Ones. These were little protectors with a lot of power. Once placed in a body, instead of making their own, they were abused and controlled harshly with vicious intent, just like Lilly and Arae.

So, the original Adamics were now being harassed and looked down on, just as was done to the Animals. In the very beginning here, in Lemuria, Humans and Animals were close friends for the most part. This Fourth Age would be different in many ways. It was time for the Original Ones to start beating everything up hard. I should say it was time for them to make everyone beat each other up hard, through their ability to control them through their Angels. They also liked to put their personal attention into some of them.

Wars began to break out all over the place. There were many issues in the war going on out in space now. These negative attitudes were brought here with the already existing and more isolated communities here. There were many who kept as far away from these issues as possible but most of the stronger colonies were becoming anxious to control the others. It was done to them but its sad how many needed little or no coaxing to do so. A short time after the original Eves and Adams disappeared, that is died off; a few of the Adamics were actually captured and turned into slaves. Some were even taken off planet.

By this time Atlantis was going into its third stage of sinking. The land there was rapidly disappearing. The Red Adamic there had become extremely aggressive now due to the interbreeding of the Annunaki, loss of land as it was sinking, and let's not forget the use of Angels to control them. This was a pot of anger being brought to boil.

The fear of their land sinking, their new aggression, their still physically strong Red Adamic bodies, and their Angelic control finally took over and turned Atlantis into a war state. What a disgrace, what a shame. The Atlantean priests, all strong and royal blood Annunaki-Adamic hybrids, took Atlantis into war for world domination, for their own personal glory.

There was a maximum of four crystal pits, or power plants, on Atlantis at any one time. Arae made the first one. It was the largest and by far most powerful one. He later constructed a form of bridge over it with one huge specially designed crystal directly over the other large crystal that covered the hole reaching down into the Earth's magma.

This is how they worked. The large crystal covering the hole in the ground focused thermos nuclear energy from inside the planet. It then spread it into the cluster of individual crystals around it which formed the basic shape of a cone. The cone's point was the lowest part of the form. This is why I call it a pit.

While the primary crystal, the one covering the hole, was radiating with energy from inside the Earth, it was also focusing our Sun's energy. This energy was also spread out into the crystal cone formation. This solar power gave additional power to the system but when the sun was covered by clouds, the device still functioned well, just not as strong.

When the bridge containing its special crystal was added, it could send this energy into the air. This allowed us to power our own craft through water and local atmosphere. The bridge was able to send out a powerful wide spread flow of energy making it possible to move ships either in air or water. Each vehicle contained a crystal which was used to receive and utilize the energy. This is similar to what many other races use today.

Arae, while still the Red Adam again, became concerned about the aggressive fighting over this power pit. The Reptilian modified Adamics were having wars now over control of the pits. The primary issue was always the first one that Arae built as it was easily the strongest.

He also helped in the initial stages of building the second pit. Once they had things squared away, understood what they were doing, he backed out. He already knew where things were going in relation to these power pits. Once the third new pit was being built he dismantled the original one he built. He would not allow his work to be used in a destructive manner. These pits would soon be used to power weapons of horrific destruction.

There was also another very important issue that the others would not take seriously enough. Every time you broke the crust, opening a hole to feed it, you were causing a slight overheating situation in the crust itself. One pit, properly designed and operated, would not cause any harm to anything. Two pits increased the chance of dangerous side effects should they be used improperly separately, more so if misused at the same time.

As usual, progress is often ignorant to anything outside personal gain. Here again, the Original Ones were helping things along their destructive way. I was aware of their thoughts. Arae has always been so very strong. This is how he was aware of what was to come leading him to dismantle his original machine.

A few years ago, when I was just starting to fire up metaphysically, I came upon a crystal in a store. I walked past it, not noticing it's difference from the others. All of a sudden I heard a strong, loud, and aggressive voice shout out "Hey, over here!" I immediately turned around ready for a fight. The voice was that aggressive.

The weird thing was that I knew it was my voice, that it belonged to me. I didn't know what to think but didn't take the time to dwell on it. I grabbed the crystal but was already talking to it before touching it. He said "Welcome Home" which felt as normal as drinking water. I often talked with crystals. I've even gone by some who called out to me in distress. One crystal was having issues with three different events it unfortunately capture, like a camera does.

Each of these images was like a short video of horrific events of people being murdered and worse. I removed them and left it with a feeling of sunlight, hope, and love. It literally sent me love as I walked away saying goodbye. That still brings tears to my eyes, even today. Anyway, back to this crystal that yelled at me.

While I was reaching to pick it up, it felt a little anxious, almost the same as I was, but not quite. Once in my hands, I relaxed with it and opened myself up. This is the same thing as saying, OK, show me what you want. When we talk with each other as Spirit, we do so by feelings, basic gut knowing, and vision made up of images that are based upon those which are already part of our consciousness.

The next thing I knew, I was myself as the Red Adam. There was a war going on involving well over a thousand Red Adamics attacking each other. They were fighting for possession of the original crystal pit I made. I was standing around fifty feet away guarding my pit. No one, and I mean no one, was about to take possession of it. This and more led to the understanding that the pit had to go.

Before leaving this instance in time, there's something I forgot to mention earlier. All of the crystals within the original pit were trans-mutated by Arae, the Red Adam. They were literally made within the field energy and then made physical. Physical material is pulled from the ground, put into the field energy, made into specific matter, and then fully replaced into the third dimension.

It's a similar process to that of making a body. There just isn't any Kundalini within it when created. Crystals can hold energy but they're not formed with a dual core energy, only that of the Planet they're from. There's actually crystals in the Pacific Ocean that are a primitive form of Silicone life. Anyway, back to the fighting.

As it was powerful metaphysical energy that made these crystals, they were very receptive to the same. With all these Adamics fighting, remember they were all very strong metaphysically, their energies started to increase the power level of the pit, making it vibrate harder than it should have been.

It only lasted a short time before it kicked itself out. It was made that way just like when I go into people's brains and work on them. If I put a little too much energy into them, I would hit some sort of breaker which released the energy I was using. This is all part of the protective agenda in Arae.

Before it shut down there was one hard release of energy inside the pit. It's the event that kicked in the breaker. A piece of the pit broke off, shooting into the air and landed next to my right foot. It had shot into the ground like a spear and was just sticking up leaning towards me.

I picked it up and held it for a moment, feeling it inside. It was struggling with all the different aggressive energies from the battle. So were all the other crystals. I took that away from it and placed a part of myself in it, my Spirit that is. Once the fighting had resided I went back to my pit and cleaned all the aggressive energy out of it. The crystals had all taken too much of a hit. I realized that not only were they abused, but that more would follow.

After a short talk this crystal and I parted ways. It was almost like a homecoming to be with it again. It still makes me feel a little lonely without it but that's OK. As soon as I return this body I'll be in it and around it. All twelve of the original "Crystal Skulls" were made the same way, by Arae. I've had a few talks with the skull called Max. It's possible for us to break off a piece of our own Spirit allowing it to become a separate being of its own.

The thirteenth skull was to be made in a cave in Brazil out of a large piece of yellow tinted crystal. This will not occur now but possibly later, due to the events occurring necessary to bring proper change to the Other Side. Arae has more important work for now, settling things over there trying to establish Creation's new format. This is the one of "Compassion, Honor, and Equality" instead of abuse. Since I've brought up the skulls, allow me to explain what the skulls were made for and why. How were they to operate, doing what?

Arae made all these crystal skulls in that particular shape for a reason. What does the skull do? What function does it perform? It houses and protects the brain, does it not? Now, the thirteenth crystal skull, once made will be put in the center of the circle made by the other twelve skulls. Once someone with a strong self-awareness asks Arae to activate the middle skull, it will fire up activating the other twelve.

This action then opens up a portal controlled only by that part of Arae within it. You can't walk into it but any person sitting nearby will be able to relax, face the center, and look anywhere in the Universe or even Creation itself for the purpose of gaining knowledge. If they are ready, they will also be allowed to astral project through it taking shortcuts directly to where they want to, accessing otherwise unobtainable information. Don't be surprised if one of Arae's physical children, with his DNA, does this at a later date. There are new metaphysically super beings coming. They will also serve and protect.

This is why these special crystal skulls with Arae's Spirit inside, not just his energy, were shaped in the form of a skull. They offer almost unlimited knowledge for those who seek it with an open heart. They house knowledge as our skulls house our brains. This is why I've always said, "The truth is usually a very simple thing. Don't put too much into it, you might overlook it." Let things be what they are and just observe them as if through the innocence of a child's eyes. Let's return to Atlantis.

The priests were still running things and continued to do so until a short time before Atlantis finally reached its final stage of sinking into the Atlantic. It's still there, in the middle of the Atlantic. The Bermuda Triangle is a sunken portion of it. Atlantis was a huge continent. It's a good thing that it disappeared. It started as a wonderful place but was very soon turned into an abusive mess. It makes simple sense. It is where Arae landed and made the red bodies. Remember, they had unresolvable issues, Arae and the Original Ones.

Before long, the Adamics were being captured, taken prisoner to be used for their abilities. This also began excessive multi species inbreeding with other races here and afar. It was not a good thing, being an Adamic back then. This started happening almost immediately but progressed into a frenzy, about a hundred years later. That's not long time in the scheme of things. And so it began, the age of war upon the Earth. Destruction on massive levels in all areas of life, soon became the norm here. It was time to bring things to a boil and keep them there. How sad, the thought process of the Original Ones. How sad their actions. They didn't care about the bodies, only growing the Souls larger so they would one day be able to release a larger number of Souls to praise them. That's not sad, it's sick.

So, let's look at what we have here now. There are many new and strong colonies on the Earth. We had the original ones which were saved within the deep ground by the N'Antids. When they came out they could sense the difference in the air, which was actually the field, the Original First Being Male. They could feel his desire to see and feel pain. This was a little more than unsettling. They wondered what they were walking into.

Then there were the immediate new arrivals from other planets after the Earth had settled down again. They came here as farmers, miners, and explorers. They had no idea how things would soon turn out for them. At first they settled in as usual, with decent support from their planets of origin but, after a short time, were also turned aggressive by their Angels.

The same happened, after a while, with the ones who came out of the Earth. They had memories though of what it was like before. They had their stories that had been passed down through the generations as they managed to survive underground. It took another couple generations but after that; they were more easily made aggressive towards everything else there. They were made to think the planet was really theirs.

Another tragedy was in the making. About a third of the way through the Fourth Age, Lemuria finally disappeared from view, that is other than Hawaii and New Zealand along with a handful of little islands scattered across the Pacific Ocean. This actually fits into the scheme of things how happening on the Planet.

Lemuria was originally a shining example of how all beings can not only survive together but live in harmony with each other. The Earth was now being made a place void of such harmony, of peace. The number four stands for fortitude. However, in this age, it was the fortitude of aggression, not compassion.

As the war in space began to grow into a much larger issue, affecting more planets, there became a need for more raw materials, especially gold. Gold was used for many things as I explained earlier but it was also used to hire strong Reptilian humanoid soldiers to fight for them or with them. Welcome Planet Earth, to the disgrace of the Original Ones, war throughout the Third Dimension.

New colonies began to be placed on the Earth. They were not farmers; they were soldiers and more aggressive miners. They were industrialists who knew how to extract the most raw materials in the quickest time possible. This was for building war machines as well as food. Gaia produced a serious volume of food. This was now a more important commodity that it ever had been before.

On Atlantis, the new Reptilian Adamics were becoming very aggressive between themselves. They were fighting with each other. This was due to their natural reptilian nature as well as encouragement from the Original Ones through each person's individual Angels and the field itself, now harboring the feelings of aggression and severe abuse. The field has a much stronger effect on every one and thing than you might expect.

In India, the Tan Adamic Race had grown very strong again. It too was eventually culled down to a smaller group than ever before. The attacks on the Adamics were nothing if not continuous and brutal. They were a more peaceful group and spent a lot of time in meditation. This eventually led to the basic general thought processes of people in that area. Here's an example of how they lived.

It was in this age that one of the more aggressive Atlantean leaders attacked these people on their way to world conquest. When they arrived in India, or that basic area, they amassed their troops in a field just outside the major city. It was a place of greater learning and self-introspective.

There was a smaller section of this great city, a town called Mathurasdas and later Mathuras, which housed a building filled with scrolls and other artifacts containing a great amount of information. Some of it made it's way to the Great Library of Alexandria. This is how I came up with the rune called Mathuras for "J'Arae's Runes of Awakening". It means knowledge, either receiving it or giving it.

Now back to the battlefield. As the Atlantean troops started to gather in force, especially having brought some of their war machines, the soldiers of this city assembled outside it also. It was more than obvious a war would have to be fought. This city was a peaceful one and therefore not prepared for any such invasion. They didn't live like that. This is also why the Atlantean troops came here before hitting other stronger targets. They wanted to use it as a base while also taking all their food and various other supplies.

When the Atlantean army was fully assembled, there was the blow from a great horn in the city. In the top of the tower closest to the city walls was one thin older man, holding up both hands over his head as if holding an invisible sphere or ball. What happened next had a positive effect which also led to disaster.

The head general or leader of the Atlantean army went limp, fell onto the floor of his erected stand, and died. Immediately following this, two more generals or whatever they were called, dropped dead also. The next thing that happened was another blowing of the city's great horn.

This more than unsettled the Atlantean army. They had one last leader who led them all into a quick retreat from the area. However, they sent someone back to Atlantis letting them know what happened. In about a month, just a little more, the troops came back but in a slightly smaller number.

This time the city's soldiers gathered and eventually pressed forward into the invading troops. Before getting even close to them there was a powerful flash of white light and a crackling of energy that still bothers me today. The Atlanteans had brought their form of atomic or nuclear weapons to the battle. They didn't do so originally as they didn't expect any problems there or anywhere else in that region.

That earlier flash of light originated from a form of mobile crystal device which received a beam of energy from Atlantis it-self, from one of the pits there. It focused the energy into a pow-erful beam that was dispersed evenly enough to cover the whole city and destroy all life within it.

There's actually some evidence of this event discovered al-ready. There were hundreds of body imprints found, all run-ning away from something in the same direction. As this weapon builds up it's energy level to fire, it crackles very loud emitting a noise you'll only ever have to hear once to remember. These men were aware and tried to get away, back to the city.

Again I apologize for now telling you more of all the events across the planet. There were many, they were varied, yet almost the same end result was found everywhere. War had broken out across the globe. The Adamics had been imprisoned and persecuted. The Earth was sent into chaos following the same occurring in space. Creation, the Third Dimension that is, was at war. What a wonderful time for the Original Ones. They reveled in the anticipation of the increased growth of all the Souls and other Spirits.

As all this was happening, so was the excessively harmful mining and mistreatment of the Earth. Different mining companies were taking more and more materials from the ground creating more and more dust from aggressive techniques. Each of these companies represented not only separate businesses put planets also.

Soldiers were sent here to deal with occasional reptile and Animal attacks, Annunaki and other groups stealing raw materials whenever they could, soldiers representing other planets and companies, and the Reptilian Adamics, mostly from Atlantis, creating great damage to the atmosphere as well as the Earth's crust, using these four crystal pits the Red Adam originally designed. Arae warned them all about it. He might as well have been talking to himself.

Without going into great detail, let it be sufficient to say that between the crust damage which actually affected Gaia's core, dust from excessive mining techniques, and weapons fire affecting our atmosphere among other things, the Earth's weather changed drastically.

The Polar Regions, cold weather that is, moved a bit with an unprecedented small change in our poles which also changed the climate of the whole planet. The Polar Regions melted and others didn't freeze into an ice age but enough to kill most of the vegetation.

At this time I have to make note that this is not the first time the magnetic poles have changed on this planet. It happens from time to time. I can tell you that all the above events were made to happen in coordination with magnetic pole movement. Remember who was running Creation, the Original Ones. They made our current Universe, the Third Dimension. Do you think they can't control events like this? They've always done so on over two trillion planets simultaneously. This is a small portion of the power of Source Spirit.

The Fourth Age now ended with cleansing by water, the great flood. The magnetic pole offset was minimal but still enough to turn the Earth's weather upside down. Sorry folks, Noah wasn't around yet. He's from the Fifth Age. This is just one more problem with the religious books. They were written around controlling concepts, not truth.

Most religious people aren't a problem. The majority of them are awesome loving beings. It's the controlling abusive religions, the philosophies about to disappear, which cause the problems, not the people. Then you must also add in the fact that the Original First Being Male and Female orchestrated the entire series of events to get the end result they wanted.

For one example remember the Crusades. One pope who just happened to be eight-seven percent negative frequency Soul Spirit, almost by himself, started a war involving thousands of people, with the Muslim folk by actually going to their own house, knocking on their door, and telling them they were going to worship a different God or they would be slain? If this is not true arrogance, what is?

Do you really think these people would have done so without their religion, their Christianity and its leaders? This situation just made it easier for the Original Ones and their Angels to make it all happen. When people are being led to do things by something else, they are not completely responsible. The thing is that some people need little or no push to be abusive and controlling.

This type of control over people has almost completely been taken away now. You will soon be fully responsible for what you do. This by itself is about to improve all your lives. It's also a very small part of the upcoming change, way less than ten percent. Strong positive and welcome change is coming. It's late but almost here.

There are millions of wonderful religious people with great love in their hearts who are just trying to find the way to something they know exists but can't see. If you live in Alaska and don't hunt, and there are only five food stores from which to buy your groceries, you're going to go to one of them. This is why I've been working so hard helping people the best way I know how, to open themselves up enough to see who they really are inside.

Once you find your true self, your Spirit inside, you are free from the abuse that exists everywhere in your lives today. You must see a problem to be aware of it. You also must meet your true self to know yourself. This will only happen by relaxing and flowing down into yourself as what you really are, a Spirit visiting this Third Dimension in a physical body made for the adventure.

Well, here we are again at the end of another age in Earth's history, the fall of the Fourth Age of organized life here. As before, Arae came back and helped save as many as possible by enlisting the help of the N'Antids, once again. The survivors were brought to places of higher altitude this time as they lived in tunnels with the ancient Ant Beings. This is why I say we owe these N'Antid family members a show of gratitude. A warm feeling from your hearts will actually touch them, even where they are today. Like I said, heart energy is very powerful.

The Fifth Age
(750,000 Years Ago – 12/21/2012)

This now brings us to our time. It was about seven hundred and fifty thousand years ago that the Fifth Age began. The seas and oceans had settled down with the settling of the small disturbance in our poles. I guess I shouldn't say small as it caused so much harm, but it was a much smaller pole shift than we've had here on Earth before.

One more and final time, the N'Antids brought our people back up to the surface, the few there were. The number of people returning to the surface was greater than ever before but little in comparison to the amount that was about to appear. Things would be different in settling the Earth this time.

We had help from our friends in space, our family members now in different bodies. We've all had lives in most of these differ-ent bodies but there was a surge of reincarnated Spirit, previously having had recent lives here, coming back. This initially caused a small issue with the Original First Ones but was easily settled, as they could control the major decisions of any physical brain.

There is a dedicated group of beings from many different Planets that have come together, as a community, to help each other as well as new comers who prove themselves non-aggressive towards others. I call them the "Federation". I use this name because as we know things a federation is a group of people who come together for a like cause. This particular cause is a positive one. They have been protecting the Earth for just over one mil-lion years but never as they do now.

The Earth has been placed on notice as a Planet no longer ac-cessible to anyone not having permission to visit. There are strict guidelines for this as well as harsh consequences, such as your ship being boarded or destroyed. Remember, there's a war going on out there in space. This Federation helped the Fifth Age get a better start. Here are more people we would thank, were we aware. For now let's get back down to life on the Earth's surface.

The Adamics came one last time, all five pairs. This time they were not taken as slaves or creatures for breeding. They were once again respected for who they were. Their colonies grew quickly once again. Actually, their growth was unprecedented. The Adamic Race was repopulating the Earth at a rapid pace.

At first, this was a wonderful time for the Adamics. However, after a thousand plus years, they started intermixing with the different races here from other planets. This soon became the norm and the true Adamics started to disappear. Along with them went our stronger physical and metaphysical abilities. This was made to happen by the design of the Original Ones.

It was happening, more often than not, from the control of their thoughts by the Original Ones through their Angels. It's not that it was a bad thing, just made to happen, that's all. It was necessary to make the Human Race here weaker. The Adamics were just too strong physically and metaphysically. Too much effort was necessary to control them.

The Atlanteans had wreaked havoc with the crust of Atlantis itself through the excessive overuse of their crystal pits. With them, enough was never enough. They wanted to feed their war machine, to extend their control over others. Instead, they sank their homeland. They never accomplished their arrogant quest for world domination. They merely destroyed themselves.

Remember if you would, that it was the Reptilian Adamics that did this, not the clean original Adamic Race. They were a loving and communal group of people happy to help everyone and thing, not conquer them. They wanted neighbors, not subjects. They lived in harmony with all life, supporting and nurturing, not destroying.

By now Atlantis had just completing its fifth and final major stage of sinking, falling to the bottom of the Atlantic Ocean where it's now part of its floor. It's not under Antarctica or anywhere else. It sank straight down, more or less. The other smaller islands quickly followed suit. There were seven sinking events in all. Many Atlantean devices are still down there although the American government has stolen as many as they could recover. With their new starships they can do more but they're being directed into space instead.

The havoc in the Bermuda Triangle is due to equipment still down there having issues from time to time but usually from other starships coming here through multi-dimensional flight, that is to say leaving another dimension and entering this one. It's about the only way they can sneak around the grid to access us without permission from the "Federation" that protects the Earth now. Actually, they have for over a million years, but never as aggressively as now.

Lemuria was completely gone with the exception of Hawaii, New Zealand, and a few high mountain peaks of previous smaller islands. What a shame, what a loss. This seems to be a reoccurring theme in physical lives, doesn't it? When something is nice it disappears after a while, usually through one means or another. Eventually this too will change for the better. There will be more positive things happening in your lives that will grow roots, so to speak. Let's get back to the Fifth Age.

The land masses continued to move, a little more than usual, but things soon settled down to normal so far as the land went. Other problems were now beginning to heat up. By now there were serious issues with slavery here. I'm not talking about that of the Earthen humanoid races you're aware of between ourselves, but those you're not yet able to see, all the beings of different planetary origins here in forced labor. They're also being used as what we have called "human shields" keeping the Federation away from the planet's surface.

There have been many beings, usually very intelligent ones, from other planets brought here to work on advanced weaponry, DNA manipulation, as well as a host of other topics. They are promised a small fortune to come here, given a substantial amount of monetary funds and promises for their families, and brought here to some of the underground bases. Once they're inside, they stay there. Many are underground under the ocean floors. They have nowhere to go if they could get out.

This is a major deterrent keeping our friends, our protectors, in space from just coming down here and "beaming" them out. There are HAARP field systems surrounding the different bases anyway. When a starship appears they can turn them on to keep anything or one from being removed. This always causes the death of any living creatures which come into contact with this energy field. It crushes them from the inside like all the Red-Winged Black Birds that fell from the sky dead in Arkansas December 31, 2010.

A government laboratory actually had the audacity to say that fireworks scarred the poor birds to death. It's amazing how mentally lame the U.S. government perceives its people to be. Of course this is a continuous thing. Here is only one example of the mindset they have. If you think this is arrogant you're correct but only barely touching the top of the subject matter.

Our governments, especially that of the United States of America, have been accepting technology from the Annunaki running this planet as payment for "staying out of their way" regarding them having access to not just livestock but all the people they want. I'm only touching a strong topic here because it's part of your history. This situation will soon be dealt with by the one thing that can. Anyway, back to the program.

The Annunaki running this planet have control over all the mass monetary funding which occurs across its surface. Over ten percent of all monies involved in transactions, worldwide, winds up in their possession one way or another. This is then used to pay off other individuals for their services creating disturbances of one kind of another.

It also feeds their assassination force, their drug manipulation group keeping Earth's people as ignorant and sick as possible, and is responsible for many sicknesses as well as other forms of depressive control over the populace. They are not the cause of all problems here, just the vast majority of the major issues.

This is where we'll leave off. We're not going to go into our most current history here. The information available to us, especially for our children in public schools, is completely dis-informative. The history of a culture is always written by the victor. Seldom is it accurate at all when you're in an aggressive society. Such is the case here with us.

There are FEMA installations here which have lower levels, usually close to or over twenty of them. There are many different functions being served there. Did you know that Human clones are being grown across the planet, almost here in the Americas? They are sold through a form of black market, across the Universe, to various Reptilian Races, for personal consumption.

Jesse Ventura, here in the United States, has had his picture taken with some of the black plastic containers that can fit three people inside. People have seen and taken pictures of stock piles of these things off of a highway or railroad track in desolate areas. They are then quickly removed. Well, now you know what they're for.

The first time I heard about them, I went to them to see what was happening. I could see the bodies in them being kept frozen and why. When I say went to them I'm speaking of looking at them as Spirit. I wasn't there physically. I could also see many chambers where the clones were being grown. There was no Spirit inside them, just that necessary for physical life to grow. There wasn't Spirit from Gaia in them either. They were growing, that's all.

There are many advantages to seeing things as I do. Being able to see energy in all its forms brings one to a rapid process of truth, simple emotionless truth. The same mental conditioning is necessary when you're trying to release your personal Spirit from your body to see things as they are. You must relax and watch, look, and feel what is happening with absolutely no desire for any outcome. You must remove the majority of your Spirit from your body.

You are not able to remove all of your Spirit from your body, just in case you were concerned about that. You've been attached to it to have a life and it's impossible for you to leave it until it ceases to function, when it dies. This was made so by the Original Ones so you would have to stay in it, being forced to receive the abuse they designated for you.

Here is a good place to stop for this age. You now have the most important missing information to help you understand the basics of what's happening to you now. I could spend months talking about this age alone but only have a few weeks to finish this book.

The Sixth Age
(12/21/2012 – Today and Your Future)

The Sixth Age is occurring right now. We made it from the fifth to the sixth by Aramaeleous stopping the turning of Earth's poles. At least he did that for us. I'm hard on Aramaeleous, who is now gone, because he was very clean Source Spirit that went bad, took the wrong path.

As all Spirit became used to the abuse format that Creation was built around, he became arrogant and followed the example of the Original Ones. Lilly and Arae did not as they were having lives which allowed them to understand the concept, the values, of compassion, honor, and equality.

Here lies the great sadness of our Creation, the empty hole feeling that lies within Arae and Lilly. There is a momentary feeling of failure from not having been able to do anything about it until this time. This is because Arae had to systemati-cally destroy the Original First Being Male and Female, Lydia and Armaeleous, Lillith and Aramaeleous, almost all the First Angels, and a lot more.

They all kept attacking him trying to keep him from destroying the abusive control system on the Other Side as well as stopping this information from ever being released. Arae used their individual arrogance against them. Each of them, the next in line in the power triangle on the Other Side, would allow the current "controllers" to be killed so they would be next to play God.

They just kept coming at Arae attacking him so he kept taking them out, cleaning their energy and storing it or destroying their energy completely. To be correct, I had to deal with this personally, as Arae is what's in me and I was consciously doing this myself. Here's the part of these two books that bothers me the most, exposing myself.

I know what I am inside, who I am, where I came from, and the individual parts that make me what I am this life. The part of Arae that is inside me is the part that keeps having lives one after the other. One of my favorite expressions is that I am no better than a stick in the mud. Let me explain that.

All in Creation are of equal value. Nothing is better than anything else. This will be maintained on the Other Side as well. It's time for equality everywhere. This is not only a correct thought process; it is the stability for all communities. There must be equality among each other that keeps no one from taking over another's freedoms whether personal or as a group. If all at least agree on this than harmony is possible. Without it, there can be no freedom to be who you are and do what you want allowing you to grow into a larger form of who you really are inside, the sum of your different frequencies.

This is a small part of what I left you my last life, as Gandhi. I wanted all of you to see who you really were inside, Spirit that was meant to be free. I just didn't talk about the Original First Being halves. It wasn't time. I also asked you to remain calm, non-aggressive. I knew strong change was coming but couldn't see exactly how it would happen. I was still under constant heavy attack from the Original Ones and their Angels, as well as others.

I'm now teaching other people who have Source Spirit within them, those from Lilly and Arae, how to put their energy into stones as well as physically enhance the brains and bodies of others. Only Source Spirit is capable of this. There are now over one hundred of them here and about twenty of them will be able to do this within the next five years, that being 2020.

Until this, I'm the only thing anywhere that could. The reason for this is Arae being inside me. He's just that strong. This makes me better than absolutely nothing. It just allows me to do what I do in serving Creation. This is why I was created in the very beginning. I am as I appear today, the "J" man, like a janitor. I fix the things that break, clean up the messes, and take care of the people in the building with them usually not even knowing.

Doing my job properly is my happiness, performing according to the format for my existence. Don't think I'm without love. My animals always ate before I did. Everything everywhere is my reason for existence. How can I not have the deepest form of love for everything?

The Lillies are finishing their recuperation from the effects of all the abuse they've been put through in their over eight trillion lives. By 2020 they will be completely healed, loving, and powerful as no female Source Spirit has ever been. You will feel them in your lives every day. They will be everywhere doing what they can to make things happen smoothly and properly.

Remember, running lives was always done by the Original Ones. They would never allow anything else to attempt it. It was part of their maintaining control over things. Arae will set up the new format and enforce it. The Lillies will help things happen smoothly and quietly. Then your councils will be set up.

Creation will run itself, or I should say, y'all will run your own lives as a council from the Other Side. You're not young Spirit anymore. Other than having to maintain the non-abusive format, you will not have controls put on you. The Lillies will continue to help everywhere they can, as any loving mother Spirit should. Arae will simply keep protecting while fixing broken issues and cleaning up messes when they happen.

(Basic Upcoming Events)

There are some things that will happen, which I want to briefly discuss now. In the next one hundred years, some powerful events are going to change your daily lives forever. With the new change in Creation's format, new things will be brought forward for everyone and thing. Strong change however is almost always brought about by powerful events. This is always true when there's an aggressive race controlling a planet's activities. This new change will be smoother, softer.

In 2016, there will be massive attacks on hidden bases on the ocean floors as well as under them. This will be done to physically bring them into the open for you to see with your eyes as well as destroy some of their encampments. This will happen first in the Pacific Ocean, just a few hundred miles off the Californian coast. We'll discuss this further in the Prophecy chapter.

This is aggressive action but is necessary to begin the cleansing of this planet of its abusers. There will be a minimum of loss of life, but it will happen. Remember, we're only in these bodies a short time anyway as they're not ours to keep. We have them on lease only. They belong to Gaia, the Earth. I'm not making little of Human life. Never think that. I feel sad at the loss of other's lives as most all beings of compassion do. To have compassion gives you strength.

One example of Animals leaving is the massive deaths of the Saiga Antelope in Kazakhstan. There have been over one hundred and fifty thousand of these ancient antelope found dead now. There are fields of them found dead, lying on the ground together as they all simply ceased to live. This seemed to appear in late March of 2015, in the news anyway. I was already warning people that Animal Essence was no longer having lives and there would be massive instances of Animal death. A few of my videos even have this information in them. One of them was in made in February of 2015, just before this Saiga Antelope occurrence.

This is a very sad thing for us in body. My understanding that this needs to doesn't take away the pain from the event itself. You see, Animal Essence has been abused for than any other Spirit save Lilly and Arae. They were actually being forced into bodies to have lives serving everything else. This was stopped in early 2013 by Arae but Animal Essence continued coming as much as needed until now. This was their choice, their decision, no one else's. They have always served with great fortitude and heart energy.

Animal Essence has new jobs now. They will no longer be coming into Animal bodies so the vast majority of Animal bodies will be disappearing. There are new bodies for Spirit to have lives in that will be available soon. They are energetic forms. Everyone will have them but we'll talk more about them in a few chapters. Let's get back to the next one hundred years.

After everyone has gotten used to this, the fact that there are other beings on this Planet, they will be ready for the next surprise. As the timeline is planned now, and this is never a permanent fixture, it will be about 2018 or 2019 when our friends in space actually come down here and say hello.

There will be a sudden appearance of starships over many of the major cities, all across the globe. There will be no doubt that they are real. You'll understand they're non-aggressive. A few of the Earthen starships might be sent to attack some of them, possibly not, I can't say right now. I don't expect so but we'll find out later.

Then, about twenty or twenty-five years later, the Fae beings living here in the four dimensions below ours, will come up and say hi. You will see energy start to take form. Then, after a brief moment, you'll see it take an actual physical form. They can make a body, shake your hand and say hi, and then leave again as energy.

This event has more importance than you might realize. The new bodies that everyone will be having lives in will be very similar to these Fae bodies. You will be able to produce physical bodies but not able to maintain that form for too long. That will be fun for you, having the ability to float through a wall, make a body inside and sit down, then revert back to energy and float out again. Heck, who needs doors?

The important reason for this is that you will no longer need physical mass consumption to maintain the body you're having a life in. While in a Fae body, I can live for one month on the energy I receive from one apple and a thimble of honey. In one month's time I can help Gaia and the Plants produce hundreds of such small morsels for consumption.

When you have children you put your Spirit energies together and, with the help of Gaia, produce a few smaller energy bodies. There is no pain involved what so ever. This happens in a matter of minutes, not months. An average of seventy-two to seventy-eight percent of all abuse in lives will be eliminated. Everyone will be like this so you'll be used to it as that's all there is, except for an occasional exception if any.

Over the next thousand or so years the physical bodies will decrease in number until only about thirty percent still exist. Within two thousand years, maybe ten percent will remain. These are approximate figures and the future is continually changing. Here's something else to keep in mind. Although Lilly and Arae have had so many lives, they're going to start doing this for the first time. Also, having so much desire to give y'all the best life possible, they will be constantly changing things to make things better for you. This does include making mistakes too.

Now we have to add to the equation that all of you will be running your own lives just as soon as Lilly and Arae have it figured out. You will all learn how to do this for yourselves soon, not just as individuals, but more importantly as a family. You will have to do this together, deciding your own future paths. This is a wonderful thing but also difficult. Remember, everything alive makes mistakes, its called learning. The difference is that now there will be no allowance of the abusive treatment of others. This is how we move forward now.

This leaves the rest of the future what it should be, an unpaved road that you will all make for yourselves and travel upon. There is just one last thing to mention now. There are four new "First Beings" growing in the First Dimension or "Origin" as it's often called. Lilly and Arae will deal with that directly. Actually, it'll be Arae. That's his job, his responsibility, his reason for being. He takes great pride in the opportunity to do so. He was made for this and he loves everything. How can he not?

CHAPTER 12

THE SLOW DESTRUCTION OF GAIA, THE EARTH

B efore I start this chapter there's a few things I need to say, prevalent thoughts which are part of my Core Spirit. These are paramount to me and you as well. They are about Gaia, the precious Planetary Essence of the Earth, which literally demands our attention if we're to survive here on her. She will survive, but the Human Race will not.

Gaia is an incredibly beautiful being and all these bodies have a piece of her Spirit, as well as her energy, within them. Remember that Spirit is sentient energy but there is also non-sentient energy flowing off of it. This energy is within all the matter which is originally of this planet. It's all a part of her. Nothing here belongs to us; it belongs to the Planet, including these bodies. They are merely on loan to us.

A stone has energy within in. Each different stone's energy is a little different. The only Spirit that you can actually talk to inside it is that of the Planet it's from, it's origin(s). Having said that, sometimes part of another Planet or even a Star, comes here and will either blend with a part of Gaia's body or sit upon it, like Moldavite or tektite.

When part of another planet's body comes here and blends with it, the same with part of a cold star's body, you can talk to both Spirits within it merely by touching it and talking to it in your head, through thought alone. You simply ask if a certain Spirit is inside it and it'll answer, not with words but with feelings, image, or understanding.

Two such stones are Essenite and Star Essenite. These stones are very important to your awakening process. They increase the strength of your Core Spirit Stream, or Kundalini, in your body. I found their energy, actually Spirit, a long time ago. When I picked up a piece, I felt an almost electric charge come from it.

It was Gaia and Gaeira saying hello. Gaeira is introduced, described, and explained in full detail in the first book of the Creation Series so we won't go there now. I will say that she was the largest Planet to ever have life on her. She was two hundred and seventy times the mass of Jupiter. She is very powerful and here now.

Gaeira's Spirit and energy, if in a stone, will flow through the skin in your fingertips, through each arm, and into your Core Spirit Stream. Using the fingertips of both hands is the quickest, most sensitive, and powerful means to absorb and understand stone energy.

Although this is not a commercial, I want you to know this powerful stone is available at StarEssenite.com or SpiritualSymposiums.com. If it's not from here, it might not be the genuine article. Michelle understands stone energy and can talk to all Spirit. She's Source Spirit inside. She was also Sekhmet, a loving mother Spirit. She's also very protective.

Anyway, let's just mention Moldavite. Many people have felt the energy within it. That's because Moldavite is part of a Planet.

Every piece of Moldavite has a part of this beautiful Planetary Essence inside it. This is one of Gaia's visitors that I mentioned earlier. She doesn't blend with other parts of Gaia, she stays separate.

I once asked a gemologist, well respected in his field, if he or his colleagues could name the elements within Moldavite. He said it was only composed of the elements it combined with. I got a kick out of that. I mentioned that it doesn't mix with Gaia's material at all. Then I explained how I spoke with stone. He just smiled, wanting to be nice to the "gentleman of fantasies" in front of him, and said it does mix.

I smiled back and replied "If it mixes with other materials here on Earth, then why is it always the same color? It's always green in different shades due to the thickness of it. It always looks the same because it doesn't mix with anything. It's a simple physical observation."

Then I told him, as I speak with stone and actually see all the frequencies inside it, I know Gaia's not inside the stone. The only Spirit in Moldavite is the beautiful Planetary Essence of it. The stone Moldavite comes from another Planet.

By now he was a little perturbed. I was being polite but treating him as he was, ignorant of something and needing to be exposed to what he wasn't aware of yet. Ignorance is a completely innocent thing. It simply refers to the state of being unaware of something. I'm not aware of everything, are you?

Anyway, before he could leave I asked him one more thing. I held out a stone that I asked him to identify for me. This is a very special stone of which there is only one in existence. It's a stone made of dirt by the Fae at my house. An Elf came up to me one day, as Spirit not physical body, and told me they had a gift for me at the tree.

I knew he meant the Fae White Beech Tree just outside my back sliding glass door. I walk past it a few times every day, at least

I used to. I always look at the ground beneath it. I know what's there. I can see when something is different. He said it wasn't ready yet so I waited until the next day and there it was, like the other things they've given me, barely poking up out of the ground.

I felt its energy which was different, more soothing while still being grounding. There was also a strong feeling of Fae Love in it. Physically it was hard to distinguish from the dirt around it, but it felt different, more alive. When I dug it out I realized it was made of dirt. I found the little Elf, using my abilities, and said "Thank you, I'll be sure not to wash it." I was afraid it might fall apart, just being dirt held together. He was confused after I said that, but didn't reply. I left him with a feeling of deep compassion and gratitude.

The longer I held it, the more I realized that this thing was solid, like a rock. I went inside and washed it. It was turned into a rock, a solid stone. When you held it you instantly calmed down. When I first received it I could feel all the Fae Love inside it. I could see and feel all the beautiful beings that had put their love in it.

Unfortunately, my energy flows into everything near me and it started flowing into it, changing the energy inside. It was still calming grounding love but it was very strong now. I increased its abilities but lost the separate feeling of love it gave me. The gift of love has great meaning to me. I realize the same is true of many of us. Anyway, back to the gemologist, geologist.

Once I put the stone into his hand for him to analyze, I gave him a few seconds to do so. He looked quite confused because he was. He didn't know what to make of it. After the wrinkles had been on his forehead a while, I told him it was simply made of dirt, that the Fae had made it for me. He became annoyed and placed it firmly back into my hand. I was merely trying to make a couple points to him. Whether or not he was ready for them, he had them.

Now, there's one last thing I wanted to say before getting to all the abuse the Earth, Gaia's body, is suffering from now. This is about aggressive protection. Arae, the Spirit I'm composed of, is the strongest protector in Creation. He's stuck in this body, or rather I am, and is anxious to get out. I talk with Gaia all the time. Different parts of her work on manipulating my brain almost continuously, trying to help me finish my last job in body as proper as possible.

It's hard for me to describe my appreciation as well as my love for her. I have love and respect for everything. Being ninety percent Arae's Spirit inside, I'm very much a part of the big thing. His feelings are my own. I am aggressive protection. How can I not be?

I've been fighting this fight, against all the abusive Spirit on the Other Side, through this body as it's been continuously attacked every hour of every day. This is how I understand all this. The fight was brought to me personally.

Our family called Creation has been suffering from abusive treatment not only in body but also on the Other Side, since the beginning. If anything this information reflects on the lack of ability I've had, being that of Arae, by not having been able to fix this a long time ago. When you're stuck in body you are very easily controlled. This final life, however, things would be different for Arae, and the Second Dimension.

I have an understanding of some sort that I had to wait until now. That doesn't help much. I still have that sick feeling of failure every moment I look around me and see everything suffering. Joy is a wonderful thing to feel but it doesn't last long as I still feel the abuse and its effects all around me. I feel responsible for it. Arae was made to be the final line of protection in the true beginning. How can I look, and worse feel, around myself and not think myself as having failed?

The Source Field that Gregg Braden, David Wilcock, and Dr. Bruce Lipton talk about is an extension of Arae's Spirit, his energy. It's attached to, or part of, me. There are many beings on many Planets, over two trillion of them, all having abusive lives.

It's amazing how all the bodies here actually belong to Gaia, yet so many Spirits in body here abuse her so quickly, unconsciously, and harshly. People don't even think about it. The Human Race has become very abusive. This is partly done to us from all the lives we've had and a little help from the Original Ones through the original Angels put on us at birth.

The ones who received the most abuse were the Animals. They have been abused, controlled, butchered, and sacrificed for this false God concept since the beginning. This is why they are coming home with me. Their new home will be in the Second Dimension at the M66 star cluster, in the heart of the Leo Constellation. This is the "Home" that Arae built, a very long time ago, for the family Lilly and he created.

Animal Essence is already there and no longer being forced into bodies. There's actually very little Animal Essence coming back into bodies now. It's time for their new jobs. They will not have bodies for this. They are Creation's new Sentinels.

Animal abusers have already started being put into Animal bodies to have lives. They're not the only ones though. Human and Fae Essence as well as Human and Fae Souls have been going into physical Animal bodies for a while now. Let's look at which bodies they've been going into.

Dolphin have had Human Essence in them, on and off, for a long time now. It used to be an occasional thing at best. Now it's the norm. Over one third of Dolphin now have Human Souls in them. Almost every single Dolphin is born with a Human Soul now. There are still a few being born with Animal Essence. Animal Essence does this of their own accord to help the Human

Souls deal with these new lives. A similar event is that of parts of Arae now here in a few different Animal bodies to help them leave. The Animals will all be leaving now. We'll talk more about that later.

Even now, Animal Essence is still helping everyone else, in spite of their harshly abusive treatment from others. This is the deep, limitless compassion of Animal Essence. This is the desire to serve of Animal Essence. This is the great honor of Animal Essence. This is what the Human Race, in general only, has been grossly abusing and butchering. Great shame belongs to us, as a race. I know most of you reading this book are engaged in helping them. I thank you with my heartfelt thanks. I will honor you properly when I leave this physical prison in a few months.

The Original First Being Male and Female were literally forcing Animal Essence into Animal bodies and making them have lives. They wanted more of them also, to put into the new Universes they were about to create. This seemed to go on forever, yet they maintained their honor and most of their compassion for all.

Animal Essence is very strong and more worthy of respect than almost all of the Source Spirit that existed before the Source War. This is why I have such great respect and limitless compassion for them. It's what they give. Should they not also receive the same?

Although the Animals received the worst of it, everything suffered along with them. Nothing, except most of those helping to deliver the abuse while in body, was exempt. Why does this happen if there's a perfect and omnipotent God or Spirit looking over us. Why are all these wars occurring everywhere? How could this supposedly all loving, wonderful, and perfect God we're supposed to have allow so many abusive people to trample us to death or close to it?

It's because there was never any such being, only the abusive Original First Being Male and Female, running your lives since the true beginning. That's why everything happened the way it did life after life after life. That's why things are as they are today. Everything is suffering now. That's the place we've been brought to. It's time to leave.

Plants have been suffering alongside everything else. Look at what's been done to trees everywhere. It's not just in the Amazon forest, but in your own neighborhoods. Look at how they're continuously disappearing until the mighty Human has made his dollar. That is just one of the Human Races' disgraces. Again, remember this is not an individual thing, but as a group.

More and more people are becoming aware of what's happening here and doing what they can about it. When your governments only use and abuse you and when the larger portion of a group cares for nothing other than its own wants in the same fashion as the Original First Beings, you're left with self-destruction.

Earthen Humankind is cutting down all the trees and destroying Plant life which gives it the necessary oxygen to breathe. This is nothing short of insanity. The degree of arrogance and greed by the Humans on this planet has become the greatest of sicknesses as it follows the Reptilian way in destroying this beautiful Planet that their very bodies come from.

The native tribes of most our lands had a better understanding of proper treatment of the land. This is always overrun by others, especially when they come in from somewhere else being another country or even Planet. This is a current theme on many planets but not all. Things have been changing everywhere but nothing like they're about to change now. True benevolent change is about to come.

Besides people dumping garbage on her, there are selfish senseless companies intentionally destroying the very land we live on for the sole reason of greater profit, more money. Screw them. They need to live and suffer on the barren land they're creating. They live like royalty yet force others to suffer. They care for nothing other than themselves. This is arrogant abusive greed.

While we're at it, let's not forget Monsanto Foods. These people have the audacity to call themselves a "sustainable agriculture company" when they're abusing so much land, actually now being fined for it, and bringing forth major abusive issues by trying to control the farming of all plant food on the Planet. They actually say they bring you better food through their new processes. What a joke. Here's the truth about Monsanto Foods that many of you already know about.

What they forget to mention is that the seed from this food is not viable. You have to go back to them to buy the seeds. This puts you at their mercy, under their thumb. These arrogant individuals are trying to completely monopolize your major food source. They need to be controlled, not you.

Toxic and nuclear wastes are being dumped into our oceans every day. This is not only killing living beings there but destroying an important food source given to these physical bodies to help maintain them. Why? What reason is there for such abuse, such punishment of our own selves? How can anyone justify this? How can one individual explain such reasoning? You can't. It's that plain and simple.

Feel free to consider this rampant rage. These two books are about Creation, how it came to be, what's in it, and how it has functioned from its beginning to now. This is part of our history. Never forget we were led here by something that was abusive itself, the Original First Being. However, it is now gone, destroyed. We must become responsible for ourselves now, if we want to get anywhere as a family. It's time to see what we can do with our newly gained freedoms. Let's see who we really are inside now. Let's see what we can do, who we can become, how we move forward as a family, the one called Creation.

There are many other things to discuss but let's talk about something in the forefront of our problems here now, human arrogance. I realize that we are not all like this. I'm speaking of how the whole of the Human Race, in general, is acting here on Earth. It's a good thing there are more and more of us here working hard to turn things around.

Never doubt that you're here for a very important reason. Just the fact that you're reading this book makes you one such individual. You were brought here for a reason. Actually, you wanted to come here. Almost all of you know that there's a special reason for your being here, in body, at this time. You just don't understand what it is as well as why that certain something hasn't happened yet. It now has.

(Human Arrogance and The Reptilian Way)

As a race we always love to speak of our great accomplishments. I guess it's a natural thing to think of ourselves as superior, at the top of the food chain. We often think of ourselves at the top of the pyramid looking down on everything else. Remember now folks, I said as a race. If you're reading this book there's little chance you're like this.

Still, this is something our generations have been taught here, such as the teachings in the Christian bible. Genesis states that God says "Man is meant to have dominion over the Earth." Wow, what a statement of arrogance. It would say that man was duty bound to care for this planet and all on it as he would be in smarter and more able bodies to do so, if it wasn't abusive and arrogant itself.

It should have said we should open our hearts to all else here and respect the Planet that gave us these bodies we have lives in, not abuse it and all on it. Where's the "love" in that? There is none, period. How then, can this false God be loving? How can this false God be perfect, loving, understanding, and completely forgiving when it also made a "Hell" to eternally and brutally punish those he was pissed at?

Here's something else I've often wondered about, where's Mother God at? Did they get divorced and I got stuck with dad? If Jesus was God's only son then who the hell was Adam? Why should I turn my other cheek opening it up to abuse if someone hits me? Are you trying to teach me to be docile and easily managed?

I think you want me to be one of these sheep that you say will inherit the Earth. Did you forget to mention that sheep are butchered and eaten, on purpose? If you want to talk about religions being full of holes, lies, and controlling thought processes, here's a good one to start with.

The Muslim and Hebrew religions are no better. All religions are false. You can't make something about one something or someone. There has always been a need for the mutual equality of every sentient being, even on the Other Side. Truth is always about everything and one, not one individual whether it be a person or Spirit being.

A perfect being should want you to have a perfect world, like itself. Look around. Do you see a perfect world anywhere? Yeah, I don't either. Religions are about controlling the masses into a thought process that serves a smaller group or clergy. Sound familiar? Why do they wear these expensive robes often costing hundreds or thousands of dollars? Don't they know how many people that money can feed, don't they care? They only say they care, they don't.

Many of these churches, temples, synagogues, and shrines cost millions of dollars to build. Why spend that much money on a shelter to house a gathering of people. With all that money, millions of dollars spent on the building, why are the people inside forced to sit for an hour or more on a hard wooden bench?

Is this because the church loves them so much? I think I'll take a little less of that love, thank you.

Of course, in its arrogance, the Human race began considering themselves "mini-Gods" now. Many have decided to kill off a large variety of the beautiful Animals and Plants here. What a disgusting trait. Look at all the events that have occurred in the name of arrogance, that is, "God and Country." Remember the "Crusades" where the Christians were going to make the Muslim people serve "Their God"? There's just one religion showing it's fake face.

The pope that initiated that was an eighty-seven percent negative Soul, just like Pope Benedict XVI who retired early when his heart was attacked twice by Arae in body August of 2012. August twenty-third Arae told him to leave or he would die of a heart attack soon. He publicly announced his resignation in November. He would not be allowed to stay in office.

The former pope wanted to start a holy war, like his ancient predecessor. He even spoke out against Muhammad publicly in his home town, while still in office. The Spirit of Muhammad was actually Source Spirit but he was made to do most of what he did, good and bad, just like all of us. Major events in our lives are, or at least were, controlled by the Angels put on us when we entered our bodies. They always have been. They were controllers used to make sure we did what the Original First Being halves wanted us to do. This was explained in greater detail in the Angel chapter of book one.

As I have told you before, all necessary change on a large scale will be taken care of for you, from the Other Side. That is where lives have always been controlled. The abusive Spirit over there, what many have called God, has been destroyed. Your freedom is only a short step away, like walking through a door. This is why my last life I asked you to be the change you want to see in life. This is why I asked you to stand up for yourself and just say no, without violence.

Gandhi had a lot of beneficial advice for you. It might not hurt to look at his personal words, not any religion he talked of. He actually built a community of many religions trying to show people how they could live in harmony with different philosophical preferences. Arae did that in Gandhi's body so you would be more prepared for what's about to happen here, now.

Let's not forget about your governments which have been screwing you out of your money as well as free time. They are incredibly efficient abusers. Some people applaud their country's free medical system when there are people dying that can't get treatment in time or their treatment was faulty.

Then there's other countries, like ours the U.S., where you need to spend a lot of money to get what you desperately need, especially in the way of pharmaceuticals. If you don't have the money, well, too bad. Many people, especially the older ones, have to choose between eating properly or taking medicine they need.

Then, there's also the medicine prescribed to them that they don't need. Hell, the medical doctor's association tried to take vitamins off the shelves of stores requiring a prescription for them before having access to them. Hey there doctors, trying to control us or what? The arrogance of doctors is beyond measure. I know there are many good ones and I thank them for their heart.

It's the top of the pile that controls all the good ones. The top of this pyramid will be taken down also. Our friends in space have many benefits for us, a whole world of offerings. They are not bound by a reptilian society's rules. They are free of such control. Soon you will be too. It all happens from the Other Side. Certain things will be made to happen which will bring your complete freedom. This is how it always should have been.

You see, things are not at all as you've been told. You've been abused harshly when it was neither necessary nor important to you. You're also much more than you've ever been allowed to realize you are. There have been radical changes made to Creation in the Second Dimension though. These changes were made to protect and free you from what runs your lives as well as your existence while out of body. They will soon be felt here.

Here is the heart of the information, the message of this second and final book of the Creation Series. You have always been very powerful beings of Spirit having lives for the purpose of evolving but were abused too harshly while doing so. There were consequences from this that many of you could not see and refused to believe. The abusive frequencies that all of you started to develop became hazardous to yourselves and all Creation as well. This was seen by Lilly and Arae who were very busy having lives, but waiting for the proper moment to begin fixing things. Timing was paramount and the process is now all but finished.

SECTION III -
THE ABUSE FREQUENCIES

CHAPTER 1

THE EXCESSIVE ABUSE OF ANIMAL ESSENCE

As was mentioned earlier, in the beginning of lives on Gaeira, after Lilly and Arae had shared about one hundred million of them together, Animal Essence started making bodies and having lives themselves. They have been doing so for quite a while now. They have accumulated more lives than anything else.

Their lives are shorter as they were more aggressive and abusive than the others. They were also usually forced to eat each other in order to maintain their own lives while being eaten themselves by most every other thing on the Planet. This adds to a shorter and more abusive life span.

This, of course, pleased the Original First Ones. They weren't having lives themselves. They made everything suffer continuously to facilitate their Spirit growing larger and stronger once out of body. This is what they called success. This was being done, since the very beginning of Creation's physical life process, to create more Souls who would then admire and pray to them, begging them for what little they might be able to receive.

Animal Essence just happened to be comprised of two high quality frequency forms, that of compassion and fortitude. They are not filled with it but made of it. This is what they are inside. This is why they have been able to continue being such a blessing to us all these lives, all these years.

As Lilly and Arae continued having the next two hundred million lives together they realized they had much in common. As Lilly and Arae were Source Spirit, which was actually comprised of Animal Essence itself as well as all others, they already had a link or relationship. This gave them a mutual feeling of trust.

Something new began to surface. As Lilly and Arae were still making their own bodies each life, they noticed a change in their energetic fields. Lilly felt it first and Arae confirmed it. A new frequency was forming within their Spirit. It was not part of their original selves. It looked and felt sick, for lack of a better term.

This new frequency was what I'm calling the "Abuse Frequency". When talking with people about it being in their bodies I call it the "Abuse Gene". As I look at this frequency I can see it's distortion from all the others. It sticks out like a camel in a herd of sheep.

The first time I saw it, while in this body that is, I was confused as to what it was. It had no proper flow, it was erratic and unstable. It was just there moving around bumping into the other frequencies around it, like a little piece of chaos. When I went into people to crank their brains and abilities up, the first thing I did was take that thing out.

As I did so, the vast majority of people immediately felt a release of some sort, something hard for them to describe. The same is said of how their heads feel when I work on them. When you feel something for the first time you have little to compare it to, that's all.

As the lives went on, this particular frequency became stronger with each abusive life. It was simple knowledge, with each new life, that this had to be removed, and so it was. When Lilly and Arae started having lives by being placed in bodies already produced, there came a kind of ignorance, a lack of understanding, of who they were while in that body.

This was a wonderful opportunity for the Original Ones to instigate increased abuse and more importantly control over them. This didn't happen until their first three hundred million lives had passed. It was at this point that Human and Fae Essence started having lives. The Original Ones felt they now understood how to make a sufficiently abusive life for them without their committing suicide too quickly.

As Human and Fae Essences began having lives, they quickly started developing these abusive frequencies themselves. Lilly and Arae were unable to help them, except for a few individual lives, as they were more easily controlled in these premade bodies.

CHAPTER 2

THE INCREASINGLY HARSH TREATMENT OF SPIRIT IN BODY

As time went by, the Original Ones managed to learn how to place the maximum amount of abuse into everyone's lives. They added enough joy, with just the right intensity, to keep most Spirits in their bodies. They learned how to produce and maintain a constant source of low level abrasive abuse to set a minimum standard. Then they added strife to everyone's lives where ever they could.

One such example of low level constant abrasive abuse is that of insects like mosquitoes, ticks, fleas, and locusts as well as many others. There are many different insects that plague the farmers who have always tried to make a living offering us food to eat. Different insects have been used to make our lives a little more miserable.

We also have the issues of governments overtaxing us. Doctors, lawyers, pharmaceutical companies, and many others have ridiculous prices to help us with a constant form of abuse, the need to make more money to feed the reptilian machine that runs our country. Then there are other issues.

In addition to this, the Original Ones added emotionally intense catastrophes into everyone's lives as individuals as well as a collective. This is what the number eleven (11) is about. The two ones standing side by side represented the (supposed) great mother and father God, the two omnipotent beings who were in control.

As great disasters would happen on these dates, such as 9/11 in America with the bombing attack in New York, and the 3/11 attack on Japan causing a nuclear reactor to explode and begin contaminating the whole Earth itself. This was them saying we're in control, get over it. How's that for a benevolent God? Wow, what a misuse of words. No, that's just a blatant, arrogant, lie.

These events happened at a later date, one we're about to talk about, but I wanted to mention this here, now. Let's get back to the lives being had now, by the Essence Fields now with Lilly and Arae. These lives, by the way, all happened on Gaeira's Planet. She was huge and full of life.

After the Human and Fae Essence Spirits had lived an average of over a trillion lives, it was decided by the Original Ones that Gaeira's Planet would be destroyed. They told Arae to do it. He said no. I remember this moment almost like it was yesterday. This was the first major event of aggression between Arae, while out of body, and the Original Ones. Arae was now easily strong enough to stand up to both of them with no problem, and he did. He refused to comply.

This is where Gaeira came into play. She is not just the strongest Planetary (Female Universal) Essence Spirit in existence, but wisest also. She knew the Spirits had to keep having lives in order to come to the necessary place, I should say set of circumstances, where the proper thing could occur. She knew that Arae would eventually destroy the Original First Beings.

When a Planet gives her physical mass as well as a piece of her individual Spirit to a body that it might house another Spirit to have a life, she becomes intimate with that visiting Spirit's thoughts and feelings. Lilly and Arae were not only very strong but of Source Spirit, cleaned at their initiation into being.

The particular frequencies of Planetary Essence were already part of them. This made for a very strong bonding between them and the Planet they were on. This bond allowed Gaeira to feel many of their feelings, understand many of their thoughts. Besides that, with each life the two had on a planet, they would actually feed that planet Source Spirit energy. Lilly and Arae have always had a very close, powerful, and compassionate bond with Gaeira.

Gaeira told Arae to comply. She explained to him that he was not destroying her at all, just releasing different pieces of her throughout the Universe to help others everywhere who, before long, would need that help. Against his better judgement, that of trusting his feelings, he complied and has regretted it every moment of every life that he's aware of it. It is a debt he can only try to pay, never being able to do so.

There is a special amulet I wear around my neck at all times, other when cleaning it. It is that of the one who used to be called the King of Fae, Arae. Lilly was the original Queen or Mother. He changed that title to father. The Fae still use a form of self-government with Queens and Consorts for the most part. Queen Lilly, clean Source Spirit herself, is the leader of all Fae. She is from Lilly and Arae.

Anyway, this amulet is actually a special piece of the heart of Gaeira's Planet from so very long ago. Arae has had this on his neck during many of his two hundred and twenty thousand lives here. It carries great meaning as well as weight. It's not self-abuse. It's a way to remember a grave mistake so as to never repeat it again. It's a reminder to maintain one's overall thought process to protect without excessive destruction. It's a way to carry with me a part of someone very dear to me.

I was in my back yard with one of my dogs one night when, near the roots of my Fae Beech Tree, there was a light as large as twenty lightning bugs flying around in an almost circular pattern over a small area. She was moving up, down, and around in all ways to point out a singular patch of the ground below her.

She was a Wood Nymph, or Wood Faerie. She said, in a rather stately manner, that there was something there for me that was very important. I thanked her and told her I would get it in the morning when it was light. She flew back towards the trunk of the Fae Beech and into the soil at its base.

The next morning I went to see what it was. I walked right up to it but had a horrible feeling in my gut, my Solar Plexus, as I did. I knew, in a strange way, what it was and what was to follow. I felt Gaeira in the stone as soon as I picked it up as well as the memory of a horrific event.

I went inside, cleaned it off, and then sat down in a chair as I knew I needed to. As I relaxed, holding it with the fingertips of both hands to absorb its energy and talk to it properly, it happened. I knew there was something, almost a form of ceremony that I had to go through. Nothing could have prepared me for that next moment.

As I felt the stone I relived the moment I had destroyed Gaeira's Planet. I was shaking and jerking so hard my butt was literally jumping out of the chair continuously for what felt like twenty minutes. I'm sure it was only a minute. It just seemed like a long time.

I felt all the Animals screaming at one time. I felt all the Human and Fae Essences in bodies reach a pinnacle of pain far beyond anything they had ever felt. I felt the sadness of Gaeira as her body came apart.

There was an explosion of emotional abuse. I was all but screaming in my chair. Actually, I was making a lot of noise of some sort, I don't remember. In this body I have never had any pain to compare to this. I have had no amount of sadness, regret, or failure to relate it to. All I can say is, once out of this damn body, I will never allow this to happen again. How could I?

Gaeira, right there next to me as well as in my head, reminded me that I must never allow such a thing. I could feel her anger towards me tempered by the fact that she pushed me hard to do what she thought was the right thing at the time. I know I was wrong though.

I apologize for spending so much time on this. It is however an important event related to what I'm writing about, the abuse all of you have suffered over the ages. The Original Ones told me they merely wanted to understand what the maximum amount of abuse to a living being was. It was a lie. They just wanted to do it to everything, including myself, or Arae that is. They wanted me to have a powerful guilt feeling, one that I could never get rid of, to use against me when they wanted to. Let's get back to the important thing, all of you.

The Original First Being halves now had their abusive life format to the point where they felt content with it. It was producing the desired growth of all Spirit beings while in body. They were also confident that they were ready to release many smaller and fragmented parts of their Human and some Fae energy, the Souls.

CHAPTER 3
THE FATAL CANCER WITHIN CREATION'S FORMAT

With the destruction of Gaeira's Planet, there was an end to all Human and Fae Essence Spirits having lives, as well as with Lilly and Arae. For the first time in a very long time, Lilly and Arae had the time to collect their thoughts together.

From the more than six trillion abusive lives he just had, Arae had grown so strong that he could enter the primary focal points of both the Original First Being Male and Female without their knowing. He could obtain their most basic primary thoughts. He knew of the upcoming release of the Souls and discussed it with Lilly. Lilly was also very powerful. She had already had well over four trillion lives.

It was necessary for Arae to continuously have lives one after the other as he had to keep growing stronger to perform his duties as Creation's protector. There were already smaller forms of a first being type sentient energy in the First Dimension. By keeping Lilly out of body from time to time, the anxiety felt from their separation created anguish, adding to their soft abuse.

Lilly and Arae realized where all this was going. The Abuse frequencies would now be spread into smaller and less powerful Spirit beings less able to deal with them. Needless to say, this was more than just a problem with Arae. He realized this was damaging to all Creation.

This abuse was hurting everything everywhere. It was already in every single Spirit being and would spread into any others produced. There was also new growth of not just the Spirit beings themselves while out of body, but of their individual abusive frequencies. This would not stop until every living being was sick, deformed by these aberrations of Creation. Creation was on the path to its destruction.

Add to this the Original Ones' latest addition to Creation's abusive format, intensive arrogance of all the Spirits towards each other as individuals and separate fields. You can actually see this today. People are kept at each other's throats through governments, religions, businesses, politics, even sports teams just to name a few.

Arae now had a very serious issue to contend with. The current abuse format had to be removed as well as all the new abusive frequencies inside everyone. Creation was being destroyed, all for the want of self-praise by the Original First Being Male and Female.

SECTION IV -
ENTER THE SOULS

CHAPTER 1
THE ORIGINAL INTENTION
OF SOUL SPIRIT

The Original First Being halves, almost from the start, knew they wanted to have smaller pieces of themselves running around telling them how great they were. They wanted praise just after their jealously set in towards each other. Let me explain this a little better. It's a simple thing to understand.

In the true beginning of things when the Original First Being was still just one single Spirit, it became lonely as it continued to develop, to evolve. It eventually decided to make itself two different beings, to alleviate it's loneliness, the first emotion ever felt. This was the creation of the male and female genders.

After a short while it decided to have more of a good thing, more company. This gave it reason to release from itself smaller parts of itself. As this energy would be released they decided to insure that it too would split into these two same type beings. Then there would be one like each of them every time more were created.

Before getting started they decided they needed a support system for these new beings, one which was mostly self-sufficient yet controlled by them. How they did all this is in the first book and takes a long time to explain so we won't do it here. Suffice it to say however, that after a short time after they began creating these beings, the Original First Ones started having the feelings of jealously toward each other.

This is something that maintained itself throughout Creation's history, their jealously, arrogance, and abusiveness towards all others. They wanted control over everything but also praise for just being. If you want to understand how things have gotten from the Original First Being to where we are today, this is where you need to start, at the actual beginning.

They also decided they needed to build their own dimension to eventually retire in, having others do their work for them. Then they could just relax, do next to nothing, and hear all that wonderful praise coming from all other dimensions. Gee, I can hear all the abuse and fearful praise now. We'll look at their final destination dimension where they would reign supreme over everything and be adored, in just a bit. For now, let's look at their new master plan for Creation.

CHAPTER 2
THE PLAN FOR CREATION'S CONTINUED GROWTH

There was a secondary plan in place for Creation as a whole. It involved the new Souls growing larger and eventually releasing Souls of their own. This was their final goal, a continuous self-sustaining system of growth in their praise machine. It was also never allowed to happen.

The Souls would grow by having lives eventually becoming much larger and stronger. The Original Ones had already discovered the advantage to extreme abuse to the physical bodies while Spirit was in them having lives. They could now put this to work for their advantage.

As the Souls grew stronger they also increased in mass, so far as energy can be understood to have mass. An electrical field can be stronger, have a larger field. This is a simple expression of a larger energetic mass. There is more energy to it, you just can't touch it.

Once the first Souls created had grown to a sufficient proportion, the larger ones would each be reunited with their actual

Soulmate and placed into one of the new Universes waiting, here in this Third Dimension, waiting for them.

They would release a third of their Spirit as one large energetic wave. These waves would slowly thin out until they became little orbs like pouring a cup of water on a highly polished car. These orbs would, once settling down, vibrate into two parts. One would be female and the other male, Soul Mates.

This would now give them many new Universes, over three thousand, with trillions of new Souls added to the family, their praise choir. This process would, according to their plan, keep occurring time after time after time. With the abusive frequencies building up in all Spirit already, can you imagine what this Creation would become?

It would become a war zone with excessive abuse everywhere, much more so than it is today, with the Original Ones sitting back enjoying the excessive abusive growth and additional praise from fear and desire to conquer others. This is where Creation was going. Again, this is why Arae has done what he has. Protect Creation.

CHAPTER 3

THE ORIGINAL FIRST BEING HALVES PLAN RETIREMENT

It was nearing time for the Original First Being Male and Female to begin building their retirement home, according to their master plan for Creation. They wanted to build a dimension of their own to retire in. This way they would remain isolated, kept from being bothered by anything or having to bother with anything. All they had to do is listen to all their praise from the new Souls they were about to make, according to their master plan that is.

Before having the largest of the Souls create their own new smaller Souls, they wanted their retirement house built. The energy within it was mostly a variety of all frequencies. The auric colors coming from a group of all frequencies is a soft charcoal black, the same as if you melted and stirred a box of crayons. They were twenty seven percent negative frequencies. They didn't have as many lighter frequencies within them, as most everything else did. Gray worked best for them.

This dimension was in its earliest stage of development but finished just the same, as a newly built house only missing carpet and curtains. It's now located as the Eighth Dimension below this Third Dimension we live in here on Earth. That's where Arae put it after deleting the Original Ones in their final battle.

There was also some Rustic Orange visible. This color comes from a serious frequency of aggressive compassion or the strong intention to make something happen. In short, this Rustic Aura comes from the frequencies of strong intentions. Their intentions were nothing if not strong and aggressive.

The Original First Being halves had come a long way to get where they were at. If they had a body, it would have been tired from abusing everything so hard for so long. They should have enjoyed some of what they were giving everything else. They never did though, not once in their existence.

Their plan was to have this private dimension prepared, put the largest Souls back with their original partners, their actual Soul Mates, place them into one of the new three thousand new Universes already created, and have them release as many smaller parts of their own Spirit energy as possible. These older and bigger Souls, larger energetic bodies from having had more numerous and abusive lives, would now be able to release many more Souls due to their increased size.

Each of these Souls would be praising the Original Ones now, just like all the ones already existing. Wow, what glory for these Original Ones, to be praised more and louder from having been beating everything up. To top it off, they all came from the Original Ones in the beginning. Is that sick and demented or what? Here was Creation's cancer, the broken path needing repair.

CHAPTER 4

THE INTRODUCTION OF SOULS INTO THE LIFE FORMAT

It was finally time for the Original First Beings to release their Souls. As mentioned earlier, this was the first of these major events to occur. This was the one to get the ball rolling. This initial introduction or series of waves of new Spirit had to come from them.

Once these Souls grew large enough, each of them large enough would release a wave of their own in separate Universes exponentially increasing the size of Creation. As the Original Ones were selecting the Souls they wanted to use, they would also turn the direction of Creation's growth towards one that suited them the most, more aggression.

The Souls were made of smaller portions of only Human and Fae Spirit. They were only about a thousandth of the size of Human and Fae Essence Spirit when released. The Original Ones had already given up a large part of themselves to release the other Spirits already existing. Their first release was one third of their total energy. That's a lot.

The Souls also did not have the advantage of having the negative frequencies removed first either. Remember, the Original First Being halves were both 27.5 percent negative frequencies. Due to this fact, the percentage of negative vibrations coming out in these Souls was more varied.

The way I like to explain this is to ask you to imagine having a gallon jar of water, but know that 27.5 percent of it is actually vinegar. Now shake the jar vigorously for a minute. Then pour some of the contents into a water gun.

As you quickly shoot the water gun, the drops coming out will be a mixture of water and vinegar. You will wind up with an average of seventeen percent vinegar but have many different percentages as well. Now, here's something that just is. It was merely part of the Original One's format. Spirit energy, when released, comes out in percentages ending in a seven.

The Souls percentages of negativity, as described in detail in book one of the Creation Series, are 7, 17, 27, 37, 47, 57, 67, 77, 87, and 97 percent. This is just how it is. The seven percent beings are of a higher vibration but also a little low on residual fortitude. They don't have the strength that the seventeen percenters do. They have different attributes making them special, as all things do, but not the same basic power level.

A certain amount of negative frequencies are helpful to create a field of negative energy when you need to protect yourself. For example, when a seventeen percent negative vibration mother needs to defend her child she can easily create an energy field that is eighty seven percent negative vibration, temporarily, to protect her family. This field will fall away once the threat is over. On the other hand, a mother with only seven percent negativity will have to work much harder to do the same thing.

The higher frequencies are beautiful; I love them, but they're only part of the larger picture. You see, we are all different but all of equal value. We are part of a diversified family. The only thanks I can really say we owe the Original First Being, is having been released from it. It didn't create us, it released us from it. If you take your glove off your hand, you didn't create it, you released it.

I've often told people to think of energy a little like water. If you have a bucket of water and scoop out a cup of it, was the bucket of water ever pregnant? Did the bucket of water create the cup of water? The answer, of course, is no to both these questions. The cup of water was released from the larger portion of water, that within the bucket.

This is a very important part of your base information if you want to understand who you really are. This is in no religion or anywhere else. It was kept from you on purpose. How could the Original First Beings control you any easier if you knew this and how everything has happened until now? They couldn't let you know the truth. It was against their control mechanisms. It would hurt their praise machine.

How were the Souls released? How did it actually happen? How did you go from being part of the Original First Being Male and Female to your individual selves? Hey, while we're at it, what's a Soulmate anyway? Everyone uses the term but there's no distinct definition of it. Let's look at how you became singular Spirit first, your origin.

The Original First Being halves, the male and female, came together as two hands would, and released a wave of their combined energies but only smaller particles of Human and Fae Spirit. Don't forget that by this time they had already diminished their actual size. Again, this is why the Souls had to be smaller. They were not concerned about it as they knew the Souls could be grown much larger over time.

As this wave separated from them, it thinned out and eventually formed little orbs of Spirit with its own energetic field, a natural event. These separate orbs, once they felt free of other energy, split into two parts, male and female. These two parts of the one whole are Soul Mates. They are the only Soul Mates there are. You can and do have life mates, but there's only one Soulmate for each Soul, your other half.

Each half, but pretty much never exactly half, has the same percentage of negative frequencies as the other. The percentage of male and female in each half is again, almost never the same. I've seen Souls that were 47% male and 53% female just as I've seen Souls that were 98% male and 2% female. By the way, this is true of all Spirit, not just Soul Spirit.

Now, let's look at the particular kind of Spirit within this Soul energy. We already know that only Fae and Human energy was used in Soul form. What you don't know yet is that it's almost impossible to separate the two different forms of Spirit from each other.

Human and Fae Spirit are so close in frequencies that you can't make a clean cut between them. There are many Souls out there with over ten percent of the other form in them. I call these beings Faeman Souls. The same is true of Essence. As you might expect, they are called Faeman Essence.

There is also a uniquely similar situation between original Angel Spirit and both Human and Fae Essence. It's not as prevalent but does happen. They are called Essengels. They, when aware of themselves and ready, can move about as Angels do yet maintain a solid form and have lives. They literally pop in and out of places similar to the people in the movie "Jumpers". There's no noise though. It just happens. They do so through the Source Field which is everywhere. That's part of it's job.

Many people have seen that silver thread attached to them when they leave the body, when they astral-project somewhere.

That is part of the Source Field everywhere keeping you attached to your body. It is also seen going from you upwards, usually to the right, and then disappearing. That's where it goes to the Other Side. It helps guide you home but you've always had part of the strongest and brightest Angel from the original ones, Lucifer.

Part of him has always made sure you got home safe. It's disgusting that your religions call him some kind of devil, which doesn't even exist. Well, at least that built a lot of expensive churches for them. That is nothing short of sickening. Ah, the lies of religions. Its no wonder that so many people have turned away from them. Good.

Well, now we have the most basic information about Souls on the table. This is easily a singular topic to write many volumes on but there's no time for that. However, it was imperative that you have at least that much. Now you understand where you came from and what you're made of.

Michelle and the others of the Source Spirit Family, still here in body, will help you moving forward. Might I suggest something though? Don't spend too much time worrying about smaller issues. Once you're done with your life, you're home on the Other Side anyway. You'll be getting more accomplished by flowing into yourselves to open up your inner self, who you really are. One last hint, you'll have to do so to retrieve more information about yourself anyway.

After the first wave of Souls were released, four more were eventually produced. They were very similar in the course of the event and there was a lot of time between them. Souls from the first wave are the oldest Souls and those of the second wave are usually considered old Souls too.

CHAPTER 5
THE FAVORITISM OF HUMAN ESSENCE AND SOULS

Its not by chance that the Original First Being halves released the Soul Spirit out of Human and Fae Spirit. The largest part of them was Human energy and Fae was the next. This is how they were in the very beginning. Almost all of the Animal, Plant, Star, and Planetary energy was released when they let go of their first Spirit field, the large one that was one third of their complete energy.

The Original First Ones were always more Human than anything else. This is why they wanted to tell the Human Souls that they made them in their image. They didn't really, they merely were from the larger part of what they were, that's all. This was placed into your religions with direct intention. They were proud of themselves and were making sure you had as much reason for arrogance as possible.

This type of thought process will always lead to the self-destruction of a family bond. Keeping you separate increases the abuse. I'm tired of using that word, abuse, but I'm more fed up with seeing and knowing of it.

This arrogance, once more in place on the Earth, is prevalent in your religions. Just look at your book of Genesis in the bible. It says man will take dominion over the Earth. Wow, really? That's not aggressive or negative, is it? Where's the love in that? I thought this God was a loving kind of dude. Shouldn't he have said you should care for and love all things given to you or something like that?

The truth is always in front of, or inside you. You just have to take a little time out of your life, breathe full and relaxed, and open yourself up. It's hard at first but only then. The beings on the Other Side, who have been keeping you from being able to do that, are gone now.

This is more of Arae's doing while in body. I'll tell you all about that in just a bit. As it was done through this body I can offer detailed information. For now, please understand that favoritism can easily lead to arrogance and arrogance needs absolutely no negative frequencies to grow in. It just spreads like a cancer.

CHAPTER 6
THE EXCESSIVE ABUSE OF THE SOULS

Although the Souls had already been told they were made in the image of the God thing, they were getting hammered while in a body. The time of the second great Soul wave release was coming up. All possible extended growth of Spirit energy needed to be obtained now.

The limits within Creation's format of abuse were being raised to get as much extra growth as possible before placing the Souls, with their Soul Mates, into a new Universe. The Original Ones only had a short time left before this event and they wanted to squeeze as much extra growth into the Spirits as possible. They had no care for the problems with the Abuse frequencies now rampant within all Spirit life. It helped them grow a little more so they were good with it.

The war in space was increased allowing more punishment everywhere possible. It had become an epidemic in space. Almost everyone was being pulled into it. As far as the Originals Ones were concerned, this was a necessity. They had little time left before the release of the new Souls.

The Animals, Plants, and even the Planet itself were now receiving a maximum amount of abuse also. Torturing and killing Animals where other people would see it hurt those with more compassionate frequencies. This abuse helped them grow but they were of little concern to the Original Ones. They had no use for Spirit with these frequencies.

The Annunaki here were an easily held tool for the Original Ones to increase the abuse mechanism here on Earth. This is the time we now live in. Everyone across the Planet is being hit hard with taxes, medical expenses, physical harm, small wars, and so many other things. Just look at what's happening around you. There's just enough joy, and barely so, in your lives to keep most of you here still. Suicide is increasing. Gee, imagine that.

The Annunaki portion of the abuse format here is about to be taken care of. Arae will do so out of body. He'll be shaking their hidden locations until they crumble and bring many things out into the open for you to see with your physical eyes. This is something you need to see firsthand.

You need to see it for yourselves, not just be told. We all need affirmations to begin to believe anything. Don't you feel you deserve it? It's time for all of them to be taken down now. They will be leaving and not as they care to think. The imprisoners will be imprisoned, those that survive that is. Anyway, let's look at something that has started happening with Arae. Remember, he is a thing of ridiculous fortitude. He never stops but does have patience when necessary, only when necessary.

CHAPTER 7

ARAE PROCLAIMS THE BODIES HAVE RIGHTS, AND MORE

By now Arae has had to deal with abuse too long. It's a little like someone pushing your friend around. They never kill them but keep pushing them and then leaving them alone. Arae was so sick of this that a serious confrontation was not only imminent, but way past due. He had waited too long to be silent anymore.

Once out of body for a short time again, he literally got in their collective faces, so to speak. Energy doesn't have a face but focal points instead as described in book one. Arae was livid. For too long he had to see what was happening to everything he was made to protect while in body having lives as well as what he perceived when out again.

While in body he witnessed first-hand, all the destruction and violence brought to the physical world. Once out of body he saw the abusive frequencies more and more prevalent in Spirit while in it's natural free form. This was not only troubling but he knew it would eventually bring about the end of Creation itself, the death of the family he was made to protect in the first place.

After having all these lives, doing everything he could to protect all he could whether in body or not, he had a strong understanding of what protection was. He learned that through compassion, honor, and a sense of equality among all that existed, he could maintain them, protect them, and allow them to flourish on their own. He was done with this abusive mess.

He, in no uncertain terms, informed the Original Ones that the bodies were now a part of Creation itself. They were separate self-replicating organisms, still part of the Planets they came from, but uniquely individual just the same. He slammed them with the fact that they were part of the Creation he was made to protect and that he would now do exactly that.

It was the female who spoke first who was immediately backed up by the male. She said "The bodies exist for us to damage to grow the Spirits within so they may have better lives in their true form, as Spirit." I was pissed that she had the gall to lie to me, like that, to my face.

I realize now that I just went from saying Arae to speaking as myself. Let me explain something. I am Arae inside; the strongest focal point of him is within this body. I'm ten percent Jay and ninety percent Arae. I have had to reason with this for a long time now, not knowing how to explain what I am to others.

I have all his memories of all his lives available to me when I need them but can only access a couple, or few, at a time. I need, above all else, to be as honest with everyone as possible. This is why I came up with the name J'Arae. This is the name of the body called Jay that is filled with the Spirit called Arae. I'm not trying to sound or feel special; I'm just trying to be accurate.

It was actually Arae that was saying and doing all this. I just remember it like it was yesterday, that's all. I can still feel his rage at what he was still putting up with. I was not yet able to take on the abuse system that had been running since the beginning. I was close to strong enough, just not quite there. Let me explain this.

The Original Ones were no longer an issue for me what so ever. Their combined power level was nothing compared to mine. I had larger issues to contend with. Taking on the other two pairs of Source Spirit, the cleaned ones, was the issue. I also had concerns about having to take on others who would want to be the new God or Kings and Queens of Creation. How many of them could I take on? How could I do this in body? Did I have to do it while in a body, yes.

This will take a while so try to bear with me on it. I have to start with the last issue, doing it while in body. There are a few different important reasons for this. We'll take them on one at a time. It's funny I just said take them on one at a time because that's the most important part of this. I didn't consciously do that. Then again, the conscious part of our minds is always doing things we're not aware of. That might seem to contradict itself but it actually doesn't. It's also something for later, not now.

Arae and Lilly were the two strongest focal points of each of their origins, Lillith and Aramaeleous. Lillith had very strong loving energy with a better than normal amount of fortitude. Aramaeleous was sheer fortitude and power with strong heart energy. There was also the other pair of clean Source Spirit, Lydia and Armaeleous.

Lydia was strong Source Spirit. She had strong healing abilities but was never using it, very little anyway. Her frequencies had a lot of deeper green to them. Armaeleous had the frequencies of hope more than anything else. His aura had a very strong light blue. I really miss him.

When we had our first confrontation he was hurt to the point of death. I put energy into him and he came back around.

We'll go over this and more later. I do want to explain the name Armaeleous though.

The name Armaeleous actually stands for malleable armor. Source Spirit has two frequencies, actually more, that are never found in other Spirit. These two powerful vibrations give off the auric expressions of Gold and Silver. It's the Silver coating that Armaeleous and Aramaeleous had that allowed them to deal with even Negative Source Spirit without issue. It's also what Arae has to protect himself as well as everything else. The protector must maintain himself in order to protect others, just never at their expense, only his own.

Anyway, Armaeleous and Lydia were made with the intention of never having a life and controlling the Other Side when the Original Ones retired. Aramaeleous and Lillith were to have and understand lives so they were the ones to run the third and other dimensions. As they were way too large to ever connect to a body, they detached the small but strongest parts of themselves to place into bodies.

Armaeleous and Lydia would have to be dealt with as well as Aramaeleous and Lillith. All four of them had never had any lives and therefore had no understanding of compassion, honor, and equality. All they knew is that they were to become the new controllers of Creation. It was certain they would become a major issue with the termination of the Original Ones. They would be ready to step into their shoes, become the new Gods.

This would then mean fighting all of them at the same time. In one respect it wasn't an issue. Arae, through his over 10.846 trillion lives and having started as the strongest focal point of energy in Creation, would never be able to be defeated, that is destroyed. The question was, how could all this happen with as little damage to Creation as possible?

Here was not just the immediate dilemma but another series of questions. How would the other Source Spirit beings react as a group as well as individually? What would happen? Who would do what and when? Then there is another major issue of importance regarding having to do this while in a body.

The Original Ones always told everyone never to listen to Spirit when in a physical body as they were being abused and didn't know what they were talking about. This gave Arae a loop hole to work with.

It was not a built system of events that Arae would be working out of. Everything that would happen, once he woke up, would be unplanned by anyone. This was going to be a free for all. He knew he had the Animal Spirits to talk to. They would always answer him honestly. The honor of Animal Spirit is impeccable. He also knew he could count on no one else. This produced more unanswerable questions than solutions.

SECTION V -
ARROGANCE SPREADS LIKE
WILDFIRE

CHAPTER 1
ARROGANCE, A NEW CONTROL AND GROWTH TOOL

Over time, having formatted so many lives, the Original First Beings found that arrogance, when it showed itself, was a wonderful emotion to use in these abuse cycles called lives. They could apply it to many of the different types and forms of Spirit. It had a soft ability to increase the Spirits size by itself but the problems which they could bring about through its implementation were extremely beneficial to the abuse system already in place. It fit in.

So, the Original Ones began to initiate their propaganda program. They pulled everyone they could, into it. The fields who abstained were Animal, Plant, most all the Planet and some of the Star Essences as well. The others, some more than others, were easily seduced by the lies of the Original Ones.

Arrogance needs absolutely no negative frequencies to thrive. This became a wonderful tool for the Original Ones. So useful was this new tool that they implemented this system into the Second Dimension, where the Spirits lived when out of body. This was a new disease. The arrival of arrogance to the Second Dimension actually helped the Spirits grow when out of body.

When you add the already existing Abuse frequencies within all Spirit to the equation, arrogance had a stronger effect on the Spirit's growth rate. This began an era of turmoil and chaos between the different fields of energy as well as individuals. The Original Ones considered themselves quite the success.

In a manner of speaking, Creation was beginning to fall apart, to turn into a war zone. This process was alive and well in the Third Dimension where almost all sentient civilizations were either being abused physically as well as metaphysically, or at war killing each other. What a mess.

Arae was never out of body for long. He had to keep going back getting stronger. He was also evolving into something new. His abilities when out of body were now beyond anything anywhere. He still wondered what he would be able to do once back in a body again.

CHAPTER 2
ARROGANCE GIVEN TO CLEAN SOURCE SPIRIT

The first to receive their arrogance training was the cleaned Source Spirit pairs, both of them. The first of these two pairs were Lydia and Armaeleous. After they began to become arrogant with self-importance, the Original Ones' went to Lillith and Aramaeleous and set them up to come into play later. All this was done to prepare for the upcoming battle with Arae, as well as making everything grow a little more.

Lydia and Armaeleous were originally designed to control the Second Dimension for the Original Ones under their orders. They were told that they were the next Supreme Beings as the Second Dimension ruled all others. Lydia was really good with this idea but Armaeleous just went along. He had more frequencies of Hope than the others. He didn't care about controlling anything. He just wanted to help.

When it came to Lillith and Aramaeleous, who were a good bit bigger in size, the Original First Being halves used a different strategy. They explained that they were more important than the other Source Spirit pair, Lydia and Armaeleous.

They said they made them larger and stronger because they were the ones that needed to take things over when they retired. They would also be able to handle things better than Lydia and Armaeleous as they would have a better understanding of how to run lives, and asked them to just get along with Lydia and Armaeleous not saying anything about this.

Needless to say, they were both fine with this. Remember please that absolutely zero negative frequencies are required for arrogance to grow. This is a true cancer for all life. It affects us whether in or out of body. It produces a false feeling of self-importance over others which can only lead to eventual abuse of others.

CHAPTER 3
ARROGANCE GIVEN TO HUMAN ESSENCE AND SOULS

H uman Essence was the easiest field to contaminate. There are more arrogance inducing frequencies here than anywhere else. Arrogance is a false understanding which comes from firing up certain separate frequencies together. The more they are used together, the more arrogant the being becomes. It's a sad thing really.

This is more easily done in the fields of Human Essence and Human Soul than anywhere else. This says nothing bad about these fields. That must immediately be understood. It does however mean that they are the ones who need to be the most aware of this condition, that's all.

Human Souls and Human Essence were always told they were better than everything else because they were from the major frequencies that made up the Original Ones. They were played hard for many reasons but one in particular.

The future growth of Creation, that envisioned by the Original First Beings that is, was dependent on the Human Souls growing larger faster to create more of them. These were the building blocks of the new "applause" system for the almighty Original First Being halves.

It was the Human Souls, more than any other Spirit form, which would be increased in number throughout this new Creation. They were not only the larger part of them, which they liked, but also the easiest for them to control, grow, and manipulate to get what they wanted, praise.

CHAPTER 4
ARROGANCE GIVEN TO STAR ESSENCE

H ere's our next topic in the arrogance arena. Star Essence is a very different kind of Spirit and energy. It is very strong energy and therefore very powerful Spirit. If you have any question of this, think of the power of our Sun. A Planet has Female Universal Essence which is very powerful also. A Star is similar with just a little more energy to it.

They were told that without them all physical life would collapse and everything everywhere, even the Planetary Essence, owed them a great deal. They were told that none could exist without them. Almost half of them feel that way today. I just looked at it again, as I do as I write, and feel sad. All this never should have been allowed to happen.

The Original First Being was exactly that, the first being ever sentient anywhere in existence. It could not help that it was created with as much physical dense matter as it was. That's where the more negative frequencies came from. A small amount is fine, actually healthy in one regard, but it needs to be kept below ten or eleven percent for Original Source Spirit.

Arae will be making the necessary changes to the First Dimension once he's freed of this body. I'm looking forward to becoming part of this. I love to serve, or as I prefer to say to help, others. Hell, it just makes me happy, that's all. I'm no one's servant, don't think that. I don't take orders well at all. I do love to help though.

Well, let's get back to everything being made to think it's better than everything else.

CHAPTER 5

A DECISION IS MADE, NEW
CLEAN SOURCE IS NECESSARY

L illy and Arae, during one of their few short moments together out of body, had a lot to talk about. They were already
aware they needed to do something about all these problems.
The Creation they loved was slowly killing itself, all for the desired praise of the Original Ones. This could not be allowed to
continue.

The issue at hand here was how to stop it. One thing was for
certain, it would require the use of great force. There was no way
the Original Ones would just let it happen. Not only were they
Creation's original control freaks but were insistent on building
their praise machine.

This was the one thing that not only kept them moving forward as a pair but also keep from being at each other's throats,
so to speak. The Male First Being was tired, actually jealous, of
the Original First Being Female receiving all the praise. That's
why she had all the physical bodies, most of the time anyway, call
her Father God. There's also the issue that the male Human
bodies were made, not always but most often, stronger than the

female ones. They were supposed to protect the females with their life if necessary anyway.

Once the Original Ones were taken out of the picture, a new restructuring process would be necessary immediately. Creation was very busy having lives and needed to begin changing to a much less abusive format immediately but not by everything being destroyed and taken home.

The physical world needed to understand what had happened and why. They needed their foundation for the new process as well as needing to understand the existence of the Other Side as well. Lilly and Arae already knew that for family to be together they had to first meet each other, be aware of each other's existence.

The Third Dimension needed to understand who they were and what they were doing in physical bodies. They also needed to understand why they were doing it. Without this information, Creation could not move forward as a family. You have to become aware of each other, sit at the same table so to speak, at least once before you can become a family. Everyone doesn't have to agree with each other about everything, but you do have to meet.

SECTION VI -
ARAE AND LILLY TAKE A
STAND TOGETHER

CHAPTER 1
LILLY AND ARAE BEGIN THEIR DEFIANCE

The more Lilly and Arae discussed this, the more anxious Arae became to get started. He was made to protect and had not been allowed to do it once he understood compassion, honor, and equality. He felt a very strong need to perform the duties he was made for. He needed to justify his existence as well as do what always felt right to him anyway. He needed to "clock in" at work.

Where do you begin to make such a great change in such a large, complex society? One thing that remains a constant, no matter what form or dimension you're in, is that to remove a problem you have to go to its source, the cause of it. The Original First Being halves created this futile abusive system of growth through physical lives. The Original Ones had to be removed from this process. They would never just step aside. They would never agree to anything.

There was only one way to achieve the removal of this cancer, they had to be destroyed. This is something that had never been done on the Other Side. Arae had removed negative frequencies from Spirit when out of body, but that's it. However, from having done so for so long, he knew he could delete the actual Spirit within the energy itself. He could change Spirit, if necessary, back to a form of clean Spirit energy.

Here again is another question for Lilly and Arae to have to deal with. How strong was Arae's ability to do so? How strong a being could he do this too? How many could he face at what time and, if more than one, which ones simultaneously? This was a serious situation.

Nothing was near Arae's strength. Lilly's power level was very strong but she did not have all his fortitudinal frequencies. That was Arae's big advantage since the beginning. Lilly has strong energy but is comprised of loving mother frequencies. She was made for a different purpose. She was to keep having lives and be used to help others while in body but only when it was necessary to keep them in their bodies. Hope deters suicide, a simple thing.

Originally these frequencies were thought to make her weak and serve little purpose. Instead they made her the best possible Source Mother Spirit there could be, a loving mother with only the best of everything desired for her children. She will soon be doing what she loves best, what's natural for her, to care for those around her. She is Creation's new upcoming Mother Source Spirit, actually more like a really strong loving big sister.

Although their own plan to remove the Original First Ones was not yet put together, they didn't have many of the pieces to put together, they couldn't refrain from showing their dismay towards them. They had simply had enough and were tired of hiding it.

While in Spirit form we communicate with each other through a series of images, feelings, and raw thought data almost like a computer. Feelings are very strong, especially when you come from heart energy as Lilly and Arae did. They no longer held back their feelings. They did hide their thought processes thought, that and imagery. It was only a short time, as they expected, before this caused incident with the Original Ones.

CHAPTER 2

THE ORIGINAL FIRST BEING HALVES RETALIATE

The Original First Being halves had been abusing Lilly and Arae harder than anything else, save most of the Animals. They had no desire to cut back on that. Instead, to cope with Lilly and Arae's new found denial of their ways, they began a new intensified abuse program for them. Lilly got hit the hardest as they were abused through attacks to their hearts.

Lilly and Arae were never having lives together anymore, well almost never that is. Sometimes they were placed together so they could feel the love they had for each other and then have it ripped apart by the Original First Being Female. This backfired on them.

Having Arae in me allows me to understand things about his, or my, past. I'm an Earthen Human body housing Spirit that is ninety percent Arae and ten percent Gaian Spirit. My feelings are my own and they are those of Arae. We are the sum of our parts and I am part of Arae. Inside me is the part of him that has had life, after life, after life. This is how I can feel how Arae felt back then. It's inside me already as if I felt it yesterday.

Lilly and Arae came from the two largest clean Source Spirit fields in Creation. Their love is something of a paramount adventure between the two of them. It is so powerful, so dense, and always used against them for the sake of abuse in the beginning. As time went on, the Original Ones just liked doing it.

I have a hard time feeling this. I love her so much that my eyes break into tears when I think of her too long, as they are now. No words can fully describe this love. It is paramount to my existence. When I was very young I saw a picture of Lilly once, in Marilyn Monroe's body that is. I saw loving mother energy and became bewildered, then sad. I didn't understand then, but I do now.

It's like when I used to say the pledge of allegiance in school as a child. It used to make my eyes tear up and I couldn't understand that either. Man was that embarrassing with my friends around. It was a little later, when I looked back, that I could see everyone freezing to death at Valley Forge. I have horrific memories from that moment in time.

We crossed that river because we were all dying. I was not smart, I was desperate. I would have lost all my men if we didn't go. We also needed their food and supplies. I had no choice, no decision to make. I would rather myself and my men die as good people than in the cold. My life as George Washington was just another one that really sucked.

It was those young, and old, men who suffered with me there that should be honored, not George. They lost their feet, hands, and more while I was trying to put something together. It was a time of extreme abuse, of the screams coming from the soldiers who were losing limbs from frostbite. I'm leaving the personal accounts, those I had with these men who were suffering, out of this. I've been here long enough.

History needs to be rewritten. It needs to be clear and simple fact that others can make their own decisions about, like my two

Creation books. Tell it like it is and let others make up their own minds. Isn't that what freedom is supposed to be? Good luck finding that today. All of us are continuously being led, like cattle to a slaughter house. We must be given enough joy to maintain ourselves, but we're still being led around. Let's get back to Lilly.

I have unlimited fortitude, that of Arae within me, and my aggression grows to almost intolerable levels when I think of the abuse given to everything, especially my precious Lilly and how it's hurt her. She's healing right now in energy chambers in a dimension Arae created to protect all he loves as well as those who wanted to wait things out in safety. It's also a place to store cleaned energy. That's Spirit that's been deleted. This can easily be absorbed by other Spirit and there's some very strong Source Spirit in there.

There are three openings in the barrier of this dimension and only Arae's energy can get through it without being dissolved. That's how he's protected everything that came to him asking for the same, while all this fighting has been going on. There are many beings there, in a state of suspended animation, who will come out untouched as soon as Arae's free again and the war is over. Many came as a family, and so were they stored, together.

I can't wait to see Archangel Michael and Lucifer again. It's amazing how an Angel called Lucifer, who's name even means of the light, can be turned into this make believe devil creature which doesn't even exist anywhere, yet has helped build a lot of churches. They both have protected you from the very beginning, especially Lucifer.

When your body expires and you go home, guess who's been making sure you get there safely? Guess who's been keeping the negative and positive frequency Other Sides separate so you can live pleasantly over there? That's right, it was Lucifer.

If you watch some of my videos you can see me clean something and then put it into my forehead. Behind my forehead it one of these energetic filters used to protect this dimension. Another part of Arae built this years ago and later showed me what it was for. I've always known I look ridiculous doing this, especially to all who were not aware of what I was doing. I don't care much about that. I had to do it then. I very seldom stop a video to redo it. I would rather things just be what they are.

When people research me they find that I talk of things and do things that are completely ridiculous to the status quo. Then, after I talk with them for a while or go into their brains, their opinion changes. I've actually had people run away at good speed after I went into their brains to open them up, after they said to go ahead and do so. This has never happened before on any Planet. It's a little freaky to some, others love it. Most people find it very relaxing.

Many are still a bit confused about what I tell them. They have many questions, as well as some proof, that there's reason enough to consider hearing my words. If I was concerned about myself I wouldn't be running around everywhere in overalls saying what I do. I'm no big deal but my job is. Let's get back to the Original Ones who are still maxing out the most abuse possible to everyone.

After seeing Lilly come out of her lives hurt more than usual, Arae become enraged. This not only cemented his desire to destroy them but also increased his power level not to mention the rate of his new personal evolution. He has always been a determined Spirit, but was now engaged as never before. This would not end well for the Original Ones. His job was to protect all Creation but to him, Lilly was the most important thing there was.

The Original First Beings knew that they were about to have new problems. Arae's rage, his energy spiking, was nothing they wanted to deal with. In their own arrogance, they assured themselves it would be overcome easily enough one way or the other. They also had this false feeling of security that he would never rise against them other than speaking his mind. They felt that if he did the other Source Spirits would come to their aid. After all, they were the original creators, they were God. This was a fatal mistake, one of many they made, one of their biggest.

CHAPTER 3

THE "EARTH 2012" LEGEND IS CREATED

The Original Ones began to solidify their plans for Creation's new rebirth. With the new issues between themselves and both Lilly and Arae, now was a good time to make future plans solid and present them to the others. This is also where they put their arrogance format to its best use, in their eyes that is, playing everyone against themselves.

This new event would be introduced as a momentous occasion everywhere, including the Second Dimension where everything was out of body. Here is where the largest Souls would be allowed to create their own families in their own Universes, forever increasing the glory of the Original First Ones. Let's look at what all this was about.

The Original First Beings were building a larger "praise" machine to make them feel better. On Earth in the year 2012 of the Fifth Age, they would take the larger Souls and put them together with their actual Soul Mates. These two Soul Mates would then go to one of the over three thousand new Universes already made by then, and release all the smaller Souls they could from their combined energy. The larger the energy field, the more

Souls they would release. The more Souls that were released the more praise the Original First Beings could receive. There was also a need for more Animal Essence to be abused.

These Original First Being halves were incredibly self-absorbed and never hesitated to harm all the bodies they could while striving to still keep them in their bodies to continue their growth cycle. The Animals always had it worse than anyone else.

In the Second Dimension, all in free Spirit form were told that many of them would finally have their own families, release smaller parts of themselves to grow into their own likeness. Actually, almost everyone was told this when there were only a few thousand that would do it. Remember, there were many trillions of Souls.

To the Original Ones, lying was nothing more than a tool, as simple to them as breathing is to us. They did it just as easily and with no remorse. They had no remorse about anything. They did what they wanted and expected others to not only agree but praise them for it. There's a sickness for you. Welcome to the home of arrogance, as well as many other bad traits.

In the other dimensions, the third especially, there was something different being spread around. They were all told that "Earth 2012" was about all Creation finally knowing the real truth of what existed on the Other Side. The only problem was that they were never going to hear it. They were being set up for another lie, again.

The Original First being halves wanted Arae to tell everyone that there was not really one God, but two, a male and female. That was the big truth they were going to unload on everyone. This was the set up for the new Universes they had just built, a little over three thousand of them. This is where they wanted me, actually told me, I was going to tell everyone about the "Mother and Father God" that were actually what we needed to praise. There's a lot more to this that we'll cover later. Wait until you hear it, first hand.

CHAPTER 4
ARAE REINFORCES HIS ORIGINAL STRATEGIES

With the newly released "Earth 2012" event, Lilly and Arae became more focused and driven to hurry with all the details they could. It was obvious that they would never be able to completely and accurately foresee the all events that would occur from what they were about to do. By now it didn't matter much to Arae, this had to happen and soon. Creation couldn't live through this abuse and Lilly needed to be protected now. He had to do more than he originally thought. He now understood the full depth of his problem, at least as much as he could until placing himself in the middle of it.

As mentioned earlier, Arae was the strongest form of Spirit or energy anywhere. His power level was so strong that no other part of Source Spirit, not even that of Aramaeleous, could stop him. The concern here was the size of strong energies he had to contend with and what these arrogant cowards might do to anything else. They had never had a life to learn anything. They had no compassion, honor, or sense of equality.

His Spirit energy had more density than anything else. As all the other Source Spirit would come at him, no matter how large their energetic fields were, they couldn't contain him. It would be like a large hand trying to stop a bullet. Unfortunately there was much more to the upcoming battle than just that.

He would be in a body. This limits your abilities by over ninety percent. Then there was the waiting until the barrier between both energetic brain halves was dissolved enough to free his independent thought allowing him to remember who he was. He would eventually have to be freed of this barrier to perform those functions the Original Ones expected him to accomplish, especially telling all physical Creation about their loving and wonderful Mother Father God.

It was obvious that those around him, in the physical arena so to speak, would probably be attacked one way or another in attempt to control his actions, keeping him in line. This was something that could not be accurately understood until the fighting commenced.

There was also no way to estimate what would happen, in relation to the two different huge clean Source Spirit pairs, once Arae's war of abuse began. Would they all come at him at one time? Who, besides Arae, would they attack? This remained to be seen. Arae already knew they were all arrogant, except for his brother Armaeleous. His frequencies were that of hope. Arae had a lot of love for him.

Now, add to this all the arrogant Spirits in the fields of Human Essence, Fae Essence, and the largest of the Souls who were still strong enough to be a problem while Arae was in a body. You see, the physical body is like a sponge when it comes to Spirit. It's made that way in the beginning so the Spirit within it can flow freely. This is important for it to function properly.

Spirit can merely touch the body and enter into it's physical mass to find it's way up to your brain, heart, Solar Plexus, or other energy field. They especially like to hit your base Chakra to blend with your emotions, trying to manipulate your emotional responses and also enter your Heart Chakra more easily. Remember the Heart Chakra pulls in emotions from your Base Chakra as well as your brain to create feelings.

There was another thing to consider. Arae would be struggling harder than he ever had while in a body. To do all this through the physical mass he would be temporarily imprisoned in, would be difficult. Could he do it? Yes. However, just how would all this go? Would he do as much as he could and then just kill his body to return home, to the Other Side that is, and finish everything there?

Was that really even an option? Didn't the Third Dimension, the Physical Realm, not just deserve to understand what has been done to them since the very beginning but have a record of it? Didn't they need to have a written or recorded file of these events? True history is important. It's usually written by those who control them. That's why it's been rewritten so many times.

Wasn't it about time that they just had the simple truth, to understand what had been happening all along? Yes. It's important for everyone to have access to this information in order to move forward with greater strength and self-conviction. Everything should understand their true and equal value within Creation.

You should know why you were being made to do things, for so very long, against your will. You should understand why you've done things that are completely against your own heart feelings as well as who did this to you. You need to understand how you were never allowed to be yourself so you can move forward without guilt while beginning to understand who you really are.

Leaving the body early was not an option unless there were no others left. This raised even more questions to search answers for. As you're beginning to see, this was no simple task. It had to and would be done. The problem was how to go about it.

One other thing was paramount, almost as important as the cleansing of abuse, the destruction of the singular God concept in the Physical Realm. There could be no reason offered for the physical bodies to begin worshiping a new God or deity. This would only take away their desire to achieve self-awareness, asking for something instead of going after it themselves as their true selves.

There were other things of concern but there's no need to bring it all up. This is enough for this book, for your understanding of the major issues. Arae already knew that, for the most part, this would entail just going into a body, destroying the Original First Being halves, and keep dealing with whatever happened.

In the end, he really had no choice. He would have to keep making contingency plans for everything as it happened. This is where his massive fortitude came into play. This is why he knew, in the end, he would succeed. He never quits, never has, never will. Let's get back to our problems now occurring in Creation.

SECTION VII -
THE GROWTH RATE
INCREASES THROUGH
ADDITIONAL ABUSE AND
PREJUDICE

CHAPTER 1

SHORTENED "OFF TIME" BETWEEN LIVES

As things were now coming to the end of this first phase of Creation's life as a whole, everything was being sped up by the Original Ones. It was time to crank up the abuse as much as possible, to max things out. This was the last chance for them to increase the size of the Souls.

One way they did this was not only to allow but coerce Spirit to have lives closer together. Although this increased the amount of their Abuse frequencies it also increased their strength. They already knew these new distorted and abusively created frequencies had the ability to eventually vibrate them apart, to kill them or mutate them into something sick, senseless, or even inert as in unable to function.

They didn't care for the well-being of Spirit, other than being able to maintain their existence. They were completely focused on building additional praise machines. The individual Spirits within Creation were tools to get what they wanted, that's all.

This short time between lives does not allow the Spirit having had that life, to release the abusive frequencies naturally. They build up inside and when you can't release them, they build up. If you go back into a body before you do, you'll take those feelings and memories with you. This is why there as so many of us having "past life issues" now.

I used to be somewhat claustrophobic. I didn't have to have the car window open but I liked it more than just for the fresh air. I also didn't like to be in a small enclosed area. I was ok in a phone booth but was not happy when thinking of exploring caves. I found out why after doing my first past life regression.

I relaxed and told my Spirit Guide, I had one when I first woke up, to "Show me what I need to see!" He did. His name was Robert, Rev. Robert Kirk. He's the same man who's journal was made public by John Matthews in his book "The Secret Lives of Elves and Faeries: The Private Journal of Robert Kirk."

I walked past the book at a Barnes and Noble book store and it lit up, in my mind's eye, like a two hundred watt bulb. I went to my car to leave, without buying it, and he kept yelling at me to go buy it even though I barely had enough money to do so. Needless to say, I went back in and did so.

Anyway, let's get back to the past life regression. Back then I usually had my eyes closed when I meditated. There was something of a blank darkish screen with energy softly moving around, behind my eyes. All of a sudden I was looking at a large strong man who was about fifty yards or more away from me, maybe one hundred, hard to say.

I can tell you though that I saw him as clear as could have ever been possible. It would bring our current High Definition TV/s to shame. He was wearing a red lumberjack kind of flannel shirt, kaki green pants, construction work boots, and a hard yellow construction hat with a light on it. I watched him enter the mouth of a cave. I also knew that although the body was different, it was me. My screen went black.

Then the screen showed me two teenagers, one young man and one young lady, both in their late teens, who had dirty clothes and bodies. There were also a few younger children behind them. Once I saw this my screen went blank again.

I kept relaxed through all of this. I knew that I was being shown something that was important. I also knew I needed to do no more than watch, to be an observer only. If I focused too much on anything, my conscious thought would engage and take me out of this wonderful experience.

All of a sudden the screen turned on again. I immediately jumped backwards in my chair almost toppling it over. There was a huge sheet of plywood about four inches in front of my face. I could see the texture of it, so rough cut that it almost looked like wooden hair. I then realized, as the thought was put into my brain through my Crown Chakra, that it was cut by a large blade in an old sawmill.

Then I left the meditation, it was over. You know when it's over as simply as when you see the credits coming at the end of a movie. Now is when you use your conscious mind as well as the rest of you, to try to understand what just happened, what you saw.

When I looked at it I first saw the 4x4 looking sheet of wood again. I realized that it was very close to my face, and was rough cut in front of me, because it was the inside of a coffin I was laying in, facing the inner side of the top of it. It's only the outside that was sanded smooth.

Then I realized the dirty children I saw were trapped down there and eventually died. This thought process flowed right into knowing that I went down into the cave to save them but perished myself. I felt worse about it when I realized they all died but one little girl who was crippled for life. There is someone who can help all of you do this for yourselves. I'll do what I can before I leave but he's already published.

This wonderful being is named Dr. Brian L. Weiss. He's a well noted psychiatrist, easy to find, and well worth your time to do so. He is Solar Plexus orientated so he really needs more physical proof than most others. After all, isn't this how things are looked at today? He was also a doctor of psychiatry.

He never had much faith in things that were of a metaphysical nature, although he knew there were things which were hard to explain away. He soon became a believer while using his own abilities, those of a strong gut intuition, or Solar Plexus Orientated Spirit. Here's a large part of how that happened.

Dr. Weiss had an interview with a lady from China; at least I believe that's where she was from. She had become aware of his ability to help others with physical problems where medical doctors could not. She brought an interpreter with her to see him as she spoke absolutely no English and Dr. Weiss could not speak her language.

The three of them settled down and Dr. Weiss put her into a relaxed state, opening her full mind by quieting her conscious one. In a matter of minutes the three of them were calm and softly talking to each other. Here's where things were about to get interesting for all of them.

Dr. Weiss began a discussion with her about the pain in her arm. He asked her when it started hurting. She had trouble seeing it so, with the help of her translator, he guided her into her true self by having her breathe even deeper. This allowed her to become more relaxed and finally able to access her inner self. That's when all the fun started.

He asked her where she was when she hurt her arm as well as how it happened. She immediately replied to him an accurate description of where she was and what had happened. The interesting thing though, was that she replied in perfect English.

This lady had never uttered one simple phrase in English and here she was speaking it as you and I do. Her interpreter started translating her words to Dr. Weiss in Chinese and he asked him to stop. He didn't speak Chinese. Both Dr. Weiss and the translator were amazed. This could never have been expected. It turned out that she had broken her arm in her last life in another country.

Dr. Weiss now had actual proof "delivered to his front door", that there was more going on than he could have ever known from his current thought process. He's really cool and has had many lives helping and leading others towards a better life. I remember him in many of my lives in Egypt. He's usually been attached to the royals there as an advisor and teacher of sorts.

Anyway, Dr. Weiss' client's last life was traumatic and she hadn't had enough time off in between lives to release the trauma from her last one before entering another body. This anxiety was expressed in her current life as a very hard memory, strong enough to cause a psychosomatic issue.

She wasn't nuts, just suffering from a previous life injury memory. Why would a loving Supreme Being allow this? It wouldn't. This is a very small issue compared to others that have arisen from the rapid return to a physical body without healing first.

CHAPTER 2
INITIATING STRONG AGGRESSION BETWEEN SPIRIT FIELDS

Here's another tool for Spirit growth, pitting the different fields of Spirit against each other. The greatest example of this was the mistreatment of Animal Essence on the Other Side. They were the ones who did the most to serve everyone and they were treated the most harshly.

Angels, the first ones that is, considered themselves above all else under the Original Ones. They were the "first ones" created by them so they felt special. They were also told they were the most important of their creations. In a way they were. They were the ones who maintained the system of abuse installed by the Original First Being Male and Female.

The original Angels always looked down on Animal Essence more than anyone. Human Essence was a close second. These first Angels knew, in their own minds, that they were superior to everything else. Animals were the greatest servants of Creation. They suffered in body and out. Angels just ran around controlling and maintaining the abuse system made for the bodies by the Original Ones. They did whatever they were told to do. They never had to suffer in the least, never.

They had never had a life, not one of them. They are as ruthless and non-compassionate as they can be. They have always been servants completely dedicated to the Original Ones and no one else. They followed orders as if they were robots. The never hesitated to break your leg or kill you when they were told to. Some of them began to grow, to understand things beyond their blind servitude. Most of these too few Angels are not just alive but being protected by Arae as I write this.

I once met the large Archangel called Gabriel at a crystal store in Atlanta. He was intelligent, strong, a bit aggressive, and very arrogant. He had his own special place in Creation, in his own mind anyway. He put himself above all the other Angels. He was told he was superior by the Original Ones and had no problem accepting it.

Angels don't usually want to touch a physical body as it contains a higher percentage of negative frequencies than the ones they produce from their own energy. Angels, the original ones that is, were made from very high vibration Spirit energy. This kept them easier to keep in line by the Original First Being halves. Negativity can produce a stronger power level. Here's why I brought this up.

Archangel Gabriel looked me in the eye as he shook my hand. He said, "Can you see my energy?" His gaze, as well as the energy coming from him, was so arrogant I was immediately pissed off. I told him I see Angels better when they leave. Then he did so. A trail of disgusting arrogance energy followed him out of the room as he disappeared.

I was not as strong then as I am now, not by any means. Still, I knew who he was and what he was thinking. That's why I was so annoyed. What a letdown when you learn what's really happening, what's actually going on in Creation and who the first Angels really were.

The Original Ones were still alive back then, orchestrating all their "excessive abuse by design." That's not something to be proud of. By the way, Archangel Gabriel no longer exists, just like all the other big ones excluding Archangel Michael and Lucifer. Archangel Michael and Lucifer were the great protectors of the first Angels. They also never became arrogant. They will return soon.

They were also non-aggressive towards J'Arae as they already understood the great need for change in Creation. They no longer felt the same allegiance to the Original Ones. They were made to protect and in doing so learned what was necessary to take care of something. That is the understanding of compassion, honor, and equality.

They have never had a life but had to deal with everything having lives as well as being free form Spirit, which was Lucifer's job, maintaining the separation of negative and positive frequency Spirit on the Other Side or Second Dimension. There was never an Angel fight and there has never been a devil, unless you want to give the Original Ones that role.

Anyway, Lucifer could see, feel, and understand the problem now existing with all the negative frequencies and Abuse frequencies building up everywhere. Arrogance was now rampant throughout Creation. It's an expression of negative energy even though it can come from a Spirit with a low percentage of negative frequencies.

This was going to grow into a much larger problem. Michael and Lucifer were both well aware. When the other large Angels had been dealt with, Lucifer and Michael were placed in the safe zone, the dimension that Arae built for just this purpose, to protect all he could. They're both in stasis now waiting for the end of the conflict. Michael wanted to stay out as long as possible to record the ongoing events.

I know where he is. I can see him resting whenever I want, but I miss him. He's such a valiant warrior of protection. He understands. This is quite a feat for someone who has never had a life to help him learn. He follows his own personal format with such diligence, fortitude, even with a kind of grace, all his own.

Lucifer is much the same, always protecting all of you and wanting nothing in return. And the religions call him the devil? That sounds a lot like your governments talking, doesn't it? Both of these wonderful protectors will be back among us soon. They'll both return in 2016 along with all the others being kept safe.

Getting back to Aggressive arrogance between the Spirits in the Second Dimension; Human Essence had also been told that they were the "special favorites" of the Original Male and Female. They were told that since the majority of frequencies now within them were Human, they should understand this as being true. They accepted that quite easily.

They were constantly reminded that they were better than Fae Essence as there was little Fae Essence in them. That's why they said they "banished" the Fae bodies into "lower" dimensions. This increased Human Essence arrogance while adding strife to Fae Essence.

They were also told that Animals only existed to serve the Original Ones and Human Essence. They explained this as they showed them how they offered Animals to them to eat while in body and other wise abuse any way they saw fit. Can anyone with any heart energy really wonder why Arae is taking all Animal Essence out of the Physical Realm?

While we're at it, the Original Ones told Human Essence that Plants and Planets were there for them to use as they wanted also. They were shown enough to understand the truth that the Original First Beings actually did put them first, and they did. They also told them that they were better than the Human Souls who were a much smaller and weaker Spirit than they were.

Now, the Human Souls were told a very similar story but with a different twist. The Human Souls were told that they were made smaller at first so there would be more of them, and that they would grow much larger in size and be used to populate all Creation, the old one and the next expansion of it.

There was some truth in this and it was already evident. The Souls had already grown quite large and it was mostly the Souls who were about to be placed into new Universes to release new smaller versions of themselves. All these new Souls would eventually repopulate Creation with a ridiculously large percentage of Soul Spirit in it.

While this was being said, they also told Human Essence not to worry about it because they were so much stronger than them and that there would be more of them going to these other Universes than the Souls expected. The Original Ones were not just playing one Spirit Field against another but all against each other.

Human Essence and Souls grabbed these thought processes and ran with them, like thieves in the night. This arrogance concept wasn't new to them. They were introduced to it a long time ago both on the Other Side and Third Dimension while in body. Their lives being almost back to back, as well as the insertion of this concept while out of body, allowed them to maintain a strong belief in the supposed superiority over all the others.

Plant, Planet, Star, and Fae were also fed many lies but they didn't have any physical proof to back up anything the Original Ones were telling them. They pretty much said "Sure, yeah, whatever you say.", and just kept going. As a group they weren't falling for it but the Original First Being halves didn't care. These fields were a little pissed off which helped aid in their abusive growth in and now out, of body.

One exception to this was the Star Spirit from what is called the Universal Field of Essence. They believed their force fed lies about their superiority to everything else. They were told that everything in body needed their energy, their light, to survive in the Third Dimension. As this was actually a true statement, they felt their arrogance had a leg to stand on, so to speak.

Well, how sickening is this now. How would you feel if you were a caring daughter or child having to grow up in this environment? Actually, you have, since near the beginning of the Soul release. Take all the abusive lives, the continuously fed arrogance, and total lack of concern from your parents, as they might be called.

How do you feel now? This is how you've had to live. This is what you've had to go through that you can't remember yet. This is how things finally came to where we are here, just in the Physical Realm. Guess what, there's still more. We haven't covered it all yet by any means.

Now you understand the primary need for my writing the two Creation books. There's a lot more to it than that though. You've about to start having lives, within a thousand years, where you will be constantly aware of all dimensions while in a body and actually be able to quit your life and go home with no more than a thought, if you wish.

CHAPTER 3
THE ABUSE FREQUENCIES CAUSE FREE SPIRIT GROWTH

Well, by now every Spirit had Abuse frequencies within them. This was now causing havoc with their energy while out of body as free form Spirit. The Spirits were now growing faster while out of body from all the tension these sick abusive frequencies were producing.

The Original First Being Female and Male were not able to do much about this, neither were they willing. When these abusive energy frequencies first appeared they played with them a little, trying to understand them. They could separate different frequencies to some extent but lacked the sufficient power level to deal with these accurately.

These were stronger and more embedded in the Spirit's other frequencies, like thread through cloth. They might have been able to do this if they worked together but they had no desire to try. I doubt they could of and they never wanted to show themselves as unable to do anything, so they never tried. They needed to always be seen as the ultimate omnipotent controllers.

CHAPTER 4

FREE SPIRIT STARTS TO SHOW AGGRESSIVE EMOTIONS

This new growth while in free Spirit form gave birth to a new issue, one that pleased the Original Ones. The arrogance and strife between the different Spirit energy fields, added to all the Abuse frequencies in everyone, was now bringing more than a soft rage into play within the Second Dimension.

There was a stronger issue of "better than" between many of the individual members of each separate field of Spirit as well as that between the different fields. This added to the already progressive chaos in all Creation. Gasoline was being put on the fire fueling chaos everywhere.

What happens in the Second Dimension, that of Spirit and energy only, directly affects what happens here in the Third Dimension. The Source Spirit field, being that of the current Father Source at the time, has all this abusive and negative intention energy flowing through it. This is similar to being a fish living in a toxic environment, or I guess like us breathing our polluted air, just worse.

At this point, Lilly and Arae were concerned that they needed to hurry their plans along. Things were quickly falling apart while the Original Ones just bathed in the chaos. Arae was aware of what he'd have to go through but now understood it was going to be more difficult as time went on. The water was coming to a boil.

CHAPTER 5
WHERE THIS EXCESSIVE ABUSE LEADS US

Let's take just a moment to look this entire mess over. We have a controlling pair of Source Spirit that the others came from and they were aware of it, reminded constantly. "You owe us and belong to us." was a common statement from the Original Ones, the projected current thought process for free Spirit to accept.

They were putting Spirits, already damaged, into physical bodies to have abusive lives which actually made them sicker. Their Abuse frequencies increased. This was slowly destroying their personal frequencies by intertwining between them and changing their vibrations. This was literally making them sick, and in some cases, a little crazy.

One such example of this was the Spiritual Traveler, a special operations Spirit that always did what he was told, that was put into the body of Stalin. When I went back in time to look at his Spirit I was horrified. He was riddled with these abusive frequencies all through. They have been removed and he's healing now but this actually brought tears to my eyes.

How could anyone ever do this to someone? Where was the concern for this Spirit, one who had done what he was told to do over, and over, and over again? How could this ever be allowed? It doesn't even make sense to let someone who is doing so much you ask to get like this as it destroys him.

One thing was certain, nothing benevolent would ever do such a thing, only a sick monster of a being. Man did this crank up my protective issues. Here again is what everyone, including myself at a younger age, calls God. I'm so glad they're both dead. I'm expressing a lot of aggression here; it was my job to do what I did. Hell, I was attacked by them both together until they were destroyed. I only regret it haven taken too long. Sorry, let's get back to Creation trying to find its way through this mess.

SECTION VIII -
LILLY AND ARAE TAKE ACTION
OF THEIR OWN

CHAPTER 1
LILLY AND ARAE DECIDE TO CREATE A FAMILY OF THEIR OWN

I t was obvious by now that Lilly and Arae had to build a support mechanism of their own. They needed to break off or release some of their own Spirit energy to have lives and grow. This created a new series of issues but needed to be done.

How much Spirit energy could they release and still leave themselves what they needed to survive? Arae had to maintain a very high power level not just to do his job but begin the task soon at hand. There was also the question of which kinds of Spirit to release.

They needed to bring new life into Creation that would help them straighten it out. They already knew that they needed smaller versions of themselves who would hopefully learn to work together doing the right things for the correct reasons. They would be getting a large dose of abuse until Arae could begin his cleansing.

Neither of them could know for sure how bad the new ones would be abused. It would be severe but within what limits? They had to have lives to be able to understand how to become what was already a part of them, Lilly and Arae's knowledge. Would they be corrupted? If so, what problems would that cause? What problems might they cause?

They would also need a place to keep their family, a home of their own so to speak. Arae found a good place for that. The current home for the Original First Being halves was in the Second Dimension at the location of the M3 Star cluster. This is where the Original Ones' special little group of worshippers lived. They wanted to have a praise machine nearby at all times. They needed constant fuel for their egos.

Lilly and Arae looked for a location for their new home. Lilly placed things in their correct order as Arae built it. They would soon be ready to bring new beings into existence.

CHAPTER 2
ARAE CREATES A HOME FOR
HIS NEW FAMILY

L illy and Arae decided on the location which is now called M66, the middle galaxy or Star system in the Leo Constellation. It's the heart of the Leo Triplet, how appropriate. What's also funny is that there are two neighboring galaxies now, on either side of it, pulling at it.

These galaxies exert a gravitational force on it which alters its shape a little. They exert negative pressure on it from both sides. Again, how appropriate. That's similar to how the Original First Being Male and Female always pulled on or abused Lilly and Arae. Life is full of many little coincidences, or are they something else?

Scientists have stated that there are some peculiar things about the M66 Galaxy. It has a strong density not found in other regions of space. It's different. I can tell you that this is where the new home of Source Spirit is. Animal Essence is also living there now.

Lilly and Arae got busy creating their new home. Lilly placed things in their correct order as Arae built it. They would soon be ready to bring new beings into existence. This is a simple enough process to understand when you keep it simple. It's a matter of expanding heavy or compressed matter and shaping it as you do.

Arae used strong heavy particular matter from the First Dimension to build M66. It only takes one small such piece to produce a Planet or Star. It takes many such pieces to build a Universe though. This Universe wasn't built from one small piece of heavy matter as many tend to think, but many instead. M66 was built the same way as the Universe was, which we covered in sufficient detail in book one. Arae did the heavy lifting and Lilly put everything together. They work very well in unison. Why not, they are the two parts of the one whole, just as Spirit Mates are.

Once Lilly and Arae finished putting their new home together, they went to filling it. It was time to release a large amount of their Spirit energy in order to create, to release, a family of their own. It's how they separated their Spirit that really makes it creation.

CHAPTER 3
LILLY AND ARAE CREATE NEW SOURCE SPIRIT

I t was finally time to decide what their new family would con-
sist of although they already had a good idea of what they were
going to do. They also knew there was a limit to the amount of
Spirit they could release. They needed a family of their own,
actually, Creation needed it. Things would never change unless
they brought the process to it. There was a lot of work, and for
Arae fighting, in their near future.

They needed smaller beings that were similar to themselves
to help later to keeping the new Creation flowing in the right direction. They were also going to need new Angels to help guide
everything along, not run the bodies. There was one more Spirit
field needed, that of Animal. Animal Spirit is made from strong
fortitude and heart. That was what Lilly and Arae were made of
from the beginning.

This would mean new Angels made from their energy but
very different from the first original Angels. These would have to
be much stronger, with strong heart, and have an understanding
of having lives to perform properly. They would need to already

know how to handle different situations correctly and with compassion. They were not to be made as mindless servants. These would be unique beings filled with full Source Spirit which came from heart energy frequencies more than others.

They also knew that the existing Animals deserved protectors and guides, helpers of their own energetic form, similar Source companionship. There was a new job awaiting all Animal Essence in the future. They would become Creation's new Sentinels, continually observing everything everywhere to help keep everything moving in a direction that helped all Creation, not any one part of it.

I realize I've said many times that Animal Essence is made of very powerful fortitude and heart frequencies. I only do so because it's not just true but very important to understanding why they've been treated so poorly for so long, what they've been doing to help you, and what their jobs will be in the future.

They're anxious to get started. They were never commanded to become sentinels. They enjoy helping just like all of you running around with all the beautiful heart energy flowing out of you, not to mention your fortitude to keep going while the world around you is still so abusive and aggressive towards you.

They decided to release about one hundred and ten thousand smaller orbs of themselves which would each separate into male and female. They would also release their own Angels which would be about fifty five to sixty percent Angel Spirit and the rest would be their particular clean Source. There would also be Animal Spirit released having that same percentage of Animal energy as the new Angels and the rest, forty to forty five percent, would be full Source Spirit.

This made these Animal and Angel Spirits incredibly powerful. Each of these Angels is over one thousand times stronger than the original ones. The new Animal Spirit is equally stronger also. Lilly and Arae were the strongest focal points ever to exist within Creation from the moment of their separation becoming themselves. Add to this the increased growth from many trillions of abusive lives and you get the picture. They were huge with a lot of power.

Maybe the most important issue with these new Animal and Angel Spirits is that they come from Lilly and Arae who were powerful heart energy to begin with. These Animals and Angels already have the understanding that comes from having many lives. This was done on purpose. I don't have Spirit Guides like others do, but I have very powerful folks to talk to.

Once these new smaller parts of them were released, they would be subjected to the excessive abuse of the Original Ones while in body. It wasn't time to take on all the big and powerful Source Spirit in Creation yet. How would these new beings grow within this sick environment?

They would be incredibly powerful as they were released from Lilly and Arae. Lilly has wonderful and powerful loving mother energy while Arae, from all his abusive lives, was an almost limitless supply of fortitude. Would their smaller released parts of themselves have the same loving mother and protective father energy format? Neither of them knew. It made sense they would but how much of what would be in each of them?

Lilly and Arae came into each other, their energy fields that is. This is always a beautiful moment for them. As their love powered up, their total energies merged and became something of it's own. This is nothing that can be maintained for too long but is a magnificent event.

Then the Spirit wave was released. This happened a little different than with the Original Ones in the true beginning. This one wave was very dense and beautiful with many different energies flowing in and around and out of each other, each one expressing their own individual Auras.

There were different shades of red, blue, green, yellow, white, gold, silver, orange, and more. Literally all the different shades of all colors you could image were flowing, glowing with a pulse. You could feel its being alive. I've never taken the time to look at it until now. I should have.

I've spent my last seven years continuously fighting everything night and day. I don't remember what it's like to have a life anymore. I'm not here for that anyway. I'm here for the job and this book will finish the last imperative portion of it. I'm anxious to finish it, drop this body, and go home to get started over there. I should say finish it over there. Ninety percent of the Spirit mass in the Second Dimension is gone now.

Your new Creation is about to start. You will have councils, each individual Spirit energy field will, and you'll run your own lives. Your only limits will be to stay within Creation's new anti-abuse format of compassion, honor, and equality, that's all. You'll all have the strongest protection there is as well as a loving mother or big sister Spirit keeping things going as best as possible for everyone with everyone in mind.

Getting back to this Spirit wave from Lilly and Arae, as it was released the clean Source Spirit Animals came out first. Before they finished the new Angels began coming out. The smaller individual parts of Lilly and Arae were also coming forward before the Angels finished.

It was one continuous wave that, while being released, came out in the form of first one large bulge, then a second, and then the smaller pieces of Lilly and Arae's combined energy that was less dense and immediately spread out like water over the hood of a highly polished car.

It was one wave with two large sections coming out of it and then finished with a large group of shining orbs which soon split into male and female parts, Source Mates. The new Animal Source Spirit followed suit and began to divide into male and female. The Angels, characteristic to their particular Spirit energy, stayed as one, both male and female. This, as I described in book one, is what the Other Side calls Zhe. That's not a misprint. It's the word she with the "s" replaced by a "z". It's pronounced as if saying "ghee".

The newly released portions of Lilly and Arae would begin having lives, at a faster pace than usual, but the Animal Source would not. They were here, as mentioned earlier, for something else. They were so strong, just as these new Angels, that nothing was dumb enough to bother them. I've no words to express the power levels involved here. This includes the Original Ones.

As they were part of Lilly and Arae, they were composed of stronger energy than anything else and, having been released from them, had Arae protecting them. When something strong came near any of them, Arae fired up. They didn't need his help, it was just a natural thing. Lilly and Arae understand family, love, compassion, honor, equality, and above all else protection.

CHAPTER 4

THE LEARNING PROCESS
BEGINS

The new individual portions of Lilly and Arae need a name
for us to understand who we're talking about as we talk
about them. In physical human terms we might call them children but they're not. In many ways, energy flows almost like water and has similar characteristics. Let's look at things this way.

If you take a bucket of water and scoop out a cup of it, was the
bucket ever pregnant? Heck no. The water now in the cup is the
same thing that's in the bucket. When you have an almost limitless amount of different energetic frequencies you'll have some
variation, but it's still water from the bucket.

Let's just call them children for the ease of our understanding. They also had certain similarities to children. They were
now independent individuals. They were now separate unique
beings and needed to learn things for themselves. Unfortunately,
they were alone doing most of this. Lilly and Arae were still very
busy having lives, waiting for the "Earth 2012" event to occur.
That was when they would take charge of Creation's misuse, remove their abusive controllers.

As soon as Lilly and Arae went back into bodies again, the trouble started with the Original Ones being too hard on these children, abusing them almost without limit. Each time Lilly and Arae came out of their latest body and saw what was going on, the trouble started. Arae's energy actually started growing, increasing in size and power level when out of the body.

CHAPTER 5

HOSTILITIES INCREASE WITH THE ORIGINAL FIRST BEING HALVES

Finally Arae reached the point where he had had enough. Each time he returned to the Second Dimension he watched the abuse being handed down to the smaller parts of himself and Lilly. As this was intentional, and done with malicious intent, Arae's energy level spiked as never before. He decided he'd had enough, period. It was time to do something final about all this.

He finally fired up at the Original Ones to the point of almost destroying them. His intent was not to destroy but subdue. He always used the minimum amount of force necessary to accomplish the needed action. This time however, he was protecting his family. The other clean Source Spirit halves, Lillith and Aramaeleous as well as Lydia and Armaeleous, got in the middle of it and asked Arae to back down saying they would look after the children while they were in body.

Arae had no faith in their words as he knew they had no honor. He did realize that there would now be less aggression towards the smaller young ones. That would have to be enough for the moment. The "Earth 2012" event, when the Souls were supposed to go to their new Universes to release smaller parts of themselves, was close enough to hang in there for now. At least, that's what they thought.

It became painfully obvious that the smaller ones would have to be extensively healed when the fight was over. They were already having some issues with excessive back to back lives and abusive frequency build up. They were very strong beings but not yet developed as individuals. They were trying to understand, to become, who they were. This was not the time for their heightened abuse.

It was also obvious that the two large clean Source pairs would become an issue when the fight began, or at least somewhere along it's path. Arae is a loving being, just as Lilly, but he was made for one purpose only, to protect. He now knew his family was in more stress than he and Lilly expected originally. He was ready to fight, anxious actually. He wanted Creation cured and fixed now. Lilly and he had a bigger stake in Creation's welfare, their own offspring, so to speak.

How could he not be extremely aggressive over the abuse of his personal family? He was also having to deal with the issue of never having been able to protect anything properly, as he was having so many lives back to back. Arae did so for a reason, to become what he now is, strong enough to finally achieve his goal.

He also now understood he had something of a chess match coming up with more than just the Original Ones involved. He had to deal with the other large Source pairs as well as any others who wished to join them. He was ready to take on anything and everything but having to do this while in body would be an issue. Arae was very patient but was way past his limits. Something had to be done and soon before everything fell apart, including his new family.

He's had to watch others suffer, as well as do so himself, to become what he needed to be, to finally change everything. He could never protect Creation until it was free. He was the only thing that would even want such a thing to happen. That's maybe the saddest part of all this. It also helps describe the feelings of necessity for proper action that Arae had inside.

He and Lilly were not alone in these feelings. Most of the beings in Creation were tired of the abusive treatment whether in or out of body. The others were not strong enough to help, could only be hurt. It was Arae's job and he was made for it. That might be the greatest mistake the Original First Beings made, aside from their choice to be abusive for their own wants.

This is where my frustration comes from in some of my videos about abuse towards Animals as well as everyone else. I can't stand it as a Human being but, as I'm Arae inside, it infuriates me beyond measure. All this abuse was wrong. I say was, even though it's still happening here, because it's almost completely removed on the Other Side which controls all your lives.

After the other Source pairs convinced Arae to release the Original Ones, Aramaeleous went to them with a proposition. He suggested that he and Lillith attach part of their energy to the bodies of all the younger ones while they were having lives. This way there would be more abuse but at a lower level than before.

These little inserted pieces of Lillith and Aramaeleous would be controlling the emotions of the smaller ones while in a body, making their lives there harder than they should be without as many drastic events. This isn't why Lillith and Aramaeleous were to be destroyed, but sure added to it.

There are only small pieces of them hiding and coming out to take potshots at me, and then die. Their Spirit will be completely destroyed within 3 seconds of Arae's settled arrival back home on the Other Side, the Second Dimension. All arrogant Source Spirit will be either cleaned or destroyed immediately upon his arrival back home. This will be within six minutes of his return. He will have his true form, not stuck in a body. This is also the last time he will ever be in one. He needs to remain himself now.

The Original Ones felt Aramaeleous' idea was a good one, especially since they planned to surround the younger ones with more arrogance. They would continue to feed them selfishness, in and out of body, until they could be turned against or at least used in the fight against Arae. Remember, they were not yet solidified in their own uniqueness, not yet grown individuals who were able to understand who they were. Impressionable youth is the expression that comes to mind.

The same thing can be said of people and their children. We can't make them something other than the sum of their basic frequencies but arrogance needs no format to grow in. Neither are negative frequencies necessary to produce it. It does have a negative effect on the being and others nearby, but it doesn't change their actual frequencies until over a very long time.

As Lilly and Arae came out of their lives they could still see what was being done to the younger ones as well as the changes apparent in them because of it. Many were becoming arrogant and selfish, self-absorbed and tending to think a little more like the Original Ones as well as Lillith and Aramaeleous. They had become aligned with the concept of abusive lives and them eventually being the controlling factor.

You can image how this made Lilly and Arae feel. They were heartbroken while also furious, especially Arae. They could only hope for the best for their family in the upcoming events. Arae already felt the aggressive arrogance, in many of the young males, aimed right at him. He knew how this would most likely end, with their cleansing or maybe even their deletion. This brought on a sadness that he could not allow to settle in.

The Original Ones noticed this feeling in Arae as he initially had it. They were festivious over it, couldn't be happier. For

Arae, it increased the depth of his resolve that it would never be allowed to happen again, anywhere to anyone. He turned inward and put his thought processes to motion as never before. He never had to plan attacks or wars. He only acted and reacted to protect. This was both different and paramount.

Arae was a machine in motion, just waiting to unleash what he had inside. He would never stop until it was finished. Even in body, he could do nothing but succeed. The only problem was how to do things properly with as little damage to everything, and to remove this cancer completely. The war was already on. He was merely the only one who realized it.

CHAPTER 6
LILLITH AND ARAMAELEOUS CREATE A FAMILY OF THEIR OWN

This information is not in the first book. While writing book one I was not sure if I would ever finish book two so I left this part out. I shouldn't have, it's important. I don't really care much for my actions being part of this book. I don't want anything to be thought of as about me because it simply isn't.

This is your book, your information, and necessary for you to understand some of what you'll be seeing for yourselves in the future. It's imperative I leave you a simple map with a legend on it to understand the different features (beings) on it.

As you awaken, rather hard over the next one hundred years, you will be able to refer to this information to understand just what it is you're seeing and feeling all around you. They are Spirit beings, part of the huge family you belong to. Everyone is about to be free, to do almost whatever they want, as they should be.

Let's get back to Lillith and Aramaeleous. They decided they wanted smaller pieces of themselves running around, just like the Original First Ones, to praise and serve them. They never made any Animal or Angel Spirit as they planned on eventually taking over the ones left by the Original Ones when they retired. They just wanted personal servants with energy similar to their own.

These smaller pieces of themselves would also be very strong. They would also have no concept of what it was like to have a life. There is one nice thing about them though, many of them learned of the abuse and neglect from the Original Ones by watching it happen. They were able to see the events occur, the affects they had, and that it did nothing positive to serve Creation.

They were also left alone by the Original First Beings as to them they were of no consequence. They had too much to do with everything else anyway. The last thing they needed was to deal with Aramaeleous and Lillith too. Remember, Arae and Lilly came from Aramaeleous and Lillith. They were all very powerful Spirit energy.

Many of these smaller beings from Lillith and Aramaeleous have actually done what they could for Lilly and Arae, especially helping Arae maintain himself during the conflict. Once a very strong female being from them was left nearly in disbelief when she witnessed the extent of Arae's fortitude.

He was willing to do whatever was necessary to finish killing the first ones, including his readiness to leave his body to return home and finish the job there. As she left his Spirit's area, she was shaking her head in disbelief of what she had just seen. Black Panther and the White Tiger just looked at each other smiling, kind of laughing. Black Panther said "She doesn't know father very well, does she."

It's one of those things that you really need to see for yourselves. I probably shouldn't even mention it in this book but it was one of the better moments I've had while having to do what I've been doing. I was going to go home and just be done with it. Lillith and Aramaeleous will both be completely destroyed.

Just a note before we leave here, many of these smaller beings from Lillith and Aramaeleous have been saved and are waiting for the cleansing to finish. Arae is protecting them, along with so many others, in that dimension he made solely for that purpose. He does whatever he needs to in protecting everyone.

Sometimes that has a disastrous effect of something but only because that something was attacking something else and would not stop. Lillith and Aramaeleous, as well as all Spirit attempting to maintain the abuse format, will be completely destroyed.

This is done out of compassion for everyone and the understanding that all are equal. Everyone will be allowed to live the way they want without interruption, as long as they're not abusing anything. Abuse will not be tolerated. There will be few limits put on everyone but it will be the same for everyone.

We need to move forward as a family with respect for each other's rights, not taking them over. This is known to be the only way we can survive as a family, as a Creation.

SECTION IX -
ARAE PREPARES FOR WAR

CHAPTER 1
ARAE BEGINS TO FORMULATE HIS ATTACK PLANS

(Taking Down A Dynasty)

Arae put his thoughts together about how to deal with all the different Source Spirit beings individually as well as how or even if, they would combine to attack him. Which ones would combine with each other and how would they go about attacking him.

He knew they wanted him to stay in the body so there was a limit to what they would do. Once out of his body Arae would explode with his energy killing whatever was coming at him. He wasn't the largest energy field but much stronger than anything else. As I mentioned earlier, at least I think I did, trying to stop Arae is like holding up a hand to stop a bullet. As the saying goes, "Just Ain't Gonna Happen!"

However, this also meant they would be doing the best they could to control him. Yeah, they didn't have much luck with that either. Here's how that works. As we learned from book one, regarding how Spirit is placed into a body before birth, there is a wall of Female Source Spirit that separates the two Spirits within the body. These two Spirits are what the older civilizations here named the Kundalini. I simply call it the Core Spirit Energy of the body.

By keeping this wall not only in tact but dense, stopping any communication between the two Spirits, that of the Earth and your own personal now visiting the Earth in that body, you are kept almost completely unaware of who and what you are. This was the big deal about 2012. That wall needed to be removed as much as possible in everyone. Arae did it in April of 2012 instead of waiting for December 21, 2012. It was done a little early as everything was such a mess due to the war. The Animals were awoken first, then the Humans.

Animals are now more aware, more sentient than they've ever been. More people are talking with them and they're doing more than they've ever done before. There is a new communication between us and them. They only seem smarter, because they are. They've been progressing well but took a large leap beginning 2013.

Everyone needed to begin the slow process of waking up as early as possible. This is also where my "Crank-Ups" come in. I awaken people's brains and abilities, while actually increasing their size. This is a physically and medically proven fact.

Anyway, Arae was done waiting and anxious to get started. He could easily see what the final event would be, the cleansing or destruction of all abusive controlling Spirit throughout Creation. It was time to begin. Let things fall as they will. It just needed to happen, immediately.

CHAPTER 2

LINES ARE DRAWN
THROUGHOUT CREATION

E vents having occurred as they did up to this point, everyone knew a "show down" was about to happen. The vast majority of Spirit beings were done with their abusive treatment. They were tired of it and wanted it removed permanently. They were also done with the Original First Beings. They abused everything while demanding praise.

Arae felt the larger Source Spirit had to either be taken out of their command stature or permanently deleted. Not being complete idiots themselves, the other Source Spirit beings were aware of this and started to make plans of their own. They knew what was coming and who was bringing it.

This started a series of agreements between different fields of Spirit as well as individuals in these fields. The funny thing though, is that none of them trusted each other. Too many of them wanted to become kind of the hill when the Original First Beings were taken out.

There were other issues at hand also. All the Fae beings were forced to live in lower dimensions than the Human Spirits. They were tired of this and rightly so. They also had their own issues between themselves, as all things do. This is how things were made to develop between the beings from the start. When I say that Creation was made wrong, this is a very big part of it.

The Stars were also very arrogant kept away from most everything else. They put themselves in their own category, that of superiority. When I found this out I was surprised. The Planetary Essence beings are almost all loving mothers. It's amazing how Creation has been led so far off track for so long.

Plant and Animal Essence had nothing to do with any of this arrogance and abuse. It was not something they were taken into at all. Their frequencies were not compliant with any of these negative or abusive tendencies. Plant Essence beings were left alone and Animal Essence was strong enough to make it through with much less damage than the others.

There was now aggressive anger towards the Original First Being halves, arrogance between most of the different fields of Spirit as well as some of the individuals within each field. Everyone was running around with an excess of abusive frequencies in them that most weren't even aware they had.

Chaos was the rule of the day and a whole lot of anger went where it belonged, to the Original Ones. The other large and clean Source wanted to replace the Original First Being Male and Female, becoming the supreme overlords. There were also many others who were getting ready to fight for higher ranking in the "pecking order" so to speak. They wanted to be as "high up on the ladder" as possible, to be considered part of the elite.

Community can only exist when there is a feeling, or at least understanding, that equality between all is true. I spent so much time my last life trying to prove that. Every time I turned a good corner the Original First Being halves were there to disrupt what I was doing. People, who think Gandhi's life was wonderful, need to take a deeper look. It sucked.

CHAPTER 3

THE ARROGANCE OF THE OLD ONES COMES INTO PLAY

The Original First Beings used arrogance to split the others up, put them at each other's throats. This was about to work against them as well as all who were so aggressively arrogant. This was something that Arae considered probable to happen and it did, even better than he could have hoped.

The Original First Being halves, still retaining their arrogance, didn't think anything would ever stand up to them, just Arae. On this, they were correct. However, something they expected to happen, didn't. We'll explain that in just a few minutes.

By pitting all the Spirits against each other, the Original Ones created a large rift that they eventually tripped over. They knew they would have their hands full with Arae and planned on the others performing different tasks for them. They had a battle strategy that didn't go like they wanted.

They were, however, the experts at forming contingency plans. They were the only ones to ever run lives and had done so trillions times trillions of times. They knew how to make changes in the middle of things. That only helped them a short time. The other Source Spirits were ready to take their place at the top of the hill called Creation. They now wanted to rule and to receive praise.

CHAPTER 4
MORE OF LILLY AND ARAE'S FAMILY ARE CORRUPTED

More of Lilly and Arae's recently released small but full Source Spirit beings, were becoming overly arrogant now, even a little abusive. This was a problem that would eventually become a serious issue. You'll read of it's sad conclusion later on.

They were having too many lives back to back to back. You can't do this without building up a lot of abusive frequencies. They were also being fed constant lies to feed their arrogance. They were all being told that they were the ones who would soon run all the new Universes and be Gods there, worshipped by all existing around them.

They also had small pieces of Aramaeleous attached to the male Spirit in bodies and Lillith in the female Spirit bodies. This was similar to what Lilly and Arae were put through. It was also another source of Arae's increasingly growing aggression towards the Original Ones.

CHAPTER 5
IT'S TIME TO FREE CREATION

Arae had no question in his mind of how to handle the Original First Being halves. Nothing less than complete destruction would be sufficient. Every bit of their energy must be destroyed. It can never be allowed to exist anywhere. This must be final.

There was no more time to plan or prepare. Something needed to be done now. Creation was sick and at it's own throats now due to what was being done to it by both halves of the Original First Being.

The Original Ones were about to release all these new Souls, already full of abusive frequencies, into the new Universes. This would instantaneously create a much larger family already infected with this disease. It could not be allowed to happen. There was no time left. It had to happen now. The Original First Being had to be destroyed.

It would happen while Arae was in body. As everyone on the Other Side already knew, in a body you would do almost anything so that might help maintain a decent attitude there. Arae was also hoping that this way he might minimize the damage due to the loss of direction over there. This would not be easily done while in a body.

SECTION X -
THE SOURCE FAMILY
GOES TO WAR

CHAPTER 1
ARAE PREPARES THE PHYSICAL BODIES (GANDHI)

A rae needed to have two more lives, that of Gandhi and Jay Essex. He needed to prepare the physical world for the new lives coming. There was about to be a great change in the course of Creation.

The Original Ones had the understanding that the physical bodies were about to become aware that there was actually a mother and father God, not just a father God. They didn't know it was going to be about their removal and a new format installed in the Creation they started.

Gandhi was a simple man who actually made his own clothes. His attire was very plain, a simple cloth setup. As Jay Essex I have been known as the "Old man in overalls", again a simple and plain man. It was time for everyone to become aware of who they are and understand the need for family.

Arae had many recent lives, leading up to this final point, where he tried to prepare the Human bodies for what was about to happen. He had already started to prepare the masses here on Earth, for what was about to happen. Our family members in space were also aware of all of this. They have access to almost everything happening down here. Here's a couple lives where he tried to move things along.

When he was Quetzalcoatl, he was a tall white skinned man who brought his people, the Toltecs, to a new age of civilization. Their science took off to make their daily lives much better than before as well as create a much stronger community. They were far advanced over any of the neighboring communities. He also built a large army with excellent weapons to defend themselves, not attack others.

The priests were not happy about things. They were Annunaki hybrids who were in charge of religious type issues. They eventually took over the Toltec government by staging a fake raid of the city where the regular soldiers dressed up as another group and attacked the city.

Quetzalcoatl's private army grabbed him from his sleep, picked him up, and ran out of the city with him. Once on the outskirts, one of his private guard captains told him he had been ousted and the priests had taken over. He was told he would be killed should he return.

He wanted to do nothing else but return but he was literally shut down by the Original First Being Female. She said she had something in store for them and to leave them alone. She was speaking about the eventual fall of their empire by bloody battle.

As the next few months went by, he was left alone by the Original Ones. He had time to reflect on everything happening there physically as well as metaphysically on the Other Side. He'd had enough of the Original Male and Female messing with him and everything else. It was time for him to leave, to die and go home.

He left on a raft, headed into the East, and said he would return one day with the rest of the knowledge his people needed. He also stated that he would fix what was wrong with Creation or destroy it. I remember being really pissed and a little helpless as I could not do what I knew needed to be done, not yet.

As Pahana, I also walked away from my village telling everyone I would return from the East with the wisdom of what Creation really was, Creation's own story as it was phrased. We used to keep history alive in story and song back then. I explained that I would help all live together as brothers. That was meant to be taken as family. I remember that life extremely well.

I have met the clean Source Spirit that was in the body of my wife then, once again a beautiful Hopi woman, as well as the Spirit which was in our daughter. I had white skin but was not albino. I was very different; tall, strong, and light colored skin. I was also aware of who I was. I was awake and closer to finishing my work having lives in physical bodies.

I was always trying to teach everyone to get along with each other, to understand who we really are, family. Still, as the Original Ones controlled everything, I could never create such an event while they were still alive. I always did what I could. What else can anyone do?

When I was Pachaquti Inca Yupanqui, I taught people how to get along and built the Incan Empire with such speed that historians today are still amazed. The rapid growth of the Incan civilization came from the strongest source of power ever used to build a community. This was the implementation of compassion, honor, and equality. Here's how it happened.

One day I was told by the Original First Being Female that I would become a great ruler and needed to obey her. She said I would build an empire of stone that would last a very long time. She said I would be known as a great conqueror and rule with an iron fist over many lands.

One day, I was told that this event was about to begin. There were about six thousand troops amassing to take over our village. The great kind, my step dad or something, was already running up into the mountain tops with about 1400 of the royal guards to protect himself and his newest son. I refused to run.

At the top of a long hill, I stood with three hundred and thirteen men to take on the invaders. I met one of them working at Gino's Pizza near my home in Georgia. His name was Fred. He was having a life in a similar body again. He was from somewhere near or in South America.

He and I saw each other and he immediately stopped what he was doing and came over to me. He looked at me funny and said hello, it was great to see me again, and who am I? I remembered him also. I could see him in the clothes he was wearing at that battle at Machu Picchu. We've been friends ever since.

I started lifting things telekinetically the day before the battle was to begin. I felt my energy flow through my body as never before. When the human body becomes telekinetic, your core energy or Kundalini, fires up from your spine/pelvic area and then flows up through your body like a tank through a water hose. It travels up your spine inside and out. I don't know how else to express it.

Anyway, that next morning we were all there, three hundred and fourteen of us and a good six thousand of them. About fifteen hundred began running up the hill in a very long deep line. The closer they came the stronger the energy built up in my back. What happened next was what I guess we'd call instinct.

There were many walls of stone that we Inca built. It would hold soil and water for vegetation on the hill sides. The invading soldiers were about a third of the way up the hill when my whole body felt like the power plant at the Hoover Dam. I've no words on this one.

I raised both arms up in the air at my sides. When I did I lifted many boulders, about one hundred to two hundred pounds, in the air. They were the large stones which the long wall behind me was made of. Then I threw them into the oncoming wave of bodies while they were still in the air. In a sense they were flying.

I moved both of my hands together, apart, together, and apart. I was throwing these boulders in and out of each other in a wave created with each hand. As the stone waves moved through each other I was crushing bodies like they were paper. It's really disgusting to look back on it. It was also necessary to protect my people.

Needless to say they all ran to regroup at a safer place farther away. I guess it's not hard to understand them freaking out a bit. The next day the rest of our army joined us and we did away with the intruders. It was a disgusting sight. Things were different back then but it still disgusts me to look at it now.

This was the battle that created the legend of the "Stone Soldiers" that saved the Incan Empire before it's great expansion. They say I called the stone to make soldiers who saved us, not quite but whatever. It was important that our country was protected. We were about to bring in an age of peace and prosperity for many people, to the demise of the Original Ones, especially the female. Here's why.

I soon took over the Incan Empire from my father the king and began to unite all the smaller towns and villages. Many of my lives have been about putting people together. I've been in as many as three bodies at one time but only one as Gandhi and Jay.

Kamehameha the first of Hawaii was one such life. Part of me was already in another body before I died in that life. I need to be mostly in one body to function right. It's hard to explain and really not important anyway. Now back to the Incan Empire's expansion. This is cool as it was the right thing to do and it really pissed off the Original First Being Female.

I put our army together and started marching from town to town. People had already heard about what I had done so they were a little skittish to start with. Few people would believe what they had just heard and I was no longer telekinetic so I couldn't show them that anyway. The Original First Being Female had already cut off my power supply, so to speak, by having that part of Aramaeleous attached to the bottom of my spine increase it's control over my emotional energy.

The first town we came upon there was a short but fierce battle. Back in those days, when a town was conquered the soldiers were placed in a circle made of the winning soldiers, and walked on like a rug. Then the king or chief had his heart cut out, etc. What happened here not only confused the town's people but really pissed off the Original Ones.

No one walked on any of the other soldiers. I walked up to the chief, looked him in the eye, and told him that he was now part of the Incan Empire. He could practice any religion he wanted but, when it was time, he would help support his new family. He didn't really trust what I said, but said nothing. He was still waiting to be killed.

I then gave him a basket of rare jewels, food, and left them with better weapons to protect themselves while reminding him, as Incan, they were all entitled to our protection. I welcomed him to the family and we left.

This was no ordinary event. It was a whole new thought process, one that would bring others together, not keep them apart. As we came upon other villages, they almost all just welcomed us and joined the Incan family. As time went on, runners were telling everyone about the new Incan Empire which was now huge, powerful, and family orientated.

As Gandhi I tried my best to show you that we were all family, no matter what religion we were. I tried to get you to put your religious books down for a minute and stand shoulder to shoulder. When you did I asked you to notice that you were now standing heart to heart.

I proved that you could live together as a family no matter what skin color or religion you were. I told you that you could bring change best by just saying no. I asked you not to be physical in doing so also. This was to prepare you for the events I knew would be brought to you now by the Original Ones. I also explained the importance of understanding Animals to be an important part of our community, our family.

Most of the horrific events which were scheduled have been stopped, and some altered. We still have had to deal with 9/11 in America and 3/11 in Japan. Notice the "11" involved here. That stood for the Original First Being halves. It was their arrogant way to tell you that they were in control, not you. The two "1"s next to each other represent each of them standing next to each other. How sick.

This last life as Jay was where Arae would have to wake up on his own and fight the Original Ones as well as everyone else that attacked him, trying to keep this information from coming out. Once this information is released, nothing on the Other Side will be able to play God, to reign supreme. The truth, with Arae backing it, will set everything free. You have to become aware of a problem before you can deal with it.

I apologize for the length of the events described here but it's important, to me anyway, that you know there has always been something on the Other Side that has been trying to do what it could to help you in whatever way it could. Arae is a strong protector and Lilly is a very loving mother Spirit.

You need to have this brought to your attention. These are the beings who will make sure your lives are what they should be, not filled with abuse. They are selfless, not selfish. Creation is about family, the whole, not just a part of it.

CHAPTER 2
THE ORIGINAL FIRST BEING HALVES CREATE LAND MINES

As the Original Ones were aware Arae would not comply with their desired events, they set up as many separate events and situations as possible to serve as road blocks for him. The busier he was the less trouble he would be for them.

They also set up the lives of those who, now in body, would help him in any way. They arranged for their parents, or at least one of them, to be cold, arrogant, and very controlling. They made sure that their lives would keep them suppressed into believing they were little things which could never stand on their own.

They beat them physically as well as psychologically, to keep them in control. They also made sure that they were not able to become aware of who they really were. This was eventually repaired by Arae outside his body, which we call J'Arae. If things seem a little complex, it's only because it was, a little complex.

These issues would be easily handled, changed by the Original Ones when they were ready, yet more than problematic for Arae while in body and fighting them. They felt that this, along with help if necessary from the other Source pairs, would assure their success. Little did they know how things would actually turn out. You'll see it was their arrogance, more than anything else, which worked against them.

They expected Arae to attempt to imprison them, trying to keep them out of the picture while he was in body. They had already discussed this possibility and solution with the two clean Source Spirit pairs. They all agreed to make sure the Original Ones would be freed if necessary. It would take Source Spirit, and a lot of it, to release them from Arae's energy sphere.

The two large clean Source pairs assured the Original First Being halves that, if it came down to it, they would back them in the fight with Arae. This was something that had no honor behind it. The other two large Source pairs had intentions of their own. They had learned deceit and dishonor from the Original Ones themselves. It was time to turn the tables on them.

The Original Ones had already set in place many things to keep people from awakening metaphysically. There were governments and laws who abused those who would admit to hearing voices by confining them to institutions and putting them on medications. Not everyone institutionalized fit this category though, just saying.

They also had religions leading people down the path of servitude instead of enlightenment. They wanted people to awaken a little but not a lot. By having Arae only release a small portion of the Source Spirit metaphysical wall separating the Spirit energies within the brain, left side and right, they'd be able to control everyone's abilities keeping them to a desired minimum.

This would help others see them better while still keeping them mostly in the dark about what was really happening on the Other Side. They always had to maintain full control over everything. That was getting harder and harder to do, especially since everything was growing larger and stronger as well as having "personal" issues.

Then they brought the many "New Age" concepts into play where people were waiting for this new "Light" to come and change everything, to save them. The eventual proposed understanding of the "Light" would be that of the new mother and father God. They wanted everyone everywhere to know there was a mother and father, a male and female.

There was also the resurrection of another false hope machine, now called the law of attraction. Wow, is this an enlightenment killer or what? It attempts to make people think they can just learn how to ask for something and this Universal power is going to make it happen. That's more than a bad joke, it's a revolving table that never stops.

It's a self-perpetuating lie that keeps you looking for the "right way to think". What it really does is empty your pockets. Many people have spent money they didn't really have to spend, on courses, books, and other information trying to learn how to do this. It's put many people in harm's way but has also made some of the people at the top of the game quite rich. What a scam.

What was expected to happen with this was everyone one eventually realizing it to be the scam it is and then fall on their knees to the new mother and father God. That's how the Original Ones planned it anyway. That's not how it would turn out though. This lawless act of attraction will eventually fall away as people wake up to themselves, who they really are. Once they do, they will understand things for themselves using their newly found and accessed abilities. They will learn for themselves what exists.

There are many other numerous examples on both a large and personal nature but not really necessary to mention here. This is enough to make a point. That being there are many things which have been brought into your life to keep you from ever becoming fully aware of whom you are, allowing you the freedom you've always deserved.

CHAPTER 3

INDIVIDUAL ESSENCE FIELDS ARE PROMISED FULL CONTROL

While Arae was back in body, and not doing as the Original Ones really wanted him to do, they were busy trying to "cement in" their own plans against him. They began a campaign of arrogance that was like none ever seen before. They started convincing all the different fields of Spirit that they would become the new rulers which would be in charge of their own Universes or even all that existed.

It was a well-known fact the Original Ones were already building a new dimension to retire in and that they would remain in charge but wanted to isolate themselves from everything, letting others do everything for them. This made their empty promises a little easier to swallow, at least for some of them.

Fae Essence

The Fae never felt for this, not at first. They became an issue farther down the road after Arae had already deleted most everything else. That's enough about that for now. Let's not jump too far ahead. As the Fae were always put down, told and shown they were inferior; they were not so easily taken.

Universal Essence – Stars and Planets

Many of the Stars were happy to comply with this thought process. Their arrogance was already well settled in. They felt all needed to thank them for their work keeping life going in the Second Dimension. They were large and strong. This helped them down the lost road of arrogance. Let's look at Human Essence.

Human Essence

Here was probably the most arrogant group out there. Human Essence had always been told that they were the closest thing to the Original Ones. They were led to believe this by the male and female Original First Beings themselves. There's nothing like being fed pure arrogance from the source of it all.

The Human Essence Spirits were well taken care of. It's a fact that they were a little more like the Original Being Male and Female than anyone else. They were also told that they'd be running the Souls in all the new Universes. The Souls had been told they would be running all the Souls released from them, in that Universe.

Animal and Plant Essence

Both Animal and Plant Essence were not falling for anything the Original Ones said, not in the least. They were always used and abused. They were never appreciated nor given thanks one time for what they kept going through, only being given the attitude that they needed to do more.

Animal Essence was continuously being forced, not placed but forced, into physical bodies to serve all that was. This is probably the ultimate abuse. This is why they have endured the most. This is why I have such a strong desire to protect all of them.

They have always needed protection the most, them and my Lilly. Their lack of proper protection is probably my greatest failure. And people sometimes wonder why I'm so anxious to finish my life and leave. Once free I can finally perform my duties properly. I don't belong here anymore, just to finish this book.

Plant Essence has great patience but it's not without it's limits. They're anxious for Gaia to evolve again so they can all leave their bodies. They stay in them a long time as trees and more. They have been having many lives back to back also. Their abuse is second only to Animal Essence.

Last year, in 2014, I was on a boulder in the Chattahoochee River talking to the water beings, the water itself, to Gaia, the Fae, and all else around me. I opened up to everything. As I was leaving I was back on shore walking up the stairs away from the river when someone said something to me in a very strong and collective voice.

I heard, "Father, when are we leaving?". It was the bank of trees on the far side of the river. I was surprised to be talking with them collectively. I was also sad at the frequencies coming from them as they questioned me. I could feel their strong desire to be free of their bodies and concern over nothing being placed in the future yet for their departure.

I didn't know what to say. I sent back my love, my sadness about them having their own, and that I was doing all I could but was not able to respond properly yet. I did say I was taking care of it and it would happen. I just didn't have a date yet.

Back to the previous time line, Arae was building up strength in all his frequencies. He was still growing, increasing in size and power as all this was happening. The Original Ones were hitting him even harder now trying to subdue him in body hoping to leave him with a submissive feeling, emotional life hangover, once out. He never did.

Arae would always just leave his body, give them a very hard glare, and flex his energy as we would flex a muscle. He wanted them to know. I wanted them to understand that they were nothing to me other than an obstacle I would walk over.

They were so arrogant that they returned to me the frequencies that are in the thought process of "So what.". I liked that. That was just what I wanted to see. Their blind arrogance was one of the tools I would use to take everything on, one last time, in a body.

I realize that I'm switching back and forth from saying Arae and then myself. I am Arae in a body. It's a little confusing to understand and I apologize for that, I'm doing the best I can with it. When my emotions fire up I remember all these things happening as if I'm right there because I am. I just go back and look at it, feel the memories flowing through me.

There's something I haven't mentioned yet. The Source Field everywhere is not just part of me, it also holds what many call the Akashic Records. You didn't think there was actually a physical library did you? Remember, the Second Dimension is comprised only of Spirit, energy, and random pieces of dense particulate matter flowing around.

CHAPTER 4

ARAE REFUSES TO COMPLY WHILE IN BODY

(The Introduction of J'Arae)

H ere's something else that can be a little confusing at first but needs to be expressed, understood now. It will help in the following pages. To help you understand what I'm trying to say, exactly who I'm talking about, I need to explain what I am inside, three different individuals. All of us are like this; it's good for you to know.

What we are, our energetic composition as individuals comes down to three different things. We are the physical body. This is a gathering of mass which is quite alive and full of energy. We are a living physical being with two separate Spirits within it.

The mass of the physical body originally came from materials within the Planet itself. This is a group of elements, as well as other mass, which is put together into a living creature, whether Human, Animal, Plant, etc.

Now, there's also the two different Spirits, actually sentient energy forms, flowing inside them. One of these Spirits is that of Gaia. She actually puts a long removed part of her own Spirit into your body. This usually represents about forty percent of your Core Spirit Flow.

The other sixty percent of your Core Spirit Flow is you, the Spirit within you that is visiting this Planet to have a life. Having said this I need to modify the statement a little. The primary controlling part of your mind is the visiting Spirit but the other forty percent from Gaia is also very much a part of you. You just have the controlling percentage.

So, now you have a base understanding of how the Spirits and energy work within your body. The body itself has energy, not Spirit. The two Spirits inside you make up what you are, how you feel, etc. These two Spirits, flowing up and down your Core Energy Field within you, work together as two hands clasping each other to perform a given function.

They stay separate as their Spirits are different, as the two hands which separate when they're done performing a task together. Clapping is a short example. The two different Spirits can work together without ever combining into one. You can blend water and dirt together to make mud but the water never actually becomes dirt. Because of what's inside me, I'm just a little different.

The visiting Spirit within me, Arae, is Source Spirit which is already composed of all the frequencies expressed in the Physical Realm and more. When I'm put, or rather Arae is put, into a body the Source Spirit starts to bond with everything else.

Arae created three different beings from itself a long time ago to assist him when leaving a body, in order to try to release as much of the Planet's Spirit as possible. I met them a long time ago when I was prepared to leave this body to deal with things head on, on the Other Side.

This bonding action makes me a lot more Arae than anything else. Because of this it's often difficult for me to explain

who I am. Therefore, I came up with the name of J'Arae to describe myself, the Human body with Arae inside, Jay with Arae.

I try to say Arae when I talk about him before being put inside this body. It's just a little hard to do so since I have become part of Arae. You can see my confusion erupting from time to time, especially when I go into protective mode. From now on when I talk about something I've personally done through this body, I'm going to try to use J'Arae as the defining term.

Just a note for you now; insects, fish, reptiles, and other smaller things too numerous to mention, only have one Spirit flowing within them, that of Gaia, the Planet's Spirit. Well, let's get back to Arae having issues with the Original Ones.

(J'Arae Rebels)

Well, J'Arae started things, as he was still awakening and not fully self-aware yet, talking as Sylvia Browne used to, about the great Mother and Father God, who was actually both parts of the Original First Being. Everyone has been calling the female part of the Original First One, Father God, from the beginning.

As I continued waking up I began to see more and more of the Original Ones, who they were and what they were doing. I was at a point of my awakening where I wanted to meet the Original First Being Female that I could already feel and Sylvia Browne had talked so much about. I was a little confused about the difference between what I felt and the words which Sylvia used when speaking of her.

I meditated and asked the Original First Being Female to come to me. I got nothing, no reply, no feeling, just nothing. So, I did what felt right, I demanded her appearance. Something was off and I wanted to understand it.

She appeared to me, through my Pineal Energy Field, as a woman dressed in thin see through material, floating less than horizontal. Her clothing was of light purples, violet, shades of red and pink, and more. They were pretty much flowing together. She also had a sword in her right hand.

As she approached me, with her sword pointed directly at my chest, I was looking into her eyes. I saw something I didn't like, I saw trouble. Then, I took my eyes off hers as I felt her sword piercing my chest just on the inside of my heart. I looked down and watched it happen. Then she just disappeared, faded away into nothingness.

I somehow knew her sword was 4.5 feet long and I knew that it entered my chest a depth of 4.5 inches. I realized who I had just met but not talked to. It was the supposed great Mother God that Sylvia called Azna. I also realized she just stabbed me with a sword. Gee, do you think there was anything behind that?

The event left me a little calmer than when I was demanding her appearance in the beginning. That was supposedly the true intention of her stabbing me. I just didn't like the aggression behind it. A soft touch to the heart would have worked just fine. She chose her particular delivery method for a reason. It wasn't compassion. There was one very important issue I now understood from having met her. I found it in her eyes, her negative frequencies.

With over ninety percent of my Spirit being Arae, I have the ability to read negativity like nothing else. It's part of my frequencies, what I am. The protector has to be able to read this properly. It's necessary for my format to function correctly.

This Mother God being was 27.5 percent negative frequencies. Twenty seven and a half percent negativity is not a good thing in something that has that much power. I began to open up a little more inside becoming a little more aware of my relationship with her, if you can call it that. She and I had issues. That was for certain.

Then on February 23rd of 2010, I became aware of Lilly, my better half, my Source Mate. I was in a meditative state about

9:00 am, and all of a sudden realized I loved this beautiful woman more than I could even understand. I had to see her immediately. I refused to do anything for the Original Ones until I did. The next thing I knew I was at the M3 Star cluster but in the Second Dimension. There she was, so breathtakingly beautiful, so full of life and love, so amazing and fulfilling.

She saw me immediately. The smile on her face was nothing short of divine and exhilarating. My heart was way out of my body. I floated above her from one side, saw her smile, and floated to the other side to see her smile again.

I could feel her heart energy all through me. Wow, what an experience. The joy, the pure love that was exchanged in that brief moment, was the thing that civilizations are built on.

I had to return to my body right away. I was only gone about nine seconds but what an incredible nine seconds. I could now move forward. I had something to hold onto, my love for Lilly and hers for me. When she looked at me her eyes were glowing with a very deep, sincere, and personal love. There's no way to ever forget that.

Once that was settled, I immediately fired up my displeasure in what was being said about Lucifer. Poor Lucifer, the Angel that had been protecting everyone and thing since the very beginning, has done more for everyone than any of the other Angels, and was treated the worst. That's the Original Ones for you.

They turn everything upside down and then twist it into something they can use against you. Who do you think was the real architect of our present governments? The Original Ones put the thoughts into the people's minds and put things in the order they wished for the results they expected.

When necessary they would use the Angels to physically control the people. Things were going to happen their way and only their way. That's how it had always been, up until now anyway. The one non-compliant component was Arae. Here's how that went, while he was still in body.

Back in the year 2008, the Original First Being Female finally released some of Arae's power level in his present body, Jay Essex. She needed to do so if Arae would ever be able to do some of the strong things he was supposed to. This was also the time when the Annunaki here noticed his energy spike using their equipment. Our close friends in space, that we haven't even met as a race yet, also picked up on it. Some of them already knew anyway. Arae had finally begun to come alive.

Things started happening in and around me. I noticed myself changing. I felt stronger somehow, not physically but in a way I didn't understand. It was soft but quite definite. Certain things had started to make sense that I had never thought much about earlier.

I've always known there was life on other planets. Somehow I knew that to be truer than earlier. It was a kind of gut feeling. I had always seen things but now they were feeling normal and to be expected, as if everyone did this. The change was gradual, soft, and fluid, so much, that I hardly noticed it. What had happened?

It's simple really. The metaphysical barrier between the two parts of my brain had been removed almost completely and I was now aware of all of myself. When a horse is plowing a field, and has those blinders on to keep him going in a straight line, he sees a whole new world once they're removed. He awakens to what is really out there, not just what he was being forced to see.

I had many lives speaking of 12/21/2012. When I was Pacal of the Maya, I made a really big issue of this. The same was said as Pahana, Pachakuti Inca Yupanqui, Quetzalcoatl, Nostradamus, Leonardo Di Vinci, and more. I kept telling you that after 12/21/2012 you would never see the world in the same way, that's all.

I didn't say the world would split into two, be destroyed by a comet, or any such other non-sense. I only said you'd never see things the same. The reason for this statement was that I knew the Source energy barrier would be removed from the middle of your brains so that both halves could talk to each other openly allowing you to awaken. By this I mean that both the Spirit from Gaia, the Planet's energy, as well as the visiting Spirit, your own personal, would finally become aware of each other and communicate.

You would then be able to more easily understand the real world around you; your blinders would be off. Your abilities would become stronger and you would now be able to "see" into different dimensions and more. This is why you'd never see the world in the same way as you'd be able to see all of it, or at least a whole lot more. Your understanding, that is your wisdom, would grow immensely. You would come alive.

The power in my core was flowing stronger now and better than ever before. By the time 2012 was here I was already deep into the war with the Original Ones and things were a mess everywhere. I knew 12/21/2012 was a bust. In early April of 2012 I removed the Source barrier in the brains of all the Animals here.

Near the beginning of May I did the same for all the people here. It was the only thing I knew to do to help everyone. It would at least help most people come to terms with the fact that there was more going on than what they had previously thought. This also made it easier for me to talk to them later about such things as what we're covering now.

Getting back to my issue with the Original Ones while in this body, I was told to do something that I didn't agree with. It was in early February of 2010 that I was told to tell people about the new "Mother and Father God" like Sylvia Browne talked about. I had issues with that.

That's the month that I met Lilly, initially told the Original Ones no, had things start moving around the house on their own, and an assortment of other things not necessary to go into.

It was a variety of daily events, my new way of living that had come into being. It all got serious when I refused the Original Ones.

I told them that they were a very important part of Creation, heck almost all Spirit came from them, all but the Energans who came out before the First Being finished becoming itself. That's a very important fact. I did explain though that Creation was about family, all of us being one very large family. They simply said "No.". They said it was to be all about them, the great Mother and Father God.

I was initially a bit polite about it but again, I just told them no. I had absolutely no hesitation or crack in my voice when I said it. I was serious and they knew it. They then tried to coerce me into doing what they wanted. That's why they opened the door for me to see Lilly before finally becoming aggressive with me. They didn't care to even try to understand. Everything was about them and only them, period.

J'Arae, the only way I know to call myself, had put his feet down. I was not fully aware of all the details. My power levels were still low. My abilities were nothing compared to now. I was able to see a lot but not use my energy to do what I can today.

I have so much of Arae in me now that I'm a large constant glow on the Annunaki and NSA scanners used to show metaphysical energy across the planet. It's Arae that does what I do. I'm just part of him, that's all. Like I've always said, I'm just the shoe with a big foot in it.

The Original Ones started their personal control strategies into play. Remember, I was not self-aware back then. They had told me I was Avatar, Centurion, and something else I can't remember. I looked up the definitions of these things and got the basic picture of what they were saying. I told them I was no better than anything else and they got pissed.

The situation was a little strange yet funny also. They actually thought I was going to tell everyone to praise them, unreal.

Shortly afterwards the lies came in hard and fast. It was pretty much all they ever did anyway. They were good at it but as soon as I realized more about myself and trusted how I felt about them, I knew where I stood, against them completely. I finally knew a big fight was coming.

They kept lying to me about little things, one after the other. I was still under the impression that they wouldn't do so because of who they were. Soon I realized they always did this because of who they were. All the religious books and philosophies weren't worth the paper they were written on. The Original Ones were abusive. I could always see a lot of things going on everywhere. It was just part of who I was.

After a short while, my ability to see had become more than just an annoyance to the Original Ones. I heard the Original First Being Female tell her male counterpart that I had extremely sharp clarity, as in too sharp. He agreed and said he'd take care of that. That night, while I slept, he physically altered my brain to try to destroy my ability to do so.

He did damage my brain's ability to see. Gaia has tried to fully restore it but she can't. Arae's already told me that the only way it can be fixed is to completely rebuild it which isn't possible while I'm still alive. My vision, as thousands of people already know, is very strong yet still not what it should be. Anyway, it's no big deal. I can always get all the information I need to take care of everyone I'm talking to.

Those bodies here now with Source Spirit inside, Lilly and Arae's children, are very powerful and they will no longer be bothered and attacked. They will be supported. I just have to drop this body to do so. This is part of the reason why I must get back home to the Other Side. I need to become my full self again, not this piece in a body.

Anyway, the lies came one after the other, the aggression grew between myself and the two Original First Being halves, and things began to come to a boiling point. J'Arae was stronger. The Original Ones had become aware they couldn't trick or control me. The next step was obvious. What I am inside, Arae, was now beginning to come out into me more and more each passing day. It was time to move forward. The more Arae came out, the more I became what I am, J'Arae the shoe holding the big foot. It was time to kick something real hard.

It was time to remove the cancer from Creation, one way or the other. All abusive controls had to be removed from Creation in order to save it from these abusive frequencies now growing rampant within everything. Didn't everyone deserve this anyway? Yes they did. Compassion, Honor, and Equality are necessary to properly protect beings. This would have to be the new format for all to exist in. There was no other choice, no other solution. The cancer had to be cut out, every last little piece of it. It also had to be done now.

CHAPTER 5

J'ARAE IS ATTACKED BY THE ORIGINAL FIRST BEINGS

Initially there was strong communication between J'Arae and the Original Ones, mostly the female. There was a short time that J'Arae was learning a little from them. It was always imbedded in a controlling format yet it was eye opening just the same. J'Arae grew in understanding as well as power level. Then the abusive lying began.

It came out of nowhere. One minute I could trust them and the next they were going out of their way to show me that they would lie to me whenever they wanted and I could do nothing about it. I tried to find ways to explain it off at first, but then I couldn't hide from the facts anymore. The Original First Beings were lying to me.

The more they did it, the more I was feeling aggression towards me. I was confused at first but that didn't last long. I went to the Original First Being Female and slammed her. I said, "You lied to me!" She said, "That's right, and I'm going to keep doing it so get used to it!"

OK, now that blew me away. How could this be happening? How is this possible? This was the Mother God that Sylvia Browne always talked about. She's not supposed to be like this. Everything I knew and had seen up to this point, had led me to believe there was a large hidden agenda with the Original Ones. Well, it just showed it's ugly face.

I was asked to go to a Whole Foods store nearby, so I went. When I got there I sat at a table outside and relaxed for a minute. Almost immediately after doing so a woman came up and sat down at the table next to me. It was an Angel who had made a temporary body. I see energy so I knew what it was. Then she started to talk.

She started telling me blatant lies, one after the other, about herself as well as everything else. She, actually I should say Zhe as that's how they like to be called. They are neither male nor female, they are both. All Angels are like that and they call this particular form Zhe.

So, after enough lies were dumped on me, I got up after giving her a hard time back. I let her know her arrogance made me sick. It's safe to say she understood this and more. I was so disgusted with everything over there now. I finally was aware of how things happened over there. I finally understood those bad feelings I had in my gut, my Solar Plexus energy field.

Well, as time went by the dissention grew. I would have nothing to do with them anymore. I'll never say I haven't lied or done something wrong, I have. However, once I was self-aware, that all stopped. It was never a big issue but for me to ever lie again would have changed who I finally knew I was.

The desperation of the Original Ones intensified. There was no trust or love lost between anyone. I would never allow them to control me. They would never stop trying. It was obvious I had to deal with them directly now, get in their faces so to speak. They just wouldn't ever leave me alone.

It was already obvious that J'Arae would not comply with their wants or demands. It was time to force control upon him. At least that's what the Original Ones thought. Yeah, good luck with that. It was the arrogance of the Original First Being halves that initially put them in this situation. They created their own problems.

They made something very strong to protect them. Then they continuously made it stronger. The kept beating it up, forcing it to watch them hurt others. They actually thought he would never turn on them when they made him to protect against their own actions. The more he learned, the more he understood, the more danger they were in.

Arae only wanted to stop them initially, but they were not like that at all. He already knew this to be the case but he tried to go down that road anyway. He imprisoned them twice but the other problematic Source Spirits later let them out using their combined energies. Then they attacked him over and over again. That was enough of that. It was time to handle things in a more decisive manner. They had to be destroyed. There was also now the question of why the other Source Spirits let the Original First Being halves out.

The Original First Ones decided to increase the frequency of their attempts to control him. They were attacking J'Arae while he was sleeping now. That's when he was most vulnerable. Remember, these beings had been running many trillions of beings lives for well over 2,863 trillion of our years, here on Earth.

J'Arae's Black Panther Animal Spirit Guide told him what stones to wear around his neck to help protect him at night. He was happy to comply. It helped but would not stop the issue. Black Onyx is a stone of personal power and great benefit when dealing with such issues.

Being that J'Arae was Source Spirit, his energy was continuously feeding into every stone on him as well. This almost acted like a reservoir of his energy while he was asleep. Again, this was no cure but it did help. To be at such a low power level and have to deal with the strong Original First Beings, was more than just a difficult task. At times it felt impossible. Actually, I should have said many times.

The Original Ones were not only experts at controlling lives by now, but the only ones who had ever done it. This helped them stay at the top of things. Many beings wanted to keep having lives and had to go to them to do so. To say they had a monopoly is an understatement. Also, no one could take over if they didn't know how. They were not stupid, just aggressively abusive and selfish in all ways.

The attacks on J'Arae became more and more aggressive. With each following assault they thought themselves to be closer to success only to watch themselves fail again. J'Arae's energy kept getting stronger. More and more of him kept coming out. He was always able to take the pounding, heal, and come back at them.

They physical brain in J'Arae was also continually changing now. I'm talking about its physical shape. His brain was continually growing and the skull would do the same to match it. His friends picked up on this, themselves. One of his friends at a Starbuck's coffee shop once said "We should take plaster molds of your head every day." Her name is Amy. She's really cool. She's been around a long time and has been a good friend over many lives. The man she's with is also a really cool dude. He's an Energan inside, his Spirit that is. I call him a dimensional dude. I'll not give out too many personal details here. There'll just really good people.

Anyway, J'Arae would wake up with the Original Ones, either one or both, in his head trying to run his body. He then had to mentally wake up, go after them, and kill whatever part of them he could find. When we're stuck in a body we are severely limited in most all ways. These physical bodies are more a prison than anything else, at least to me.

It took so much energy, so much thought process with aggressive brain flexing, to do this that J'Arae's brain would be in physical pain after having done so. After one of these incidents, Gaia would have to come to J'Arae's aid to fix it. I remember that pain like it was just yesterday.

The brain, in many ways, is like a muscle. You can flex it, use it in different ways as you flex different parts of it. I realize that in many ways I'm a bit of a freak, a singularity. Still, many of you are growing larger brains right now and will learn how to use yours to your benefit. You just won't have to do what I've had to. That was part of my being in body one last time. I'm the janitor. I clean up the messes.

In the earlier stages, while still very weak compared to now, I would grow very weary of all this. I just wanted to come out of this body, go home, and destroy the problems immediately without the hindrance of this body. I already knew how strong I was. I was tired of fighting with my brain's hands tied behind my back.

I was at a McDonald's with a good friend, Fran S., one night. I would often walk down there with her after she finished her work at a nearby vitamin store called Good Nutrition in Norcross, Georgia. She's moved to North Carolina now where she was needed to be for a while. I was sent to her to help me understand the upcoming changes in my energy. She is a very close, old friend of mine. We've had many lives together.

She's an iridologist while also many other things. She's a healer and a damn good one. She can see into the body energetically but also physically. She is a dual phase doctor, so to speak. She's complete as she uses both her physical and metaphysical abilities to help others heal.

Anyway, we were sitting and she saw me dealing with both the Original Ones at the same time, in my brain. I was really pissed

I could never be left along for even five minutes. When in free form, out of body, you need no rest. You're not attached to a physical body needing sustenance and rest. You're free of such things, thus the term "free form Spirit".

I got pissed from the female putting pressure on the left side of my brain and the male doing the same on the right side. They just wouldn't leave me alone. I fired up my energy with massive aggression and literally blew the two of them off of me. Fran looked at my head directly then. She could see the energies everywhere and she knew that although not yet myself, I was very powerful.

After blowing the two of them off, the female looked at the male and sent the thought process which would be behind the spoken words of "Look how strong he is already." With no other words spoken, that is thoughts produced, they both attacked me again. It was only a short time later that the male Original One went into my brain while I was sleeping and physically damaged my brain to destroy as much of my ability to see clearly and pull my brain apart. He did damage that cannot be repaired while I'm in this body. It has been fixed as best it can be though. Anyway, back to sitting with Fran.

I had reached the end of my limits. That was it. I had had it with all this crap. I was going over there to kill both of them now! I went into my brain and started to physically separate it down the middle. I'm talking about using my abilities to physically separate my brain into two halves. I knew this would kill my body so I could leave and do my job.

I wasn't fully aware of myself yet but I knew what I was inside. My reason for existence, what I am beyond all else, is "Protector". I have great compassion but its coupled to strong power that I didn't understand yet, nor was I able to access it properly. I just wasn't there yet.

I could feel my brain straining as I was pulling at it. Fran literally screamed "What are you doing? You're pulling your brain in half!" I never mentioned what I was doing to her. She could see all this herself. She's an awakened Spirit, strong too.

I explained what I was doing and she politely gave me a hard time about it. It's good to have friends. I had just had enough, that's all. I had to death wish. I have not just the strong desire but the actual need to do this, the need to protect and my primary issue was with these beings. They were my primary target. I didn't understand the extent of all this but I knew I was anxious to do all I could to remove these things in their entirety.

It took a couple weeks for my brain to heal. It was almost finished before the Original Ones came back to me. Above all else, they did not want me out of my body yet. Nothing over there did. That was a given. The war was on. Once out of this body I will totally remove all parts of this cancer. They knew that. They also knew they couldn't deal with Arae's main focal point in this body let alone the fullness of him flowing out of and attacked to, my Crown Chakra.

As I continue to grow, becoming stronger and more self-aware, I realize more of what I am inside. This is what I want for all of you. I can understand more and more each day as more of Arae comes into this body. I apologize for jumping around speaking of myself in a third person and then singular, or however you express this. I like to say J'Arae but that's me, what I really am. We are all more than one thing you know.

Arae is a huge being now with a few different focal points. One of the issues with powerful energy in large amounts is that it cannot fit into a body. The most common analogy I use here is that of trying to pour a swimming pool into a balloon. Yeah, good luck with that.

The same is true of trying to place your intelligence into a physical brain. There's just no way. It's like trying to press the water from a full five gallon bucket into a coffee cup. It just won't fit. I try to impress upon as many as I can that the truth is much simpler what others have been trying to explain to you.

Why do you think the bible has been rewritten over seventeen hundred times and there are volumes of other books trying to explain away all the proven faults in it. All of you have continuously been fed lies, one after the other, in an attempt to control you.

I'm not just picking on the bible either; all your religious books are like that, the Qur'an, Torah, as well as the rest of them. They were written to control the masses, not enlighten them. The only true enlightenment for you to find is already within yourself. If you do not find or see something for yourself, what do you have?

You'll find you have a message or possible truth waiting for you to look into for yourselves, that's all. The problems within your religions come from your abusively incorrect philosophies, not those within them having love in their hearts, just trying to find the right place to express it. It's about the right way, not place. It's about flowing down into your true self, becoming aware of yourself and what's around you, that will free you from your religions.

There is no name for this other than self-awareness. How can you have your own truth when you don't find it for yourself? I don't mean you read something and others tell you, "This is true and what you must do or you'll be punished forever." That's only abusive misleading control. That's not truth. When you can feel with your heart, see with your mind, and learn to use and trust your gut, you can finally awaken to the fullness of who you already are. Find your own truth, own it.

There have also been things stopping that from happening. They didn't want to allow you full disclosure of what was being done to you. They only wanted you to see them in, as they said, all their glory. The truth needed to remain a secret. You could never be allowed to understand the abuse you're given in a body.

They did want you to see them being worshipped by everything else in the Second Dimension though.

Now that you understand all this, it will be easier to understand their reasons for what they did. They, the Original First Being Male and Female, cared nothing for the welfare of others, only their desire for worship and praise. They were literally destroying the Creation they built in order to have that one disgusting thing, arrogant selfishness.

Arae, through J'Arae, has destroyed over ninety percent of everything needing to be removed in order to initiate and maintain the new format of Compassion, Honor, and Equality. Still, I have to keep dealing with problematic Spirit on the Other Side. There is so little left that my systolic blood pressure, the top side of it, has decreased well over twenty psi.

I just saw my doctor a few days ago, 7/31/2015, and he thought he had put me on blood pressure medicine which didn't make sense because I told him I couldn't take any, it made me aggressive. Anyway, that's how my blood pressure dropped, less attacks. It's still twenty four hours a day and seven days a week but it's not as continuous or aggressive. I've always taken out the strongest stuff first. That's what always came at me next.

All of these Spirits kept coming at me. They all thought that they would be the ones who would finally "tame" Arae. They all watched me delete everything before them yet, in their own arrogance, kept coming at me, like flies to a zapper. It's never ceased to amaze myself as well as others who are now strong enough to see it.

Arrogance is a serious illness now being handled in the Second Dimension. Arae will deal with the Third Dimension, our own, as soon as he's out of this body and his true self again. The time for change, as almost all of you already understand, is long overdue. Now, let's get back to the fighting between Arae and the Original First Beings.

J'Arae had the ability to go into the main focal point, or any other, of any Spirit and listen to it, know it's thoughts. This turned out to be quite the advantage. At one point the Original First Being Male went into J'Arae's brain, as we've already mentioned, to try to remove this ability. He couldn't take it away from him.

J'Arae was watching a DVD one day, the movie Avatar, and before the first five minutes was up, he had run through about every single emotion there was. I remember waking up to what was happening. I went straight into my brain and there was the Original First Being Female pushing buttons in my head.

I focused on her and she turned around to look at me. She was actually surprised that I caught her doing it. I told her to get lost and she did. This is one way that Spirit controls you, by getting under your emotions. It's also how they try to adjust you after making your brain stronger. Feeling this emotional mix-up is not a reason for concern. The situation was a little different for me, that's all.

These attacks were persistent and would easily take a few hundred pages to discuss but, why bother. It's just more of the same, different ways in which I was attacked day after day and night after night. The only important thing here is to know that it kept happening. It never stopped. This is enough to drive one crazy.

Each day passing found me stronger and more aware. I would fight during the day, relax and get repaired by Gaia, and then be attacked again while sleeping. In the morning it would all happen over and over again. It was very frustrating. I tired of it quickly. There had to be a way for me to deal with this.

CHAPTER 6
J'ARAE ATTACKS THE ORIGINAL ONES

I was tired of being attacked. It never stopped and I had had enough. I had tried everything to get them to stop. I understood how they were, being able to feel them inside as well as read their basic thoughts. It would never stop until they were gone, out of the picture. It was time to go on the offensive. I needed to either imprison them or permanently, and completely, destroy them.

I found them, one at a time, and placed them within a box built from my energy. It kept them there for a while. I watched them try to escape and they couldn't. I kept a good eye on them to make sure. It was nice, just for a short while, to be left alone. They weren't pounding on my head anymore trying to get in. When they did it was very hard getting them out.

If necessary I would flex my brain, as if a muscle, and put all I had into it. That would always work but left my brain a little damaged, like a sprained muscle. I was doing all I could, and trying to be careful, but it was really hard for me to do in a body. I always knew I could take care of them easily out of body but there were a few things I had to do that I wasn't aware of yet. I did get there was something about a book, information, but that's all I knew. I was still waking up.

Well, the Original Ones weren't imprisoned very long. When I awoke the next morning, they were running around causing issues but trying to hide while doing so. I was a little more than confused, more that pissed too. How the hell did they get out? I felt them try to escape earlier. They couldn't. I felt their anguish as their attempts failed, their frustration from being held captive the first time in their existence.

I didn't know I could do it yet but I went back in time and watched everything happen. They were let out. Armaeleous and Aramaeleous used their combined energy to dissolve mine and let them out. Lillith and Lydia were also there, just watching though.

OK, that pissed me off. I wasn't sure what was going on. Why would they do that? Why would they want them free? They were clean Source Spirit. Didn't they understand that the Original Ones were responsible for so much harm, disaster, and abuse? My anger was overcome with disbelief, confusion.

I asked both Armaeleous and Aramaeleous why they let them out. I received no reply what so ever. Armaeleous was just thinking he did the right thing because I didn't know better, part of being in a body. Now Aramaeleous was a completely different issue. He was trouble. As strong as he was I could still get into his head, so to speak. It's actually the primary focal point of his Spirit energy.

He had plans within plans on how things would go until he was in charge of everything. He was going to be the new God, in his mind anyway. He already knew how he was going to play everyone against each other until he was left at the top of the hill with no one standing against him.

I could also see where he felt quite confident that I would never be an issue. Either I would follow him or he would destroy me. This was a little confusing as I knew he wasn't able to do so. However, he actually thought he could. More important than that was the fact that he was willing to do so with no regret or remorse what so ever. This left me feeling a little sad that he would feel this way about me but more importantly I immediately understood I had to take him down and the quicker the better. I already knew he wanted me to get rid of the other Source Spirit pair first. Here's where I began to learn about arrogance in a whole new light. Here's where my sadness of Creation's current condition set in. Why, as Arae, had I waited so long?

Armaeleous was a being of strong hope. He just wanted everyone to be happy. I still think back on him as a brother and miss him. The Source Spirit involved here that I was most concerned about was Aramaeleous. He had just proven himself to be a serious problem. He was the strongest thing out there, other than Arae that is. He was also the largest Spirit form in existence.

I felt him, read him, and realized what he had become inside. He was clean but filthy from arrogance. He was self-serving and waiting to be king. That's when I realized that Arae was the only protector, Aramaeleous never had that format. I felt sad, alone, betrayed, and then ready to pursue the battle on a much larger front.

I knew nothing could kill me. That was never an issue. My biggest fear is that as J'Arae, I could screw up and let something else control my body allowing them access to Arae's power. To be the protector, knowing and understanding what you are, and have someone else control that to do as they wished, would be the ultimate destruction of my own format. I would never let that happen. I would rather get out of this body and free Arae.

As time went on, the Original Ones realized I was willing to do so; I made it more than obvious. I had to let them know this was a fact. They couldn't read my mind as I could theirs. Arae's that strong. This was something they not only didn't want, but would never be able to handle. Things having become what they were now, I would immediately and easily destroy them once out.

Now the Original Ones were more cautious around me. They would hide behind the energy of others when they attacked me, making it more difficult to get at them. It was hard to see them that way. Their determination, as well as that of the rest of the Source over there, was relentless. Theirs was more so though. They were very strong with those additional negative frequencies inside them.

This helped me learn how to see things a little clearer and definitely deeper on the Other Side, the Second Dimension. I had already been damaged by the Original First Being Male while sleeping but I could still see things quite well. It just wasn't like I was looking through my own eyes over there anymore. The section of my brain that produces the Scanner field was damaged. I lost my ability to see things with high definition clarity. I still saw things, just not as easily. Think that didn't piss me off?

Anyway, eventually I managed to catch them again, one at a time, and imprison them. Once again, they were let out by the others Source Spirit pairs while I was sleeping. I didn't need to see this happen a third time. I didn't have the time, nor the energy, to waste on it. I had to do something else. It was also time to address this new issue with the other Source Spirit over there.

By now I could easily feel what was going on with the other Source Spirit over there. I could get their primary thoughts when I wanted them but it wasn't necessary. They weren't trying to hide their feelings. Once again, arrogance was showing it's ugly face. This was always as sad as it was helpful.

Both of the other Source pairs were starting to talk to me more now. They though me ignorant to their end desires. I understood them so it wasn't too much of an issue to see through their actions. They were not a big problem yet, not until the Original Ones were removed.

They hit me with lie after lie after lie after lie. Man, nothing over there would stop lying to me, other than the Animal Essence I was talking to. They were the only beings that would never lie to me, that and the new clean Source Angels and Animals which came from Lilly and Arae. Everything else was happy to lie.

The Original Ones had always done so, they established this format for the Other Side. This made it appropriate for everything over there, especially both of the other Source pairs who had never even had one life, to lie. They never had to learn about compassion, honor, and equality. They also never wanted to though either. Why should they? They were always told they were going to be the new Gods when the Original Ones retired and they were about to do so.

Once, early in my awakening, I was attacked by some of that Negative Source Spirit which was removed from that large field of Original First Being energy which became the other two Source pairs as well as all the different fields of Essence. He was doing what he was told. He wasn't there because he wanted to be, because he didn't.

The Original First Being Female brought him to me and told him to grab my heart and squeeze it twice. He was careful not to kill my body. He and I knew each other well. He helped keep the Negative Source Spirit field in check. He was powerful Negative Source Spirit but had no desire for aggression towards anything. He was made from negative frequencies, that's all. That's not anyone's fault.

I always have, and always will, protect all beings within Creation providing they are not aggressive towards anything else. This being could not help being made who he is. It was by no choice of his own. The fact that he is made of such strong negative frequencies, and doesn't want to attack anything, actually says a lot of good about him. True compassion is not selective.

We have been led in many bad directions through all our lives. This will all change now.

Actually, to beat a handicap like this is awesome. That says volumes about a person. He's the head council member that runs the Negative Source Spirit Field and keeps it in line. There are many other and very powerful protective measures in place here. That's my business alone for now. I apologize if that bothers you. I'm releasing many personal things about the horrors in my last life but there are things that are relative to Arae only.

I've always been doing all I can for everyone. Now that I'm staying out of body forever I can finally do what I was meant to do, take care of your environment properly so you can become the awesome beings you already are. You just need a safe house and yard to live in. You need to be left alone to be you. You're not children any more. That stage of your lives is long gone.

Well, the fighting was still ridiculous between the Original Ones and myself. However, things were about to come to a head. They finally decided they were better off trying to take me on out of this body. That was not a strategic move. It was the beginning of their end.

On July 10, 2012, at about 10:23 pm, they came at me with an army of their own choosing, negative Source Spirit and Souls. There is a place where negative frequency Souls stay together. Some religious people would probably want to call it a hell. It's on the Other Side in the Second Dimension just like the Other Side of positive vibrations, what many would call heaven.

It's located around the first moon off of Uranus but, as I just mentioned, in the Second Dimension. The moon's name is Miranda. If you look it up you'll see how it's born from conflict, a collision between two large inert masses which became one. That's where all the negative Souls are kept out of body. It's their home, that's all. Lucifer always kept everyone in their perspective areas to avoid conflicts with each other. He's a protector, a peace keeper. Well, back to the conflict.

I was sitting in my downstairs free used office chair looking out the sliding glass door. There was a horde of negative stuff coming at me. That's all I could see at first. I saw negative Souls and even Negative Source coming to me from that general area. Then I saw something I didn't expect, although I really didn't expect this either.

There was energy, seen in my mind as two sets of arms with hands, reaching through the varied negative energy field or cloud in front of me. They reached towards me but didn't touch my body. They did however start pulling at the Silver protective coating I have in my energy that keeps negative energy away. This Silver coating not only makes me slippery to those frequencies but not also disintegrates it.

As this coating was being removed I noticed that I could feel the Negative Source Spirit starting to reach into my heart area with the intent of killing this body and getting me out of it. The two sets of arms and hands I saw belonged to both of the Original Ones.

Only Source can do that to me, or at least back then. Nothing can do it now. I guess the Original Ones actually thought that they could hold me and somehow contain me. That proved to be a grave error in judgement.

I looked inside said to the next layer of what I thought was my Spirit energy and asked it, "Are you going to help me or not?" He didn't answer so I told him to just keep his little wussy butt out of the way so he didn't get hurt while I took care of it myself. The next thing I knew, Arae and I went after everything in a way that's difficult to describe.

The whole event took less than nine seconds, three seconds for me to attack the Original Ones personally and then another three seconds for Arae to join me and finish the job. The last three seconds was for me to look back and try to understand the extent of what had just happened. It all occurred too fast for me to be able to realize in the moment. Remember folks, this is energy we're talking about. It doesn't flow as slow as the speed of light.

The next thing I knew, I was trying to understand everything I had seen, everything I had felt. The Negative Spirit around me was not only gone, it was destroyed. I looked for it and couldn't find it. I went back again to watch what happened and saw it completely destroyed in a flash of energy. That's the only way I can describe it.

I can see, hear, feel, and understand all forms of energy let alone Spirit. I had to be sure of what I was looking at. We have to know for ourselves whether or not something is real. I had a few affirmations regarding the reality of what I saw. I had none against.

When I look, see, hear, and feel things in order to understand them I'm actually there. I'm not going by hearsay, but by experiencing it for myself. I'm literally there while it's happening. It took a few years for me to accept what I was learning to accept. It's not like holding an stone in your hand, but in a way it is.

If you look out the window and see a mother and a child walk by, after they're gone, are you sure you really saw that? You can't go back and run outside and touch them to be sure. However, when you see them a few times, in different situations, and then talk with them instead of at them, you begin to understand that they are real.

When you ask Spirit a question to which you have no answer, and you have to think about what their reply, why would you believe you were talking to yourself? When Spirit answers you, using words you don't normally use or need to look up the meaning of, why would you push yourself down that road that asks, "Did I hear that a long time ago and decide to fool myself with it now?"

Why would you do that do yourself when all you wanted was the truth of the situation anyway? You wouldn't.

This is one way that you learn how to start having "faith" in yourself. This is the first true faith that you must have in order to move forward becoming more of yourself than you've ever been, in all your lives. This is how you start to become you, to open like the Lotus flower as it feels daylight again.

Well, here's what had happened in the fight we were just talking about. I immediately went after the male and female parts of the Original First Being. I hit both of them with a hard blast of energy, enough to burn theirs up, and all of a sudden my brain was stressing less and the power I had put out was enormous. I managed to kill about two thirds of each of them, but I didn't do it alone. Part of my Spirit out of the body, Arae, had just joined me. It's a quiet part that has always helped protect me but only when my physical body was about to be destroyed. Other than that, I've always been on my own when fighting.

The last third of both of them was removed from immediate sight and hidden. I found them but knew not to be concerned with them at the moment. For now they were not a threat and I would look at that again later. The next thing that happened was relative to the Negative Souls that had surrounded me earlier.

I found myself at Miranda, Uranus' first moon, and saw the damage being inflicted over there as many of these aggressive Souls had run back home, so to speak. There, a portion of Lucifer, one we named Luke, was already protecting about six thousand and eight hundred non-aggressive Negative Souls from the upcoming event.

Arae simply released a burst of energy and deleted all of them there, other than the ones Luke saved. There were about five hundred million of them. The Earth has been polluted with Negative Souls for a long time now and that's where they stayed when out of body.

Then we, Arae and I, were at the Negative Source Field. He, or I should say we, hit that one also but were more selective about it. There were many there who were non-combative and non-aggressive. They had every right to be left alone. They were not responsible for having been made what they were. That was the fault of the Original Ones.

Well, that's the first fight. It was in May of 2013 that the final fight between Arae and the Original Ones occurred. This is where Arae finally finished destroying the Original First Being halves. This was a permanent event. There were no pieces of them left anywhere. It's also where Arae's Spirit energy mutated into something with new abilities as well as power level. This had the NSA over to my house the next day. Their satellites showed them something they had never seen before. We'll go there in just a bit.

The Original Ones had been wearing the energy skin, a thin piece of other energy, trying to look like something other than themselves. That was a little confusing at first but easily distinguished once I did it a few times. It's like using a mask of someone else but it was a piece of their energy. I found that a little disgusting.

Anyway, I had both of them, what was left of them by now, hiding in different sections of my brain and body. I had already taken out a lot more of each one of them without larger Arae's help. He only got involved when my life had to be preserved, as I mentioned earlier.

I finished taking out the female first and then the male. Neither of them came to the aid of the other, much at all. They had no honor or understanding of compassion. They had never had a life and only lived to please themselves no matter the cost to others. All that mattered was their individual happiness. That probably sounds like a few people you might know.

When I finally finished burning out the last bit of the Original First Being male, something happened that has never happened before. As I was putting everything I had into it, my energy changed. It morphed into something else as I was putting it out with everything I had. It twisted a little and took off from me faster than it ever had before. The Original First Being Male's Spirit as well as energy was now burned in front of me, my pineal gland that is. This was very strange.

My friend had come over to visit me when it happened. He had been Confucius, Hannibal the Great, King Arthur of Camelot, and many other prominent people in our history. He was sensitive to energy and very good at understanding it. When the last blast happened he was sitting about ten feet away from me. As my energy changed it literally blew him half way over the arm of the chair he was sitting in.

I was almost always under attack as soon as I had to place my conscious thoughts on other matters. If I was getting in the car to take off and go somewhere, I would be attacked as soon as I started driving. After a while that didn't matter as I adapted and learned how to disintegrate Spirit while doing so.

Also, once I started talking with someone, often at a cash register or similar situation, I would be attacked again. So, I just waited until I was done and then took care of it. I used to be confused as to why they would watch me delete the other attackers yet keep coming at me. I thought it impossible for intelligent life to do such a thing. They just kept coming out of arrogance.

I had to go back in time and into their heads, or energy focal points, to listen to their thoughts in order to understand what they were thinking before they were deleted. They kept coming out of arrogance. All of them were expecting me to fold, to quit, to give up when they came at me.

They all thought themselves to be the last straw that would break my back. They expected that their attack would send me packing and I would start obeying them. Arrogance was all I saw, simple arrogance. I realized that were led to think this way.

Unfortunately that mattered little to me. If they attacked me, and wouldn't stop, they were gone. They just kept coming. Is that sad or what? It was for me.

Well, so much for the Original First Being halves. They were now gone completely. I searched for them everywhere. I went back and watched their destruction again and again looking for any piece of them having escaped that blast, and there was none. I felt for any of them having survived at the scene of their demise as well as anywhere else in Creation. I felt nothing and watched once again as I saw all of both of them destroyed.

Finally my Solar Plexus or gut intuition told me they were gone also. That still wasn't enough so I asked all the Animal Essence Spirits to help me. They all watched the same thing happen so I left it alone. I later kept feeling for them in all ways and then stopped as I was wasting my time.

While these battles had been occurring there were also skirmishes with the other clean Source Sprit pairs. They didn't want to help the Original Ones. They stayed clear of that mess. Few Spirits, other than the different Source Pairs, got involved in the fights. Each Spirit was anxious for the last one in charge to be taken out so they could become the next supreme one or ones. That was definitely to my advantage.

Now let's get to the battles with the other Spirit groups.

CHAPTER 7
J'ARAE IS ATTACKED BY LYDIA AND ARMAELEOUS

While J'Arae was fighting the Original Ones he already knew that the other Source pairs would become an issue. He was not yet aware of exactly how the other Source Beings would treat him. He had no reason to expect the worst, not yet anyway, so he tried to get along with them as best he could.

Lydia and Armaeleous were the Source Spirit pair that were to be used to control the Second Dimension once the Original Ones retired. They were also told they would be the new Supreme Beings and that Lillith and Aramaeleous would serve under them. As you can guess, they told the same basic lie to Lillith and Aramaeleous.

Armaeleous was actually a good being, full of hope and desire to help all he could. He was just lost in the old way and not able to understand how to do the right thing. He only didn't understand. He was only trying to help. He just had problems believing me instead of the other Source Spirit out of body.

He and I had gotten into a big fight earlier when he attacked me. I hit him so hard it knocked him into a form of stasis, but he was also losing his energy. He was dying. I didn't want this at all so, once I realized what was happening, I filled him with some of my own energy to heal him.

I actually made him stronger than he was before. I was pretty darn happy about that, knowing he was healthy and improved from his earlier self and now hoping he would leave me alone. Heck, there were a few times he actually kept some smaller stuff away from me but eventually he turned on me again. At least we did have a few good times together. He's in stasis now being protected by Arae.

Lydia was more aggressive about things, just as the Original First Being Female was. She kept attacking every time she felt my guard was down. It's funny how all of them were so anxious to attack me in my sleep. That's when I was most vulnerable. Still, every morning I deleted that part of them they had broken off and placed in me, annoying but no major deal.

Lydia and Armaeleous finally came to me and asked to be put into stasis to be removed later. I happily agreed and did so but as I did, before cleaning and freezing Lydia, I felt her Spirit and then read her thoughts. She was gloating over the fact that I was not aware of her having brought into play a plan to keep attacking me. She had broken off a whole lot of pieces of herself which would keep attacking me.

After they were both placed in stasis the attacks upon me, by Lydia, began. There's almost none of her left now and the part of her inside the protective dimension is now destroyed completely. Arae can bring back Armaeleous in a slightly different form but Lydia is gone forever just like the Original Ones. That leaves us now with Lillith and Aramaeleous to discuss.

CHAPTER 8
J'ARAE IS ATTACKED BY LILLITH AND ARAMAELEOUS

L illith and Aramaeleous made up the other clean Source Spirit pair. They were larger and stronger than Lydia and Armaeleous. They were also being told, by the Original Ones, that they would be the ones to become the Supreme Beings once they retired. Manipulation was a specialty of the Original First Being halves. They excelled at it.

Here we have a different situation for Arae to contend with. He and Lilly came from Aramaeleous and Lillith, respectively. There shouldn't be such a big issue between them but, unfortunately, it was worse. Aramaeleous had become very arrogant and Lillith had become much the same. Lillith has proven to be diligent in her attempts at controlling me, just as what little of her left is trying to mess with my typing right now. (This was in the initial writing of this book, 2015.)

You see, this fight still remains but there's only a little of them left to contend with. It's not like it was in the beginning, not near as vicious and I'm much stronger now than ever before in this body. There have been lives where I was able to do very powerful things which I don't, won't, and can't do now. This is your new beginning, not mine. This isn't about me, it's about you, your freedom, your rebirth.

Getting back to the fighting, Lillith was very sneaky about things and Aramaeleous, although much the same, was more aggressive about his thoughts of supremacy. His feelings were strong enough that I never had any doubt of how he would act regarding certain things. That helped a lot.

Lillith and Aramaeleous had released smaller pieces of themselves to act independently now as well as later, like hiding a few land mines. They never hesitated to sacrifice the smaller parts of themselves to watch me react to their attacks. This immediately showed me that they, like the Original Ones now gone, would treat all with the same disrespect the First Ones did. That helped me seal the deal with them.

I now had a good idea how things would wind up in regards to dealing with these two. It would turn out badly for them and no fun for me either. I wasn't yet aware of what would be involved in the fight with them. I was still becoming aware of myself and waiting for more of Arae to come into me.

I was never afraid of losing, of not being able to deal with them on the Other Side. The issue was with how things would turn out over here in the Third Dimension. What would I have to go through? I already knew that there was something that was protecting my body from being killed, but it was hard to see exactly what it was. Was it a part of me I could trust? Was it Arae or something else? That was hard to see at the time. If you want to know what it's like to learn how to trust yourself or see, feel, hear, and understand the Other Side, I'll tell you.

Well, to keep from writing too much about this, covering years of events which finally ended up in a permanent solution, let's get to the center of this new conflict. Fighting with these two was more difficult than with Lydia and Armaeleous. I also cared for Armaeleous with his desire to help others much more than Aramaeleous with his aggressive feelings for "Power Over" everything. That was more like the Original First Being Male who wanted to control everything and help nothing other than his self.

Aramaeleous had also been watching the Original First Being Male as he manipulated others, especially Arae. Besides having been a good student, remember that he had been attaching a small part of himself to Arae in each life Arae had. It was always the same piece so it became quite knowledgeable in regard to Arae's feelings and thought processes, over most of his many lives. There's still a small part of it alive today. It's barely visible and extremely scarred. It knows it's almost gone now and will be finished off in a few months. Good.

When it comes to Lillith, the same is true of her knowledge of Lilly from having been attached to almost all the bodies that Lilly was in, which she didn't make for herself. This understanding of Arae's love for Lilly was used against J'Arae whenever possible. Lillith was never hesitant to abusively attack whatever she wanted to. She was like the Original First Being Female in many ways. What an abusive pair Lillith and Aramaeleous made.

Well, as you can guess, this fight went on and on over the next few years. Lillith and Aramaeleous were separately and together attacking J'Arae with smaller pieces of themselves as well as themselves in their full states. They were so large they were their own army. Arae was just stronger, denser energy. Like I said earlier, trying to handle Arae was like trying to stop a bullet with your hand, not a good idea. They never did learn though.

After a time, J'Arae had once again reached his limit with this continuous fighting. He was tired of fighting on so many fronts 24/7. He came close to ending his body's life and two funny things happened. Aramaeleous had taken off, stayed away from things. He had a good idea what was about to happen. Lillith wasn't so bright.

J'Arae was preparing to leave his body when all of a sudden, Lillith almost physically produced a large hand to try to grab Arae leaving his body. Then, knowing what was about to happen, the worthless piece of Aramaeleous attached to the bottom of J'Arae's spine literally did all it could to remove itself from J'Arae's body. I watched as he pulled as far away from me as he could, still looking at me, right in the eyes.

He had so much fear in him you could see it in his eyes let alone feel it throughout his energy field. He knew he was now dead and had nowhere to run. He was still attached and couldn't get free but that really didn't matter anyway. He was also aware of this.

Being as strong and large as Arae is out of body, nothing can hide from him. There are Spirits, just a few, which can hide from my view unless I'm serious about looking for them. I can feel their being alive immediately if they are. It's a different thing to locate them and destroy them where they are. It's easy to take out a cloud but it's another thing to destroy every last drop of water in it. That's not the best analogy but it gives you the basic idea.

Well, eventually Lillith and Aramaeleous came to me, as Lydia and Armaeleous did, and said they would allow me to put them away, store them. As I started to do so, I had already felt what was going on in each of them. They felt the only way they could take me down is to go inside the dimension housing all this stored energy and take it for themselves. They weren't aware of what was involved with being put through the barriers protecting this dimension.

I knew I could dissipate them through the filters protecting this dimension but was concerned that they might know something I didn't. If there was one thing I was certain of was that I was continually learning how to deal with different things, as well as growing stronger. I started to clean them once I put them in a large energy sphere, or orb. As soon as I did I felt them getting concerned about being able to do what they had expected to do.

They started kicking up a fuss and I just took them out, wiped them completely. By wiping I mean that I dissolve the Spirit within their energy. It can later become something else but it'll be different. They weren't up for that but had no choice. I already knew they had both broken off many smaller pieces of themselves already anyway.

Although I still have to deal with some weak smaller pieces of them today, they are almost all gone now and will be completely deleted when I'm out of here. So, I just keep going, like always.

I realize how it would seem that I'm writing this book to make myself stand out but nothing could be farther from the truth. If you built a house and later explained it, wouldn't you say "then I put additional support to the major gussets ...." or something like that? I would have preferred that I could be like the normal janitor who does his work when no one is around, just performing his tasks.

I have proven already that I can do what no person in body in the history of Creation has ever been able to do before. You have not and will not ever see me on a TV show. This is not about me and will never be allowed to be about me. This is about all Creation, not one person. That's how things got so screwed up in the first place. A book is not about page 4; it's about the sum of the book itself. Heck, I don't even have a nice cover.

Let's take a look at some of the other Spirits now ready to get involved. Although these next few sections have been broken down into different groups, all the different fields of Spirit were attacking J'Arae throughout the war.

With each new group discussed, that particular field of Spirit was the next basic group to come into aggressive contact with me. That's why they're listed this way. It's a general thought process, not entirely chronological. It was now time for Human and Fae Essence Spirits to become actively engaged.

CHAPTER 9
J'ARAE IS ATTACKED BY HUMAN AND FAE ESSENCE

(Human Essence)

Human Essence and Fae Essence had already been involved in this conflict. Now as a group they decided to enter the battle. The two large pairs of clean Source Spirit were gone now with just a number of the smaller pieces of them left alive. Some of the Human and Fae Essence Spirits decided to join the last of the smaller pieces of the larger clean Source Spirit but many wanted to take on J'Arae by themselves. They felt that once they defeated him they would be the next gods. I'm telling y'all now; arrogance is usually a very stupid thing.

The first to try to take charge was Human Essence. They were the most arrogant of the Essence fields. It's a shame but things are what they are. We can mostly work to improve ourselves but we can only help others by teaching them through example, and hope to lead them in a good way, one beneficial to themselves as well as those around them.

As Human type energy was the largest portion of the Original First Beings energy, they were more easily led into the swamp of arrogance. This was exactly what happened. As Human Essence was much stronger than Soul, they were most easily convinced that they were better than everything else, save the Original Ones.

Now that the Original First Being halves as well as the two large Source pairs were gone, they felt it was their duty to step up and take over everything. What a mess they were. I shouldn't say were because there's still many of them left. However, a little over half of them are gone now. They might have been the most insane group in Creation in regards to this arrogance thing. This was all done by the Original Ones.

One by one they kept coming at me. Each one thinking they would be the ones to break J'Arae's Spirit. One after the other came, one after the other died. It was almost like watching flies continue to commit certain suicide by flying into a bug zapper. They just kept coming. The insanity of this has always boggled my mind as well as those close to me. They could actually watch it happen in their pineal glands.

Now, some of these Human Essence Spirits were very strong. There are two who were the strongest. When Essence is out of body they can usually break off holographic pieces of themselves to do different things, like Angels. Human Essence can often do this.

The bigger they are the easier it is and the more they can release from themselves. Remember they were made larger and stronger than the Souls to start with and grew from the over one trillion lives they already had when the first Souls were released.

Of these two massive Human Essence forms, one was called Bruce. He was very powerful but there was one who, from the very beginning, was being raised to be at the top of his peers. He was told he was a king by the Original Ones who had others still in body call him that. That fed one heck of an already big ego.

He was often abused hard in body but always praised loudly when not. Out of all the Messiahs here, he was the only one that wasn't Source Spirit, but just part of Source, that of Human Essence. This many of you won't like if you attempt to hold onto the teachings of all your false books of control. This is the Spirit that was in the body of the person the Christians call Jesus Christ.

When he became physically violent towards me, he had left me no choice. Before we go here though, there are a few things I want to tell you about.

You need to at least hear truth before you make important decisions. Your decisions are your own but they're only as good as the information you have when you make them. You also have to put yourself outside of your feelings, especially when they're feelings someone else gave you.

Jesus and Arae had many lives together. In Jesus' last life here, Arae was a young second cousin, or something like that, of John the Baptist. I remember having seen J.C. at the river with John. I've always done what I could to help J.C., not give him a hard time. I've always looked after him, protected him.

Even out of body, Arae protected him from the Original First Being halves when he acted out arrogantly towards them. However, once all the large Source Spirit was removed, he decided he wanted to maintain the format of abuse and run everything himself. This could never be allowed to happen again so there now became an issue between J'Arae and Jesus.

Things erupted almost out of nowhere. J.C. came to me and told me I would no longer attack the old way of doing things, that being of abuse. I had a lot of the first Angels attacking me and I was getting rid of them as fast as they came. He told me that now, with the Original Ones gone that everyone would be praising him and that he would not tolerate my changing that.

I looked at him and asked him if he was out of his mind. I told him "How dare you speak to me like that, everything I've done for you." and asked him who the hell he thought he was. He merely replied by saying "I'll Kill You." Then he took over the muscles in my right arm, shoulder, and hand as I was cutting onions for a salad.

All of a sudden my right shoulder and arm dropped down towards the counter and my grip on the knife loosened up. As the knife hit the counter side instead of the cutting board, it should have fallen out of my hand onto the ground but instead it started to circle around like a buzz saw on the inside my thighs where that artery is that, once cut, will allow you to bleed to death quickly.

Once that happened I looked at him and he just glared at me as if to say, "Do as I say, or else." I looked at him and said fine, you've made your choice. I returned the favor and attacked him. I immediately took out the larger part of his Spirit's energy field but there was still more of him left. He was spread out all over the place. Small pieces of him were being hidden in a variety of places but, about a week and a few days later, he had been terminated.

Each of these smaller parts of himself would keep coming at me. I was more than just disappointed. I felt let down. He had lied to me before but I never felt the extent of his arrogance. I don't have the time to talk more about him now but I'll try to make a video about what happened in his life, how he lived through his crucification and physically suffered after it.

Early on, when I had gone to the past to see his life for myself, I found out many things that I wasn't yet aware of this life. I do know that when I was with the church, as a child, it really pissed me off that they would dare make a cross with him still attached to it. How dare they do that to him. They should have shown him teaching children or standing up for people instead.

He was born of Mary and Joseph through totally natural means, sexual intercourse. The Immaculate Conception was just another lie. The wedding at Cana was that of Jesus and Mary Magdalene. It was his primary Archangel that turned the water to wine. He did not die on the cross. There were many people involved and working hard to keep him alive. His arms were tied to the cross as well as nailed. Just thinking of what was done to him makes my blood boil.

When Judas kissed him is was to let him know that the soldiers were there to take him. The guards outside his tomb were bribed by two beautiful ladies who drugged them with wine while the others got him out. It was a well thought out plan but never should have happened anyway. That never should have been done to him.

I was infuriated about many things regarding his treatment in body. When he was on the cross he asked for one very simple thing that he never should have been denied. He did say, "Father, how can you leave me now in my time of pain?" The Original First Being Male never said one thought to him, not even a single thought.

Where the hell is the compassion in that? Here's more proof of this supposed all loving, all forgiving, and perfect God being nothing more than an arrogant lie, a self-serving chump. Both the Original First Being Male and Female were like that.

There are too many lies about his life which were made up to "sell" Christianity to everyone when it first started. That's all I speak of this for now. He forced my hand and physically attacked me in an attempt to stop me from changing the Other Side format of abuse.

I could easily write a novel on his life and the lies in Christianity, as well as all your other religions. The bible itself was written by the Sanhedrin, the priests of that time. They were all either Annunaki hybrids or Annunaki controlled people.

I remember how let down I felt when the Original First Being Female kept lying to me, so much that I could no longer make up excuses for what she was telling me. Then I had to deal with J.C. after all I had done for him, sticking up for him on the Other Side as well as in body.

There is little in life that is as it actually seems. In religions there is next to nothing. You can't base anything of value on false information. Genesis is a blatant lie. From there it all goes downhill. Many of us have grown up with various religions feeding us controlling garbage from birth. Our parents didn't know better and neither did theirs.

I've always said you can go to most churches and just feel the love in the hearts of the people there. It's the religions, not the people, which are a problem. They will eventually die off. There are many wonderful people wanting to find a way to express the love they have in their hearts, their appreciation for having something to be thankful for. If you live in the wilderness and there are only five stores which sell food, you're going to one of them.

The other large and strong Spirit of Human Essence was one who called himself Bruce. He wanted to be the new God now. He was strong. There were many pieces of him to contend with. Just like the others, he's now gone also, completely destroyed.

I'm for Human, Animal, Fae, Plant, and Universal life everywhere. My job has always been to protect everything. I just haven't been able to do it while in a physical body. Soon that will be fixed. I'll never be in a body again, never. My job demands I return to my natural state and stay there. I'm really tired of having lives anyway.

Getting back to the Human and Fae Essence issues, one by one the Human Essence that attacked J'Arae was taken out.

Sometimes it was in larger groups. Before it was over, there was less than half of the Human Essence left.

(Fae Essence)

Now, Fae Essence had a different outlook on things. They never put much faith in what the Original Ones were saying. After all, they were placed in the lower dimensions of almost every Planet they lived on. They were never treated with any respect so they already knew better than to listen to the lies of the First Original Beings. They always promised but never delivered, not to them anyway.

One thing they did like seeing was Human Essence being whittled down to a much smaller group. Human Essence was always looking down on them yet never hesitated to ask them for help. The Human Spirits were always eager to put the Fae down as if they were inferior. After all, the Original Ones were more Human Spirit than Fae Spirit.

The Fae have been able to do a lot to help the Planets they lived on while the Human Spirits were always tearing the Planets down. That's why the Fae really like people who work in the soil and help the Earth. They are more, if you'll excuse the expression, down to Earth. I mean that literally.

When Fae talk, their conversations are much more as a matter of fact than with the Human Spirits. They say what they mean with no bitter end attached to it, no aggression, just conversation. They often find us a little silly the way we get attached to certain ideas and thought concepts always looking for a meaning behind something. The Fae simply say what they mean. Life is easier that way.

Well, the Fae Essence that was aggressive began to try to cause problems with me as soon as the Human Essence was mostly removed. They really wanted to run things now. They had small groups already scattered throughout the Star systems, ready to begin controlling things. Needless to say, they never got the chance.

I understand that they were tired of being put down. That doesn't mean that it was their turn to tell others what to do. I had many of them coming at me but it wasn't near the same issue as it was with Human Essence or the First Angels. Queen Lilly of Fae is the boss down there and she keeps things running rather smooth. She did have some issues that needed to be dealt with but when she needed help she asked and got it.

There was a Fae war of sorts between the positive frequency beings and the more negative ones. This was stopped in mere moments as the trouble makers simply faded away. That was enough of that. They were trying to overthrow Queen Lilly. They never got close to it.

The Fae are a little difficult to deal with as they stay in energy form most all the time. They can move in and out of dimensions at will, unless there's a strong barrier that is. After a while, about a third or a little more, of them was taken out, removed from Creation. Many of them came and asked me to take them home. That meant store them in that safe dimension so they could come out when it was all over.

The strong Fae fighting only lasted a few months, maybe two to three. Then that was over. There was always more to come anyway. It never does seem to stop, not until I get out of this body anyway. Then it'll be over for good. Well, here's where the Original Angels decided to kick their battle plans into high gear.

CHAPTER 10
J'ARAE IS ATTACKED BY THE ORIGINAL ANGELS

I have to begin this section by announcing that there are two basic groups of Angels that have been produced. There are the original Angels who came from the Original First Being Male and Female as well as the new Angels. The original Angels are a problem and the new ones a blessing. They understand compassion, honor, and equality.

The new Angels are actually clean Source Spirit which came from Lilly and Arae when the Original First Being halves were about eighty percent of the way through releasing their third wave of Souls. These new Angels come from true heart energy and are fifty five to sixty percent Angel Spirit.

The remainder of their Spirit consists of all the other frequencies which make up full Source Spirit. That's why they're over one thousand times stronger than the original ones. They're already at work helping you. This chapter is only about the original Angels which came from the Original Ones, not the new ones from Lilly and Arae.

These original Angels were the biggest bunch of lying and stab you in the back beings you could ever run into. Next to nothing that you've ever heard about them is true. When your Spirit is about to be put into a body you meet the Angels assigned to you for your life.

The harder your life was and the stronger your energy, the more Angels they assigned to you. There is a good reason for this. The first Angels were complete servants to the Original Ones and controllers of your lives. They made sure you would be saved if you were about to be harmed before it was time.

They would also make sure you broke your arm or died when it was time. They would take you out themselves or arrange it. Either way they never cared. They didn't have much in the way of feelings, other than the arrogance bred into them anyway. No Angel has ever had even one life, although they have spent some time here in a body they made for themselves. This only lasts hours at a time though, never a day or more.

Everyone is told how wonderful these first Angels are. Man that is so far from true. They are cold blooded killers and protectors. There are a few which are different, but not many. Archangel Michael is one of them. Lucifer is another. They were made to function as protectors so they have an understanding of compassion, honor, and equality. They're now in protective stasis waiting for the smoke to clear from this war almost completed now.

The first Angels were covered in great detail in the first book so we won't spend too much time here talking about them again. They had their own hierarchy, functioning almost like a corporation. Those at the bottom of the pyramid knew little other than their current orders. For those who haven't read the first book yet, I want you to know they were servants who didn't care about your welfare. They just followed the orders of the First Ones, for the most part, like a machine.

J'Arae explained to them that they were now free and could have lives, serve others, or do whatever they wanted provided they follow the proper format. Almost all of them kept coming. They never stopped until they were gone. J'Arae's not aggressively abusive but will also protect himself. He has to in order to perform his job, protecting others.

So, the Angels became aggressive when they found out the Original First Beings were destroyed. That's not who gave them their orders but they knew that's where their orders originated. The Angels above them handed down their orders.

At first, after the Original Ones were taken out, they didn't know what to do. They just kept going. Soon after the Angels at the top of their pyramid decided what would happen next. It was time to decide which part of Source Spirit they would now take their orders from.

This had to be Source Spirit that, like the Original Ones, had never had a life. They had to always remain out of body. They also had to be very strong Source Spirit. This led them to Armaeleous and Lydia first. They were the ones who were never to have a life and run the Second Dimension or Other Side. That is what they were told by the Original Ones.

They also had a slight problem here because Aramaeleous and Lillith were stronger then Lydia and Aramaeleous. They needed to work for the strongest of them. So, over a short time, they decided to try to work for all four of them. As Source Spirit didn't always agree, this was sometimes a slight issue. The top or head Angels were a little confused from time to time. They were still trying to settle down and follow only one pair. They found making that choice to be difficult.

One thing that everyone agreed on was that Arae was to be punished for what he did. This suited all the large Source Spirit, other than Armaeleous that is. It also suited the Angels. They didn't have feelings, not much anyway. They did however have a sense of duty which had been taken away by Arae.

When Angels are assigned to a body, they stay with it keeping it going in the direction they're told to. Angels put their energy into your Crown Chakra and control your thoughts from there. They don't control everything you do but are involved in most of your important decisions. They were made different so that they could easily control you. This is one of the means the Original Ones used to manage your lives as they desired.

There were a little over ten trillion of these first Angels. They were made in the beginning. They had a lot of practice learning how to do their jobs in the most efficient way possible. They were good at it. They knew how to manipulate your mind as well as your emotions. They would also run their energy up your spine lighting up your endorphins on the way. This would make you feel love or divinity. It was also being done to you. It was a lie.

The clean Source Spirit pairs would send these Angels to J'Arae, usually about seven at a time while sleeping and one or two while awake. They would be destroyed all day long but there were so many of them it didn't matter. They couldn't take J'Arae out of his body. They just wanted to control him or at least wear him down. They had to make him give up his plan to destroy the old format of abuse one way or the other.

This went on all day every day, especially while I was asleep. I would wake up every morning mad from having been fighting all night while asleep. Then I would go after all the energy hanging on me and some that actually got into my head. Eventually I started taking them out in large numbers. I had to.

As soon as a body dies, and it's Spirit returns to the Other Side, the Angels assigned to it are released. As soon as they returned to the flock, so to speak, they found out that the Original Ones were now dead and learn what had been happening to the other Angels. They were easily led to come at me, all they needed was the suggestion.

To end this quickly, there are now about ten percent of the original first Angels left. They were non-problematic, non-aggressive, and being held out of harm's way, protected. They will be back when things calm down.

CHAPTER 11
J'ARAE IS ATTACKED BY OTHER CLEAN SOURCE SPIRIT

The two clean Source Spirit pairs, Lydia and Armaeleous as well as Lillith and Aramaeleous, had attacked Arae separately as well as together. Adding insult to injury, all the arrogant and now aggressively abusive small portions of clean Source Spirit that Lilly and Arae released from themselves, were attacking J'Arae, Arae in a body.

Now, there is also another event that's only been mentioned earlier. The Original Ones were attaching small parts of Aramaeleous and Lillith to the smaller portions of Lilly and Arae, at the base of their spines, to influence and control their emotions as best they could. They also were having lives back to back.

This, when added to the constant force feeding of arrogant thought, turned some of them into extremely selfish and arrogant beings themselves. Not all of them turned on Arae, but most did.

There have always been laws regarding the means by which the physical bodies were to be abused in order to control them. There was an understanding that one didn't listen to a Spirit in body as it was being abused and not using it's proper thought channels. It was under extreme duress. The issue here now was that Arae was wide awake, aware of what was going on in the Second Dimension, and aggressively affecting it.

At the same time, everything on the Other Side was also aware of Arae's power levels. The other smaller parts of Arae and Lilly's Spirit that was released to have lives of their own should have known better than to get aggressive with Arae, attempting to maintain the old format of abuse. However, they just kept attacking him. They wanted to be next in line to be the new king and queen. As soon as one or more were destroyed, more came up and attacked.

As flies to an electric bug zapper, they just kept coming. They also kept dying. It's amazing how each next Spirit thought they would be the ones to stop him, make him comply, and then control him. This is hard to understand, especially to accept, until you've had to deal with it over time. I've been doing this now for seven years, and still get attacked twenty four hours per day seven days a week.

I don't know if I mentioned it yet, but there's something else that played into the arrogance of these smaller pieces of Lilly and Arae as well as the others before them. Arae would keep having life after life after life and so on. Also, no one knew for sure what Arae would do once in body again. Let's look a little closer at this.

Arae was known for having one life after the other. He had very little time off in between lives. Since the beginning everyone in the Second Dimension watched him keep going back into a body again. It became a natural process over there, something that was expected.

Arae also knew he couldn't talk to much of anyone about what he was going to do this last life, or that it would even be his last. There was so little honor, so little trust over there, that he couldn't take the chance to mention his plans to anyone. Lilly,

Gaia, Gaeira, certain Animal Essence, and very few others were aware of what Arae planned.

When you take the fact that everyone expected Arae to come out of one body and go into another, coupled with almost no one knowing there was going to be a battle, and then add to that the arrogance of almost everything over there, you have some big issues to deal with. Finish this off with the desire for almost everything over there wanting to play God and even being told they would soon do so, and you have a hornet's nest.

Everyone kept attacking to maintain the old way of abuse where that next being would be able to play God, or be next in line. As it was getting near the end now the attacks became more violent. The rest of the Source Spirit over there in the Second Dimension was aware of what would happen when Arae returned, the death of everything that had opposed him.

They were now also trying to delay his returning home to the Other Side, trying to buy some time to figure out how to hide or stay alive when he did. He would be home any time now. Try to remember that when we're not attached to these physical bodies, our emotions are not as important as they were while in body. That is to say we don't care as much about some things,

Many of these attacks have become physical and painful. I have a pain from last night's attack that I won't even discuss here. Source Spirit, the arrogant ones, on the Other Side will not hesitate to do whatever they want to you. Your pain means nothing to them. They simply don't care.

I've received what others, for the most part, never did or will. I'm the one that is exposing Creation's abusive format as well as destroying all who try to maintain it. I should really say Arae is but it's being done through this body and I'm using my conscious mind to do so. That's why I call myself J'Arae. It can get a little confusing but it's also why I can give you detailed information about what happened.

Arae has always had the intention to bring peace to Creation that was never possible the way the Original Ones did things. He was made to protect and then never allowed the freedom to do so. He has finally taken on the full extent of his own format. Abuse will begin to be permanently deleted before the end of the year 2015, never to return once it's completely removed.

(J'Arae Is Physically Attacked)

Twice, sick arrogant Source Spirit has physically attacked J'Arae by breaking the metatarsal bones on the top of his left foot while he was sleeping. He had no bruises or cuts and never even got up that night anyway. His bed has no footing to kick in his sleep either. Of course that would have left some kind of mark anyway.

He woke up to find his foot was broken and in great pain. He posted pictures of this on the internet immediately after it happened. Each time he was on crutches for a few days. It would heal in around five to seven days. Here's what happened each of the two times.

The first occasion was the result of an outer portion of Arae, one that still had a piece of Aramaeleous attached to it, releasing the true Arae's protective energy field so he was susceptible to attack. He did this for a part of Aramaeleous that was waiting just outside J'Arae's body.

As the protective Silver energetic coating was opened, this smaller part of Aramaeleous placed his energy on J'Arae's body, the left foot metatarsal bones, and broke them. The mixed piece of Aramaeleous Spirit which was holding onto a small piece of Arae, did this hoping to make J'Arae comply with the demands of the others in order to speed up the process of Arae coming out of Jay's body and all this finally being over. He was tired of dealing with everything going on.

When J'Arae woke up, he immediately felt the pain and was taken back for about twenty seconds. He immediately looked at what had just happened. I've always told people about physical issues they had in their bodies. It's just part of what I see. Since it's always for their needed good, it's easy.

I saw all four of my metatarsal bones finely split as if done with surgical precision and there, right in front of me, was the part of Aramaeleous that had done it. He was literally marching back and forth at the foot of my bed looking outwards away from me declaring that he was the great one that had just accomplished this might feat and that he now "owned me" so to speak.

I was in strong pain but really pissed off. I took another moment to look at how this was even possible to have happened. That's when I saw another piece of Aramaeleous which was holding onto, or mixed with, a larger piece of Arae that had separated and been abused for a long time. I knew him and was shocked at what he had done, pulling my protective silver energy coating off of my foot.

He was worried about what he had just done. He not only betrayed me but he was the cause of my injuries. For the moment I separated him from my own body, near the Base Chakra, keeping him isolated from me. I had every intention of dealing with him on a very personal level but there was something more immediate I had to attend to.

The thing that just broke my left foot needed to be taken care of immediately, permanently, and in front of everything on the Other Side. I was about to send a powerful message to everything over there, even though they never do seem to learn.

I went after this arrogant idiot who had just broken my left foot. He was a strong piece of Aramaeleous left over from when I had taken the largest portion of him out. Destroying a large Spirit energy field is almost like destroying a cloud but then having to clean up all the smaller drops everywhere. As I like to say, energy is very much like water. It's not exactly the same but similar in enough ways as to benefit our understanding of it.

It was difficult to maintain a conscious mindset to deal with deleting this Spirit, due to the immense pain I had. His arrogant attitude, the fact that he attacked the protector, and my really being totally pissed off at him, was enough. Within the next twenty to thirty seconds he was dead, completely destroyed.

A short moment later I went after the other Spirit who removed my protective coating allowing all this to happen and asked him why. He said absolutely nothing, just fed back the energetic feeling that come from the act of looking down in disgrace of what he had done. Discussing the following conversation is not worthy of your time here but, needless to say, he no longer exists.

To most people, those who have never been aware of or approached by problematic Spirit, this will all seem like non-sense. I respect their not just believing something they can't understand. Then I would ask them how this was possible when I never even got out of the bed and had no marks to suggest any type of physical blow to my foot. As I mentioned earlier, I didn't even have a footboard on my bed to kick anyway.

This same event happened at a later date, once again, by a piece of Source Spirit from Lydia and a little help from another piece of Aramaeleous with a small portion of Arae inside. This event followed suit with the previous one. J'Arae's foot breaks again and both the smaller Lydia and Aramaeleous Spirits die.

The only difference is that this time J'Arae did something different to his Spirit energy. He found the Aramaeleous issue and destroyed it so it would never happen again. At least that's how it seemed to go down. J'Arae is now much stronger than he was before. I guess we'll see what happens these last few months that J'Arae will be in his body.

There were also other ways that J'Arae was attacked physically. One of his close friends was taken over, in the period of a few months, by one of the loose parts of Aramaeleous and literally driven half crazy. He was made to see and do some abusive things and then fall apart.

June 22, 2015, a friend of J'Arae's, who had been completely taken over physically, was sent to his home for help. J'Arae tried to do what he could for him but, as the next morning came, he awoke to a broken sliding glass door and a lot of other damage. His friend was send out the front door and the locking mechanism inside the door knob assembly, was broken with no wear or stress indications of any sort.

This was done by Source Spirit on the Other Side trying to do what it could to stop J'Arae from writing this book, or at least slow him down. These individual beings wanted to get to play God after Arae came out of J'Arae's body. That would never be allowed to happen.

Unfortunately, there are some very clean Source Spirits on the Other Side who, from only knowing the old way of abusive treatment of all in body as well as having developed their own frequencies of arrogance, were determined to maintain their "right" to play God. They were next in line or close to it.

Such is the way of greed and arrogance. They only lead to the corruption of the proper flow of equality. Arrogance can easily grow within all Spirit forms. It's the understanding of compassion, honor, and equality that is necessary to keep this from happening. The main way this happens is from having lives or at least becoming engaged in watching many of them.

The incredibly abusive act we just discussed was done by clean Source Spirit. He wanted to use this poor Soul against J'Arae. He didn't care about the fact that he was driving the Soul over the edge. Here's one more example of how Source Spirit is not the wonderful thing many people think. It's just very strong, that's all. It's the actual being within the Spirit is what makes the difference. It's who we are inside that matters, not the type of Spirit make up we have.

There was also an attack on J'Arae's spine where it attached to his pelvic bone. A few different Source Spirit members attacked him while he was sleeping, pushing a few vertebrae out of place to bring hard pain, in all positions, immediately. They also attacked J'Arae's stomach, making him vomit the whole next day. J'Arae received the proper medical help. This was last night and earlier today, August seventh, 2015. This type of thing will probably continue for the next few months he's alive.

There are other numerous people who are being run by these clean but arrogant and abusive Source Spirits as they desperately try to cling onto the old format of abusive treatment and control throughout Creation, becoming the new Gods. Arae can't fix all this until he's free from the body he's stuck in. J'Arae has promised to release him before November's end in 2015, shortly after having finished writing this book.

Creation is about our whole family. It should have been so from its beginning. Soon it will be about everything and everyone everywhere. Why shouldn't it be? Isn't that what it's made of? It will never be about any supposed Supreme Being or beings again. When you want to thank someone for something you can thank the councils you're about to have, the Animals and Plants that feed you now, or whoever you want. Just remember there is no longer anything wanting you praise. Actually, its going to be put down. Family should be about thanks not praise anyway.

When you come into the house do you praise your mother and father? I hope not. If they want that then you don't have good ones. As I've always told others "If something was worth your praise, why would it want it? That just doesn't make any sense." The truth is simple if you just let it be what it is, understanding through self-enlightenment.

CHAPTER 12
J'ARAE STRUGGLES TO FINISH
HIS JOB AND LEAVE

(The Books, Individual Awareness and Evolution)

J'Arae, at the time of writing this book, is now all but finished doing those things he needed to do while in body. He's ready to go home. It's time for Arae to clock into work in the Second Dimension. It's time to finish things on the Other Side so they can be changed here in the Third Dimension.

I keep getting attacked and then delete what's attacking me. It just never stops. It won't until I can drop this body. In the mean time I need to just finish what I can after this book is done.

I needed to "Crank Up" as many brains as I could while here but that's coming to a close too. It's time for these Human bodies to evolve into something new. When I go into people's brains I enhance not only their abilities but DNA also. This is in addition to the fact, not errant thought but fact that most of these people's brains are also growing in size. The skull grows to match the brains new dimensions.

There are many other people here with Source Spirit inside. They're also strong enough to do this and I'm in the process of training them now. I will enhance them further from the Other Side.

(The Land Mines of the Original First Ones)

There were many issues, land mines so to speak, that the Original First Ones planted within people's bodies and throughout their lives, especially within the controlling bodies on this Planet, the Annunaki. This was done with the intent of destroying any possibility of people awakening if they were no longer in control. It was also done to make it easier for them to limit the amount of awareness in everyone.

The Original First Being halves created the 12/21/2012 awakening to glorify themselves as "Mother and Father God" as the late Sylvia Browne used to talk about. They had also instructed J'Arae to say the same thing. He was promised many things including physical and metaphysical abilities to display to others if he complied.

When they felt the time was right, the Original First Being Female told J'Arae he would speak only of mother and father God. He answered back "Creation is about family, not you. You're a very important part of it, but it's about the complete family package, not just you."

As you can probably guess, they didn't like that at all. They demanded J'Arae talk about a mother and father God. J'Arae said no and was rather aggressive about it. This was the moment of the Source War's beginning, when J'Arae simply said no. This might remind you a little of his previous life as Gandhi. He told all of you to stand up and just say no. As Arae is protector he doesn't just say no, he acts. That's his job though.

The Original First Being halves were aware of this possibility and had made changes in the lives of almost all beings that were able to help Arae create his changes in any way. Everything possible was done to the lives of these people to make them feel insecure, weak, and unable to handle many of life's issues.

They also went into many of the brains of these people and gave them physical problems to deal with, such as ADD and other such things. This would slow them down and make it easier to control them. There were also other things put in the way. One such thing was the resurgence of the lie called the law of attraction. Another was the rise of the witch hunters who came after anyone showing any metaphysical abilities. Let's look at the law of attraction first.

The Law of Attraction

The law of attraction or, as I like to call it, the lawless act of attraction, is a bigger problem for people's Spiritual growth than they realize. It's also harmful to the rest of the Planet. It promotes the false concept that you can have whatever you want if you know how to want it right. Just listen to that. Can you not see its problem just in its description?

This whole concept is nothing less than a blatant lie, it always has been. People are reaching out trying to find a reason to be happy about whatever they can. Many people can feel that change is about to happen, but they don't understand what it is and when it's coming.

The greatest issue with this lawless thought of attraction is that it not only fires up the frequencies which can create greed but, more importantly, it removes any feeling of necessity to awaken to who you are inside. It keeps you from growing into your true selves. It inhibits not only your own personal growth but your evolution.

Another very important issue with this is that if promotes people to become self-serving. Just have whatever you want and don't worry about anything else. How can a person like Ester Hicks have so much money and not help people, other than taking their money giving them false hope. That's not helping anyone but herself. This is an elaborate pyramid scheme which promotes the wrong concepts.

It was introduced to us many years ago in different forms, through different people, by the Original First Being Female. She made it prevalent today using two married twenty-seven percent negative Souls, cleaned to seventeen percent while out of body, Ester and Jerry Hicks.

She says she's talking to some group of special beings that she calls Abraham but she's really just talking to her one Spirit Guide. There is no council over there as she says. She just makes up what she wants, whatever fits her agenda or needs at the moment.

How is there a loving group of beings that want you to have whatever you want yet don't want you to help others with it? Where's the love in keeping everything for yourself? Why isn't she doing more to help others instead of spending all her new money on herself? Most of the people involved with this latest fad have a lot of love in their hearts and fall for this spending all the money they have hoping and expecting to learn how to receive everything they've ever wanted. What a scam.

If everyone could have what they want, just because they knew how to ask for it, then everyone would have everything. This is an impossible thing just by itself. Life just doesn't work that way. What a dream to sell though, give me your money and I'll show you how to have whatever you want. Can they bottle that snake oil up?

There are many problems that most of us have to deal with today. The need for more money keeps us emotionally wound up inside. Keeping everyone excited about horrific events in the news does much the same. When people are kept in such a condition their DNA is wound up like a tight spring. This has been proven to cut off your body's immunity responses as well as cutting your metaphysical abilities down to nothing. You have to be relaxed to come alive.

There are many people who have a completely inaccurate concept of what a psychic is anyway. What is a psychic? I don't like the term at all as it already has preconceived notions. You're supposed to be able to tell the future which can't be consistently done as it's always changing anyway.

If those on the Other Side which run things haven't make up their mind, and keep changing it anyway, then how the heck can you tell the future? You can't. Yet, they say you're not real unless you can. Now that is them being unrealistic. They make a box to put you in and then say you don't fit in it and give you a bad name.

Don't ever stand for that. These are ploys of the witch hunters. Wow, like all these false religions weren't enough. The issue with the witch hunters was large enough for me to make a chapter out of. Let's deal with them now.

SECTION XI - FIGHTING THE WITCH HUNTERS

CHAPTER 1

WHO AND WHAT ARE THE WITCH HUNTERS

One example of these arrogant and self-serving people is James Randi. He's only one of many. He just happens to be a popular one. There are many "magicians" or "Illusionists" that are metaphysically duds and can't except that anyone else can be just because they can't awaken themselves. What a waste of a person.

Witch hunters can help us by exposing the fake claims of all the fakers and liars. The problem is that they are not equipped to do their job. They don't even understand what a metaphysical ability is so, how are they qualified to judge them? Here again is that box we were talking about earlier. They say they can scientifically prove that metaphysical abilities don't exist. Really, is that so?

Well then, why can't they disprove a mother being aware of their child needing her help from far away with no phone or means of communication? How do they explain a mother's intuition? How do they scientifically explain Animal intuition?

They can't explain either and these are only two of many examples. How does a policeman know when someone is looking at the back of their necks or head? Ooops, there's another one. The easiest way to shut them down is to explain that they have no basis for their arguments. They also expect you to be able to see whatever they want and that's also impossible. They are a joke, but a bad one.

They're just like the witch hunters from Salem in America's early history. They said that a witch would float if forcibly dunked in water. If they didn't, they were not. What difference would it make then, after they were murdered by drowning? Here is the basic intelligence of people like James Randi.

James Randi is a 37% negative Soul that doesn't care about compassion or the existence of anything other than what he can hold in his hand. What would he say if you asked him if he had a Soul? He wouldn't know. He can't prove he has one but doesn't care about that anyway.

The most prevalent "witch hunters" are usually at least 37% negative frequency Souls. They care more about their own "glory" than they do the well-being of others, even though they will insist they do what they do for others, not themselves.

Again such is the case of James Randi. He says he does what he does so "the young people" will understand there is no such thing. He only does this in attempt to glorify himself. He wants to be in the limelight, like a fake practitioner of lies, you know, an illusionist or magician.

Does he not use his "gut feeling" to feel out how the fakes do what they do? He uses his Crown Chakra, hypothalamus gland, and more to try to understand how the fakers do what they do. For this, we could thank him but why do that? He causes more harm than good. He has no true understanding or wisdom of what metaphysical abilities even are. Therefore, he should stop to consider what he's not yet aware of if he really cared that is.

The issue here though is that he doesn't care. He just wants to be in the public's eye.

Why does he call himself, and set himself up to be called, "The Amazing Randi!"? Is that arrogant or what? He used to be a magician, a faker, and now he still wants the title. It's all arrogance and selfishness. It's ego on a rampage.

He does what he does attempting to prove to any who'll listen, that if he can't do something it's not real. So, once again, how does he disprove a mother's intuition? He can't. So, we're supposed to think this doesn't exist?

This stems mostly from the fact that he not only doesn't understand metaphysical abilities but is a 37% negative frequency Soul. They have no desire to wake up. It's just how they are. Add to this, his desire for self-gratification on a large scale and you have the basis of why he does what he does.

As I said earlier, I appreciate his having exposed some of the fakers but I also understand the harm he's causing by not letting others think freely for themselves. He's intentionally pushing people away from considering that they are more than society has previously allowed them to believe they are.

He does this out of his own arrogance and greed to be in the spotlight. He wants praise. I find this sad. I want more for him but he'll never find it. He denies his own true self.

Awakening is hard to do at first. Once you get going it's as simple as breathing. It's getting started that's challenging. Here's where James and his type cause problems. They put you down while you're going through the hardest part of becoming alive, something they can never hope to do. They feel accomplished when they deter you from that. If they can't do it they don't want you to be able to. Once again, its simply selfishness.

SECTION XII -
ARAE RETURNS HOME

ARAE AND LILLY RESET CREATION'S FORMAT

O nce out of his body Arae will immediately discard the rest of the problematic Spirit on the Other Side. As best I understand it, about five minutes after returning home to the Other Side, or Second Dimension, Arae will have adjusted to being there again. This usually takes a couple weeks but remember how many times he's done this, over 10.846 trillion. He's also very strong.

Then, in about three seconds or less he can locate and delete the rest of the problematic beings. Once this is done he'll lay down the new format of compassion, honor, and equality. This is done by making new laws. I guess I should have also mentioned that there won't be anyone over there opposing him either.

Anyway, the Spirit Guides will not only never be asked to lie to the people they're helping through lives but they won't be allowed to. This will be a very strict rule. Lies and abuse will no longer be tolerated. Everyone will be told of this rule and it will be adhered to. When the Spirit in body is being overstressed, something must be done about it immediately. There will also be a long delay before anyone goes into another body anyway.

Then there's the issue of the amount of time required to rest in between lives. You will now have to spend twice the length of your previous life out of body as free Spirit to release all your emotional issues received from that last life.

This will cut down the past life issues that almost all of us are suffering from now. It will also greatly reduce the possibility of producing abusive frequencies within your own Spirit. It's time for everyone to have easier daily lives without all the constant abuse systems in place.

Daily lives in the physical world will lose thirty percent of their abuse by the year 2020. There is a time of action coming soon, a cleansing for the planet. This will have some tragic events but, once they're done, things will settle down nicely.

Now Animal Essence will begin their new jobs or careers. They will become Creation's Sentinels. When things are going wrong somewhere, or incredibly right, they'll let Lilly and Arae know so Creation can maintain a smooth and proper flow. They will most likely already know but it's a good system to have in place.

Animal Essence has proven itself as having impeccable honor as well as a solid understanding of compassion and equality. They are already made for this job. They also already have the newly mutated Source Spirit energy in them, allowing them to move incredibly fast and morph into many things simultaneously.

They'll often be seen as upright Animal/Human beings made of Silver with a large staff in one hand. They will seldom interfere with things other than immediate protection for others. Their job is more to relay the information. Still, they will be active in smaller matters.

Something that will happen, almost immediately, is Arae going straight to Lilly and her various focal points to accelerate their healing processes. She has received great damage from her many excessively abusive lives. She should be ready to get started by May of 2016. She is what Creation needs, just like any other family, wonderful loving mother energy.

All of these dates are as close to accurate as I can get while in this darn body. I need to be out of it and myself again before I will know exactly. I will also be constantly updating my schedules to get as much done in as little time as possible. Remember the future is not only fluid but must remain so if we are to improve on who we are and what we're doing.

Once she's up and running, Lilly will be the Spirit which moves throughout Creation, fixing many of the large and small issues everywhere. I'm not trying to tell you that all life will be like a perfect dream. I am saying that compared to what we've all been going through, it'll feel like it's almost that. Even the unnecessary bugs on all the planets will be leaving. You don't need to be bothered with them anymore. Many serve no purpose but to be bothersome.

There are over two trillion planets with over a hundred million beings on each of them. This is a rather large family to look after. She won't have any problem with that though. There is another program coming back as it's never been before, Karma. It will be different now.

When Spirits in body are being abusive, they will immediately receive the same. This will help them receive the training they need on the spot, no waiting. It will also help to protect everyone else. There need be no delay time to understand a mistake. When it continually repeats itself the Spirit will be taken out of body and dealt with. This no abuse policy will be in place permanently.

The worse the abuse given the greater the abuse received. It will be a good deterrent to keep people from abusing others. Either way, you'll know immediately. This will take a few years to implement but it will happen.

There will also be an understanding of equality between the different Spirit energy fields. It's time for arrogance to start to disappear. There will be measures in place to stop it and reduce it down to zero. There is no need for this in family. Nothing is any better than anything else.

Lilly will also be putting all the Spirits into the bodies and making sure that their lives fit the new format. There will be great strides made to produce the lives you want but remember Creation has to keep moving forward in the right direction. Now, let's see what Arae's up to.

There's been an issue hanging over Arae's head for a long time now, the new First Beings coming sentient in the First Dimension. The next one to come out is already sixty seven percent negative and likely worse before leaving. This can't be allowed to happen and it won't. There's been enough trouble with a new First Being that was 27.5 percent negative. Imagine what it would be like with one that was sixty seven percent.

The negative frequencies actually come from the heavy particulate matter in the first dimension. That's why the Energans aren't negative beings. They came out of the sentient mass which was becoming our First Being, before the heavy particulate matter became involved.

By manipulating the heavy matter there, Arae can actually help new beings come out with less than ten percent negativity. He can also adjust the negativity of the beings now growing there. That's how he can change things without destroying anything, just the heavy matter.

Once things have settled down, Lilly and Arae will be able to look things over together and decide on how to improve whatever they can. This is not the kind of thing that happens over night, but it will happen just the same.

There need to be many changes as well as new Source Spirit beings brought into existence and eventually into play. There also need to be many changes to your life formats. You need to have an out if you've really had enough and just want to leave.

I wish I could tell you more about all this but I need to be outside looking in to be aware of just what will be happening everywhere. I do have the basics though. Besides, let's leave a little to the imagination.

The next issue is a big one. It's where you all learn how to run your own lives. It's where Creation learns how to run itself. Here's how that happens.

SECTION XIII -
CREATION LEARNS HOW TO
CONTROL ITSELF

CHAPTER 1
THE NEW COUNCILS ARE CREATED

There will soon be a form of self-government consisting of a series of councils. Each separate field of Spirit will be equally represented by two councilmembers. One will be female and the other a male. The only exception for this is the two groups of Angels.

Angel Spirit is literally called Zhe, pronounced ghee. It's what they call Spirit which is both male and female. So, for the two Angel Spirit fields, there would be two representatives each being male and female.

Each field with their two representatives will be required to have a sub-council of about one hundred more representatives and one more council below it having about a thousand councilmen. This is how your councils will make their decisions within themselves. Then all the councils will work together and decide how to run things for yourselves.

If things do come to an impasse, Lilly or Arae or both will come in and explain how things need to be for that issue as well as why it's best for everyone that way. There's no more supreme beings telling you how it has to be. There's no more abuse to beat you down with and everyone on the other side is equal, as well as here in the physical world.

You're not children any longer and you need to be free to become all of who you are, whether in body or not. It's time for all Creation to be free from oppression, abuse, arrogance, ignorance, and pain.

CHAPTER 2
NEW ELDERS ARE SELECTED FOR ALL PLANETS

There will also be new Elders Life Councils selected for all Planets having life on them. There will be nine Human and nine Fae along with one more to be selected later. This will be in case of the group coming to an impasse on anything.

When people are trying to build up a life plan with their Spirit Guide volunteers, they will present the finished plan to them for their approval. Once all is in agreement, the lives will be granted for them as the proper time.

Typically these councils have always been Essence members but things will be more representative of the Spirit living on the Planet as well as the lives being had there. Once your Creation Council is set up, you will choose these individuals yourselves.

SECTION XIV -
THE NEW CREATION
COMING

CHAPTER 1
HOW DOES THE NEW CREATION START FLOWING

So, how does the new Creation start? The first thing that happens is Arae destroys the rest of the problematic Spirit in Creation. Then he lays down the new format of compassion, honor, and equality. Next he heals Lilly while he's setting up Animal Essence to take on their new roles as Creation's Sentinels as well as forming the new Spirit Field Councils.

Once Lilly is healed, she will be where she should be, in her role as Creation's Mother Spirit. She'll start helping with the daily running of lives as Arae begins to take on other protective and repair type issues all around.

After a while the new councils will be set up on all the Planets with lives on them to help everyone there put their new lives together. Now, at this point things will have settled down quite and bit and it will be time for the Souls of the Fifth Wave or Generation to be released into bodies to have lives. Most of them have never even had one.

The new bodies will be the next issue to complete. There will already be Spirits having lives in the new bodies but this will continue until there are only ten to twenty percent of the physical bodies left. This is how things will be maintained for the most part. Again, all of you, while out of body, will be making many changes for yourselves.

Isn't Creation what you're part of? Isn't it about all of you? Shouldn't it be run by you? Arae will maintain proper flow and abuse control. That will never change. Other than that, he's staying out of the control business. He's a care taker, not a supreme being. Lilly is love that will be everywhere.

The next big event coming your way will completely change everything. It's our new neighbors about to move in.

CHAPTER 2
THE NEW INITIAL FIRST BEINGS LEAVE THE FIRST DIMENSION

I've mentioned many times in many places, including You Tube, that there are currently four new First Being type beings coming into sentience inside the First Dimension. When they come out, as they're ready, everything will change. The first one to come out, as it now appears, has some very serious negativity issues. It's already just past eighty seven percent negative frequencies. That's twenty percent more than the last time I looked at it. It cannot, and will not, be allowed to come out like that. This is something that no one has any say in.

Our Original First Being was 27.5 percent negative frequencies and look at what we have now. I'm aware of all the problems involved with this kind of issue, they're memories of Arae as well as myself. There's no way in hell something like that will be allowed to come out.

It's not a destructive thing to remove negativity from any being, not for Arae. I've done it for years now, just this small part of me in this body. I'm aware of a lot about Arae, it's what I am inside. Once this being is cleaned I'll clean the other three in there. Then, once this has been dealt with, I'm going to clean up the source of the negative frequency producing material in the first dimension, dense physical matter.

This is what causes negative frequencies in Spirit, sentient energy. This is also why it can give you a little strength which you can get on your own with just a little time having any sort of lives. Arae is the plain truth of that statement. He's only 2.081 percent negative frequencies yet the strongest being anywhere.

This dense matter is very useful in creating Universes so it'll be saved for later, so to speak. We just don't need it being part of the sentient being producing process in the first dimension. We've all had enough of that, Arae has anyway. That's his call. Now, let's get back to what's coming out of the First Dimension.

(Our Creation Grows Into Something New)

There will be either three or four new sentient First Beings completing themselves and coming out of the First Dimension before too long. When they do, we will have a very unique experience to enjoy and deal with. It will be nice to meet someone else but also a little like having a child. They will be brand new sentient beings.

At first they will not understand what we do and why. It will take a little time for them to adjust. Any aggressive actions on their part can be easily controlled but they will not be harmed unless there is no choice in the matter. This is a highly unlikely event, especially with a small percentage of negative frequencies.

They have rights and will be considered family immediately, simply because they are. We all are. They will probably also like a little company. They will have their own minds but they'll also be affected by what they see, just like everything else it. Get a load of this; you're all about to become parents, in a matter of speaking.

How things develop from here, I can't tell you. This is a unique situation which has never occurred before. We'll see how things go when it happens. The youngest one there is really cool. It has a beautiful pink aura coming from it. This one has incredible compassion and will no doubt be offering just that.

CHAPTER 3
THE NEW CREATION'S FUTURE

There is no way to understand exactly how this will all turn out. We can only surmise, from what we already know, that there will always be issues as well as compromise but let's not forget something. We have all had many lives and will have our own Spirit energy cleaned before long. We will be relaxed with who we are, how we feel, why we feel this way, and how we want to act about things.

This is a stable situation for new beings to grow in, to become who they are inside. This is a stable situation for Creation to continue on the path it chooses for itself. There is a loving mother that will take care of so many things that might arise.

There is also a loving father or big brother type energy that is already much stronger than anything else, which will allow us the protection we need from everything else, to grow on our own, to become ourselves.

I can't forecast this future, no one can. I do know who all of you really are though, and that leaves me feeling confident that things will work out fine. We just need to be able to do so

without negativity hammering everyone and Arae already knows how to do this.

The one thing that I'm concerned about is arrogance. As I've already stated many times, it requires absolutely no negative frequencies to grow, to become a cancer for whoever carries it as well as anyone nearby. This can also be handled without mayhem. I'll know when I'm out of this darn body.

CHAPTER 4
THE SUMMARY OF CREATION'S EXISTENCE

Well, let's see what we have here. There is a First Dimension which has all the energies within it to create sentient energy or Spirit when the proper ones collide and hang out together. The very First Original Being came from it a very long time ago and that's where all of us came from. There are also four new First Being type energy fields becoming sentient inside it.

The Original First Being became two out of the first feeling which was loneliness. This was the creation of male and female.

Then it released some of it's energy to create family or, more precisely, company which it wanted to want it. This began the false concept of praise.

Then everything it created was abused so it would grow quicker to make more of itself and offer more praise.

Then it decided to make everything grow as a unit, the expanding of it's applause center.

Lastly it was destroyed by something it created, the protector. It made something to protect itself and all it created but it didn't realize that it would learn to appreciate things for what they were, as themselves, instead of the purpose the Original Ones had for it.

Then Creation's format would be changed and all energy cleaned.

That is a very short summary of events as well as what's actually in Creation. The first book in the Creation series, "Creation: It's Beginning and Your Origin", describes in length what's actually in your Creation including the how, why, and when involved.

When you put the information of both these books together you'll understand who you are, what's around you, how it got there, and what to expect from it. It's a hand book to yourself and all around you.

SECTION XV -
PROPHECY

CHAPTER 1
WHAT IS PROPHECY AND WHY IS IT SO ELUSIVE

OK, this is an important chapter. It's also something that has been a major influence in keeping you from waking up as a society. The general consensus is that if someone is a real psychic they can see the future. Why do the sleepers, the vast majority of people not yet awoken, think that the future is like a book and someone is supposed to be able to go to this magic book, turn the pages, and read it?

Who came up with this concept? Who started this train of thought? It was uttered from one Human body and then many others. It still flows out of people's mouths today like bad breath. Many who try to dispel the possibility of metaphysical abilities uses this as a tool against those who are already using their abilities. I'm putting a stop to this right here and right now.

Once you understand a few simple facts, and have a few questions of your own to throw back at them, you can shut them up and shut down their desire to put you in their own little "Spanish Inquisition". Let's take a simple look at one of their questions, why can't anyone accurately predict the future?

There are millions or billions of lives on over two trillion Planets, here on Earth it's over six billion. Each person is neither aware of who he really is or what they're supposed to do in their current life. There are control systems in place but things happen in our lives, especially the more traumatic ones that no one can predict.

Even though there will be something very intelligent as well as benevolent guiding our lives soon, there's a lot of change happening in everyone's life. Now, many of these people are supposed to be meeting up with each other at different times in their lives.

These events are a large part of what creates our future. When so many people change these smaller events, it affects the outcome of some of the larger and later events. This is how our future changes. There's still one more thing we need to look at.

CHAPTER 2
WILL PROPHECY IMPROVE IN THE FUTURE

W hen there is something running your lives, and it really does care enough to give you a continuously better life, than there's more need for change in your future. As intelligent as large Source is, that constitutes a whole lot of change in each individual's future. This will also have a rather dramatic effect on the future events scheduled for larger groups.

This is why the future is always changing. Recently there has been a war on the Other Side which has actually been changing the structure of who is running lives as well as how it will be handled. There's an even greater reason for diversity of future change.

Now add to this that there is new loving Spirit about to run lives for the first time. This means there is a learning curve about to present itself. If we add to this the fact that Creation is about to learn how to run itself, well, there's a whole new issue there. This will take time to learn and, although the future can never be properly predicted, it will get better. I do believe that's the more important thing to relate to.

CHAPTER 3
VIOLENCE IN THE PACIFIC ARENA

The Federation, our protectors in space already mentioned, have had to become much more involved with things here. There have been prisoners brought here to work as slaves in everything from mining to personal servants. Today, more often than not, they've been brought from distant worlds with promises of great futures and wealth, to help themselves as well as the Humans, live a life of splendor.

As soon as they go into the large elevators taking them down below some of our FEMA camps, military bases, and other installations, they are kept there as prisoners never to leave. They go in and never come out. There have been generations of them born into and living in, slavery.

These prisoners are a primary reason for what's happening here today with our family in space. Over Ninety-eight percent of the starships in space are there protecting us. It's the ones we find most often in our atmosphere that are the problem. They are most often triangular in shape. There are many pictures of them on the internet today. They're usually called TR-3's, TR-4's, and what not.

These ships are owned by our government as well as others. As I started writing the first book of the Creation Series there were only eight countries with them. Now, before the finishing of this book in just weeks, there will be ten. The Annunaki that run things here are preparing to create a great disturbance with these ships to either attempt completely dominating us or leaving here escaping as stealthily as possible.

There are many hidden bases on this planet, most of which are underground on the land as well as under the sea. The first ones to be attacked will be in the Pacific Ocean, as mentioned just moments ago. Here lies the beginning of the end for the Annunaki control of our Planet. Man was this a long time coming.

As these hidden bases are attacked by what will seem the Earth itself, not only will the imprisoners and controllers be evacuated, but many of the workers imprisoner there will be abandoned. As the mayhem continues the Earthen starships, the triangular ones, will fly out to these locations to transport the higher end officials to safety. There will also be many large groups of prisoners, the hi-jacked workers, now in peril.

Our friends and protectors in space will also immediately come to the aid of our newly freed multi-planetary visitors. There will be large starships here to beam them up directly. These are cargo type vessels and will be accompanied by smaller but very powerful attack vessels which will immediately attack most of the smaller Earthen starships.

These Earthen starships are the ones our governments wanted to use against us to create a planetary form of Marshall Law. They still want to but it can't happen now. Things have been changed that we don't need to discuss here now. Do not think these triangular ships are going to help you. They won't until the Annunaki are "removed from office" as we would say. Then they will become of great use to us. It's not the ship; it's what's controlling it, carrying out their orders.

This short series of fire-fights between the two sides will only continue until all the endangered ex-prisoners are found and removed. Some people will die in this event, but I hope not many. I know these things will be kept to a minimum, but they will happen none the less.

There will also be a few actual Annunaki on the shores. They average about six to nine feet tall and many hundred pounds. There will be people there to take pictures of them which quickly hit the internet. They will surface on the beaches near San Diego and San Francisco for the most part. People will be there not by accident, but simply made to arrive at the right time and properly prepared. This will all be done by Source Spirit on the Other Side, bringing much needed change here.

Unfortunately, there's so much garbage in the way of fake alien pictures already circulating that it'll be more difficult for people to have much faith in the actual physical proof being made available. Still, it will be there and in sufficient quantity. This is only the start of the problematic Annunaki demise here on Earth. It only gets stronger as the year 2016 continues.

There is already a contingent of Annunaki here fighting to free these prisoners. This is not so much a physical fight as it is multi-level planning with smaller incursions. Next year it will become a larger issue.

Before leaving the Pacific Ocean area I want to mention something else. There will be some smaller issues, a tearing of the ocean floors, as Lemuria begins to shake loose again. This is an event that has already started.

I remember waking up years ago watching myself, as Arae, closing many of the different fissures on the bottom of the

Pacific Ocean. This was to start solidifying the ancient land mass of Lemuria as well as start building up pressure underneath it. This was allowing the lava to fill the old seams that used to be the outer edges of the major islands or continents of Lemuria. She will rise again, period.

CHAPTER 4

UPHEAVAL IN THE NORTH ATLANTIC OCEAN

There is also a skirmish at best in the Atlantic Ocean which will follow the Pacific event. It might be in December of 2016 or even 2018. I don't know the exact year at this moment and don't really care.

None of this is about me. I'm only giving you some basic information to help you understand some of the things that I'm going to make happen once I dump this physical shell I'm temporarily imprisoned in. You need to understand who you are, how you got here, why you are, and why/how everything is about to change.

There is a shelf, on the North Atlantic Ocean floor, that extends from the Northeast to the Southeast in a soft curve whose apex flows towards the United States but not anywhere near it. It is a small section of the sunken continent of Atlantis. It's a bit southwest of the Cape Verde Islands.

This area will be shaken up rather hard. There are Annunaki installations down there, one in particular, that need to be destroyed. So, it will be. Just as in the Pacific earlier, this area will have some activity going on as starships, boats, fighter planes, and more get involved removing all the individuals that were located in these bases.

There will be a few Earthen starships taken down, not many though. There are only 10 countries that have them now. Remember this folks, the Earthen starships are not your protectors, not unless it suits the Annunaki here abusing you and destroying your planet. Each of the current 10 countries that have them also has their limits in relation to how they may be used. They are controlled. They have a loose leash, but they are controlled.

CHAPTER 5
THE FINAL ARRIVAL OF OUR FAMILY IN SPACE

Eventually, all this fighting will open the door to our family in space to literally beam down here and say hi. It won't be in one location but many. They will make sure to have such a presence that the event will not be able to be controlled by any one thing here. The events will be made to happen that will open that door for them.

They are not just benevolent; they have been protecting us for a long time. One of the many reasons for this is relative to all the unfortunate beings who have been imprisoned here on Earth for a very long time now.

There are over twenty two thousand wonderful Annunaki prisoners here and this is just one group. There are also thousands of Serpoians held captive here. They are the major race of beings that others often call Grays. There are well over sixty different races imprisoned here. This will also be stopped. They will all be freed. That will happen by force. The Annunaki that control things here will never do this on their own. These problematic Annunaki are about to be removed from this planet but not until you seem them physically. You need to know they exist.

Arae promised to do this a long time ago and it's finally about to happen. When in a physical body I always strive to do the same, in spite of how things can be controlled around me keeping me from doing what I need to do. You can only do the best you can while in a body. You don't have the freedom you might believe you do.

There is a federation, for lack of a better term, of starships from other planets who joined together a long time ago to help each other and attempt to maintain a peaceful form of security wherever they could. They are here to help. Our problems are here, deeply imbedded in the Earth.

There will be a day, right now it's scheduled to be about 2018, when many of our city's skies will be covered with starships. They will only be saying hello. This is a moment I've been waiting for, for a long time. I was hoping to see it while still in body. Oh well.

Once our friends in space introduce themselves, you'll see many different starships coming and going. There will be enough of them to where you actually start recognizing a few of them by sight. At this point you will be ready for the next event, meeting the Fae.

CHAPTER 6
THE FAE INTRODUCE THEMSELVES

The Fae have always been here, hiding in plain sight as well as in their own dimensions. They used to run around with us up here in the Third Dimension. That's why there are so many tales of them. Unfortunately, the tales are mostly false, inaccurate, and untrue to the point of gross disbelief.

The Fae are real but most of the stories about them are fabricated. The same is true of Dragons. Their breath could actually heal physical tissue. It could also cause harm if they were attacked and needed it for defense. These beings are not here today for us to physically look at, not yet anyway. Don't expect to see physical Dragons but do expect to see the Fae, up close and in person.

Their Spirit energy is very close to Human Spirit energy. They're so close that when they're separated they can't be completely divided, there's always a slight mixture of both. We used to live together and we will again before too long.

They will teach you how they make a physical body while in a Fae body. This will be important to all of you in physical bodies in the upcoming centuries when you'll be in the new bodies of energy instead of physical mass. There will already be physical records of how this is done for those still existing in physical bodies. When the physical bodies start having lives with those of Fae, as well as all the new upcoming energy bodies, they will more easily understand what's happening and how. Understanding helps maintain a calm community.

CHAPTER 7
THE PHYSICAL BODIES DISAPPEAR AND THE NEW ONES APPEAR

O ver the next two thousand years, at least that's the program for now, well over half of the physical bodies will have disappeared. There should only be about ten to thirty percent of them left. As you begin to have new lives, you'll do so in the next energetic bodies similar to those of the Fae. They will reduce the abuse in Creation from seventy two to seventy eight percent overall.

When you have children you'll be putting your energies together, relax, and then release part of your own energies to produce new bodies, children. It's completely painless and they grow fast. There aren't even any diapers to deal with. There's no labor or any such thing. It's a simple process.

You will be able to live off of the energy you can receive from one apple and a thimble of honey for one whole month. Is that cool or what? You can literally help the Earth grow stronger while you're fed as best as you can be. This is also why they Fae love those of us who take care of the Earth. The Earth feeds all of us. They just understand it better. Simple, isn't it?

You'll be able to float through a wall, sit on a chair at a table, and then float out through the wall again. You will not, however, be able to maintain a physical form for too long. That is the only price you pay. You will never have any of the physical pain either.

SECTION XVI -
A WORD FROM THE AUTHOR

This is the shortest section in the book for good reason. It's relative to having had to talk about a lot of things involving myself. The only reason for this is because of the fact that Arae is what's inside this body. As people begin to awaken, you will understand why I call myself Creation's janitor.

I prefer to work behind the scenes, not in public view. This was not possible this life, to do what has been done without mention of who did it. I tried but everyone kept asking how and not replying just shut me down. That was not acceptable. There was no way for me to explain the truth of who they were, what was happening, and why.

Like everyone else in body, I am just the sum of my parts. I am more than just a vehicle, I am the three made into one like everyone else, two Spirits and a physical body holding them inside. It's because Arae was put into this body that I'm so involved in this. This is not something that many of you would want, not after two hours of doing so.

I've had the Original First Being halves, both of them, inside me where I had to fight them off until, after years and with help I might add, were able to use Arae's energy, part of what I am, to burn them into nothingness. There are many things in the Creation books left out by design. They have no relevance to your relative understanding.

This is neither a pity corner nor appreciation day. I just wanted to explain a little about what I am and how I know what I'm telling you. It's easier for someone to describe an event when they were part of it. The best way for someone to understand things is by seeing for themselves. The next best way is by hearing events, placing themselves in the person's place, and feeling just what was happening. Then, using all your abilities, you will hold or release what fits and what doesn't.

I have had my feet broken twice by arrogant, aggressive, abusive, yet clean Source Spirit, while sleeping in my bed. I have seen things that no one else can, which allows me to explain them in their simplicity but takes people time to understand. That is also the reason for these Creation books. As everyone begins to open up and awaken their abilities, they will see things for themselves. Then my words will make more sense. They will have names for images and visions. They will feel what's real. They will have their own truth and be able to relate to mine.

I have physically evolved thousands of people and even more Animals. When I go into someone's brain and work on them, their brains physically grow in size over ninety percent of the time. This is an easily proven fact but what's important is that I did my job, as I promised I would. You were all made to stay unawake, blind, while in body.

Anyway, I've also left many videos on You Tube trying to describe as much as I could of what I'm aware of. It's important for you to become as much of your true self, who you really are. Go inside and meet yourself. I've known y'all a long time. It's time you knew yourselves better, appreciate yourselves more as I appreciate you

SECTION XVII - HOW TO TALK TO THE SPIRIT IN STONE

HOW THE HECK DOES A STONE TALK

OK now, what's all this about? Talking to stone, really? Yep. It's a simple thing and easy to do. The more relaxed and aware you are of yourself and what's around you, the easier and louder it will be. Louder might not be the best choice of words. Here's why.

The energy within any stone is that of the Planet it comes from. The different stones from the same planet will have only the Spirit, the sentient energy, of that Planet. The particular energetic frequencies of that individual stone will be different than another stone from the same Planet but the only Spirit inside will be that of the Planet or Planets it came from.

The one exception to this rule is that of Source Spirit. As Source Spirit is both comprised of all frequencies including those of the particular stone as well as strong enough to do so, it can place it's energy into the stone. It can actually place part of it's Spirit in it.

An example of this is the case of the original twelve Crystal Skulls. They all have Arae's Spirit inside them. So do a few other pieces here and there. When you talk to Max the Skull, if you really are, you're talking to a part of Arae he broke off to put into it. That's why his energy is so strong.

When you hold a piece of stone wanting to get the maximum feel of it and do so as quick as possible, hold it between the fingertips of both hands. If you can relax you'll feel it moving through your body or possibly just feel it moving inside a certain part of your body. You also might just see image. Either way, you've just begun to communicate with it.

When you're personal energy is Solar Plexus Oriented, you usually feel things in your main torso, gut or stomach area, arms and legs, as well as anywhere else. We are all different. I'm only speaking in terms of generalities here. This is a guide to start with, not finish with. The finishing results come from you inside, you personally.

When you're Heart Oriented, you will most often feel things in your chest or heart area but also, almost always, in your hands and fingertips, often your feet as well. When you start to feel the stone, before you even realize it, you'll realize you're taking a deeper breath all of a sudden. That's your body reacting to the energy before you're mentally aware of it.

When you're Pineal or Brain Oriented energy you'll always feel it in your head. You might even become a little dizzy but you'll feel it, as long as you're awake, aware of yourself. This takes a little time and everyone's sensitivity is different. Also, the stronger you become the less you feel the stone unless you relax more and open up to it, making the affirmation to receive it.

Here's how we go about talking to stone. If you hold a stone that has Gaia's energy in it, her being the Spirit of the Earth, she will talk to you in one form or another. Once the stone is in the fingertips of both hands and you're relaxed, take another full breath and say as thought only, "Gaia, are you in here? Are you part of this stone?"

If she's in there she'll say hi. Give her a second to replay but you might not need it. If she wants you to relax a little more she'll wait for you to calm down a bit. If you're ready she'll talk to you immediately. Here's what happens.

When you're Pineal or Brain based energy, she'll either give you a feeling in your head, your body, or even send an image to your Pineal. Remember that Pineal based people can feel things the easiest, with Heart energy close by. It's the Solar Plexus folk that have the most difficulty.

When you feel this feeling or see this image, she is saying hello. Sometimes people even hear a voice. It's all good no matter how it happens. The important thing is that it did happen. Gaia said hello.

Now, while you're still holding the stone, you can ask Gaeira (pronounced Gayra) to say hello. She is the Spirit from the very first Planet ever to have life on her. She is also the strongest individual Planetary Essence Spirit. She will say hi in a similar but stronger manner. If you felt Gaia but not Gaeira, then Gaeira isn't in that stone.

Then, once you're able to do this, pick up a piece of Star Essenite, a piece you know actually is, and ask by thought only for the Star Essence, male Universal Spirit, to say hello. He will.

Once you've done this you might also want to say hello to Mollae, pronounced Molly, the Spirit in Moldavite. She's a very beautiful being also. She is not an asteroid but a piece of a Planet that has had it's physical end as a large mass only.

This is how you talk to stone. It's simple, true, and very real.

SECTION XVIII - GIVING CONSULTS USING COMMUNICATION, NOT DIVINATION

This is important to understand if you want to give better consultations with your clients. Divination is about divining or telling the future. This is impossible to do on a regular basis unless you're so bland and general in your answers that they could mean almost anything. Why do it?

The future is always changing; it has to in order to keep moving forward in the best possible way for all involved. Is there a reason we would want anything less than that? I hope not. The actual future events have been changing violently these past seven years and will continue to do so, although it's for different reasons now.

Creation is at a point where it is evolving and that is the strongest kind of change there is, rebirth. If it's something in the nearby future go ahead and take a look at it. There's nothing wrong with that. Just remember, the farther off it is the less likely it is to come true as seen if at all.

THE DIFFERENCE BETWEEN DIVINATION AND COMMUNICATION

D ivination is what many people who are waking up, usually want to know about the most. When will I meet my Soulmate? When is true love coming into my life? When am I going to have money? The list goes on and on.

If you really want to help them, let them know this. The future is always changing and now more than ever. The good thing is that things are now constantly being made to happen to improve your life as never before. You should also remind them that Creation is in another learning phase of it's development.

When you help them communicate with Spirit, such as their Spirit Guides, they are getting real help today for what's most important to them now. These are real things that they can hold onto, not fluffy images which will fade like clouds in a clear sky.

Another thing I want you to be aware of is that the larger the percentage of negative frequencies there are within a person, the more difficult your consultation will be. This is for several different reasons.

First, their energy is not as easy to look at. It's more opaque, not as clear.

Second, they don't have but one Spirit Guide who usually won't be much if any help in the process.

Third, they don't have much if any faith in what you're trying to do for them. They're more selfish and just want more of everything.

Fourth, and by no means least, they will lie to you in a second as you begin to give them information. They want to feel a power over you so, when you tell they something that's true, they'll often tell you it's not just to see a look of confusion on your face, possibly one of anger after a while when you realize they're lying to you.

These are just basic guidelines for you to follow. They will help you help others as well as yourselves. The more you help them, the more you'll be helping yourself. Just don't make it about you.

As your abilities become stronger and stronger, you'll possibly go through a small arrogance phase. Don't worry about it much, it'll go away. When you don't worry about it at all, once you see it happening, then you might have a small problem you can easily get rid of. You also might have a little help with that from the Other Side, hint, hint.

You can use Oracle Cards, Tarot Cards, Crystals, Runes or Rune Cards, and many other things to help you see things for people. You can use everything or nothing other than your own abilities because that's what you're using anyway, your own abilities.

I've made special Rune symbols for all of you as a guide and assistant in your awakening process. They are called J'Arae's Runes of Awakening. I like to use the actual Runes but it takes me hours to make and I've never had the time I needed to do what I needed to do. These cards will work as well as the Runes themselves. That's why I made them.

They help you understand the different parts of your brain, your body's different energy fields, how they all work together, when you might want to use certain ones, when to protect yourself, and more.

I'm doing all I can for all of you. No one ever tells me what to do. That's always come out to be a mistake for someone else. I am, however, one who always serves out of desire to do so. I don't know how to be anything else and don't want to.

Be at peace with yourself by becoming who you really are.
Take time away from everything to flow within yourself.
Trust Animal Spirits. They never lie.
Talk to Spirit as much as possible.
Open Your Heart, Be Yourself.
We Are Family Now.
Let's Act Like It.

HERE'S A LITTLE MORE INFORMATION FOR YOU.

Initial life and colonization here started well over 11 million years ago.

First Age – 10.572 – 8.3 million years ago
Second Age – 5.2 – 4.3 million years ago
Third Age – 3.8 – 2.5 million years ago
Fourth Age - 1.1 – .8 million years ago
Fifth Age - 750 thousand years ago – 12/21/2012
Sixth Age - 12/21/2012 – Current Time